FOR YOUR

VEGETABLE GARDEN

Also by **Duane Newcomb**
The Postage Stamp Garden Book
Growing Vegetables the Big Yield/Small Space Way

FOR YOUR
VEGETABLE
GARDEN

DUANE NEWCOMB

Illustrations by Lynn Lieppman

J. P. TARCHER, INC.
Los Angeles
Distributed by Houghton Mifflin Company
Boston

J. P. TARCHER, INC.
9110 Sunset Blvd.
Los Angeles, CA 90069

Library of Congress Catalog Card No.: 81—50328

Design by Jane Moorman/Mike Yazzolino

Manufactured in the United States of America

Q 10 9 8 7 6 5 4 3 2 1

First Edition

CONTENTS

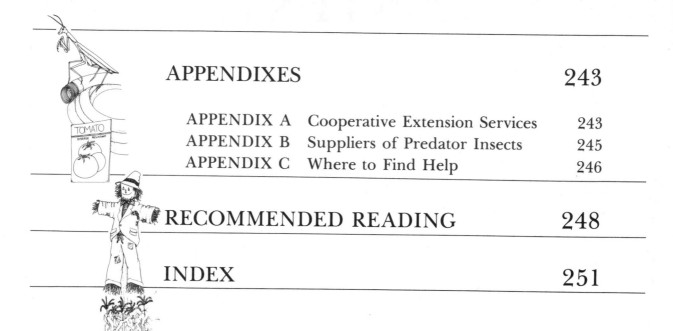

ACKNOWLEDGMENTS

A great many people have contributed directly or indirectly to this book. I am especially grateful to my editor Millie Loeb who contributed many good ideas from the inception and who added greatly to the organization and clarity of the book. Without her hard work this book would have been much more difficult to put together; to my agent Jane Jordan Browne, who is herself a serious and knowledgeable gardener and who has worked with this book every step of the way. And to Karen Newcomb who is very expert at and put a great deal of work into the charts.

I would also like to thank the following:

Norman F. Oebker, Extension Vegetable Specialist, University of Arizona; Marie L. Lavallard, Agricultural Experiment Station, University of Arkansas, Hunter Johnson Jr., Cooperative Extension, University of California, Riverside; James E. Ellis, Department of Horticulture, Colorado State University; David E. Hill, The Connecticut Agricultural Experiment Station; D.N. Maynard, Institute of Food and Agricultural Sciences, University of Florida; C.H. Hendershott, Department of Horticulture, University of Georgia; Geddes W. Simpson, College of Life Sciences and Agriculture, University of Maine; Sylvan H. Wittwer, Agricultural Experiment Station, Michigan State University; Eduard J. Stadelmann, Department of Horticultural Science and Landscape Architecture, University of Minnesota; Clyde C. Singletary, College of Agriculture, Mississippi State University; Roger D. Uhlinger, Department of Horticulture, University of Nebraska; Robert D. Sweet, Department of Vegetable Crops, New York State College of Agriculture, Cornell University; Robert G. Hill, Ohio Agricultural Research and Development Center; Charles N. Voyles, Agricultural Information Services, Oklahoma State University; H.J. Mack, Department of Horticulture, Oregon State University; Jack C. Shannon, College of Agriculture, Pennsylvania State University; Robert E. Thornton, Cooperative Extension, Washington State University.

INTRODUCTION

The very first year I planted a garden my zucchini plants formed little zucchini that promptly rotted and my early tomatoes grew gnarled and distorted.

To find out what was wrong, I called several dozen nurseries and read a number of popular gardening books. Occasionally someone had a part of the answer to one or more of my questions, but no one source ever answered them all.

Later, as I began to write my own vegetable gardening books, I discovered that almost every other gardener was in the same boat. I also learned that most people had the incorrect perception that insects and disease accounted for just about all of their gardening problems. They didn't understand that water, soil, nutrients, weather, temperatures, competition, and other environmental factors can also account for a substantial percentage of all home garden troubles. These realizations led to this book.

Today there are volumes on garden insects and on diseases, and there are general vegetable gardening books that discuss other plant troubles. But until now there has never been one book devoted exclusively to the full range of vegetable gardening problems.

This work is the result of my effort to fill that gap. To write it has required an extensive search for bits and pieces of information that existed only here and there. What I found should help provide answers to hundreds of gardening problems and make life a bit easier for both the beginning and the advanced gardener.

Rx for Vegetable Gardens is offered with the hope that it will make gardening an easier, more bountiful, and more enjoyable experience for each and every home grower.

Duane Newcomb

CHAPTER ONE

CREATING A HEALTHY VEGETABLE GARDEN

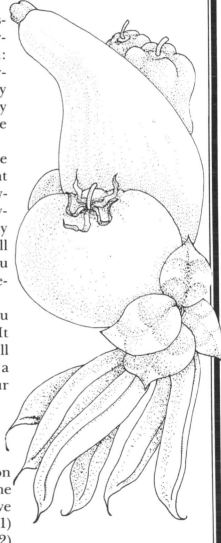

Whenever anyone interested in the subject discovers that I have written books on vegetable gardening, they inevitably ask the same question: What's wrong with my vegetables? This occurs every gardening season. Perhaps the radish leaves grow vigorously but the bulbs remain small; maybe beans blossom mightily but fail to produce pods; or tomatoes are distorted and have little zipper streaks down the sides.

These and dozens of similar garden troubles plague even the most experienced gardeners. The problem is that Mother Nature can be very unpredictable, with each growing season presenting its own unique challenges. The early-spring months may stay wet and cool; summer days may turn hot for days on end; and insects or disease may well present a severe problem during a particular season. If you don't adjust for these problems and conditions, your vegetables will suffer.

And that's what this book is all about. It will take you step by step through the major gardening trouble spots. It will explain why your vegetables react as they do and it will give you the gardening know-how to diagnose and cure a wide variety of gardening maladies. It is, in short, your prescription for a healthy garden.

THE ROLE OF PREVENTION

The book begins with the neglected topic of prevention because many problems can be avoided by adopting some simple strategies. It's no accident that some gardeners have very few insect and disease troubles. They are careful to (1) remove garden refuse that harbors pests and insects; (2) rotate their crops; (3) avoid planting at the time of peak insect infestations; and (4) grow resistant varieties and plants that repel insects, known as companion planting. In short, they do all the necessary chores that prevent pests, disease, and other garden problems from obtaining a toehold in the first place.

Some gardeners, for instance, keep corn borers from attacking their corn by planting giant sunflowers in the garden, and they discourage the spread of virus diseases by staying out of the garden when the plant leaves are wet. Those who smoke eliminate the threat of tobacco mosaic by washing their hands before working in the garden.

SOIL AND NUTRIENTS

Both heavy clay and light sandy soils create a problem. Their composition makes it difficult for nutrients to get to the vegetables, preventing vigorous growth and the production of healthy, mature fruit, roots, tubers, stalks, and leaves.

For instance, a boron deficiency produces deformed cauliflower curds and brownish broccoli buds (it's like not getting enough vitamins). A slight manganese deficiency in peas can create a brown cavity inside the individual pea called marsh spot; only the inside of the pea is affected, while the pods and vines look perfectly healthy. Fortunately, all your garden's soil and nutrient problems can be diagnosed and corrected with a bit of effort.

WATERING WISDOM

Either too much or too little water will open another Pandora's box. Ask any "garden doctor" why cabbages crack and you'll be warned about an uneven water supply. Ask why carrots are stumpy, and you'll be told you overwatered. Ask why potatoes are knobby, and you'll get the same response. Once you understand what role water plays and know how to keep your vegetables properly supplied, you'll be amazed at how easy it is to avoid most of these problems.

MOTHER NATURE'S VARIABLES

There's a good reason why farmers are so concerned with the weather. Such factors as day and night temperatures, the absence or presence of sun during daylight hours, the length of the day, and wind, rain, and hail can all help or hinder the growth of your vegetables. For example, cool spring growing conditions can sometimes help create marble-sized potatoes—a distressing development when you're hoping for eating size. If you understand weather- and season-related problems, you can learn to plant at the most appropriate times, select plants with good foliage, protect your vegetables from severe weather, and, in general, work with Mother Nature to produce the most bountiful crop.

STOMPING OUT THOSE INSECTS

A wide variety of organic and chemical methods are available for controlling the insect problem. These range from chasing away bugs with a stream of water to waging biological warfare with toxic sprays and dusts. Some gardeners kill aphids with an oxalic acid spray made from ground rhubarb leaves, trap whiteflies in a molasses-coated bucket painted bright yellow inside, and control grasshoppers with the grasshopper spore. This section of the book will give you the latest background information on the many traditional and imaginative strategies that vegetable gardeners are now using to deal with destructive insects. You will also find information on helpful predator insects that can be imported to chase the "bad guys" out.

DEALING WITH DISEASE

Most gardeners have only a vague understanding of plant pathology and of the many ways to prevent or eradicate disease. The chapter on this subject will enable you to become an instant expert. For example, you will learn how to deal with sudden bacterial wilt in cucumbers and squash by controlling the cucumber beetle that spreads the disease. Similarly, the antidote to curlytop in beets is to prevent leafhopper infestations. And common scab in potatoes can be eliminated by changing the soil pH in the potato bed. You will be given a quick summary of the major diseases that can attack your vegetables along with a description of both the organic and chemical methods to control these problems.

KEEPING THE VARMINTS OUT

Four-legged pests (cats, dogs, rabbits, gophers, and deer) can be even more frustrating than insect pests. The neighbor's cat, for instance, can wreak havoc with your emerging carrots and yet must be treated with kid gloves, and gophers sometimes harvest as many vegetables as the gardener does.

Some people find odoriferous plants effective for controlling critters; others prefer fences, traps, and even more exotic deterrents. This chapter offers a complete rundown of the many methods available for keeping unwanted animals out of your garden.

Rx FOR INDIVIDUAL VEGETABLES

In this final section you will find a complete rundown on the major problems that can befall over 40 common vegetables. You will discover why onion bulbs sometimes split into two pieces, why carrots become long, thin, and spindly, and why potatoes sometimes turn green.

Each troubleshooting vegetable chart covers environmental disorders, the insects that can harm that particular vegetable, and the diseases to which it is prone. To simplify your diagnosis, you will find identifying physical characteristics for each problem. Finally, these charts offer a variety of organic and chemical methods for correcting each malady.

Now, let's start by looking at a program for prevention, because a substantial percentage of vegetable problems can be stopped before they begin.

CHAPTER TWO

MANY OUNCES OF PREVENTION

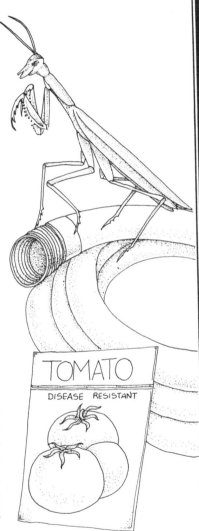

At the first sign of Spring, one of my gardening neighbors (I call her Ms. Buggy) trots out her backpack spray can, loads it with chemical insecticide, and starts spraying every plant in sight. Every two weeks after that during the gardening season clouds of insecticide rise from her garden. "Not one insect," she claims, "is going to set foot in my garden!"

Another gardening friend (Ms. Clean), on the other hand, claims it's what you do *before* the insect hordes arrive that counts. She cleans up her garden in the Fall, never plants the same crop in the same location a second season, selects vegetables that are resistant to local diseases, and in general gardens with an eye to stopping all problems before they start. Every Summer her garden produces an abundant harvest of mouthwatering vegetables. As far as I know, she doesn't even own a spray can. Prevention, she insists, is absolutely essential for creating and maintaining a healthy, vigorous garden.

As discussed in this chapter, prevention refers only to methods and strategies for avoiding problems with disease, insects, and plant competition. Environmental problems will be covered in the three chapters that follow. There is a certain amount of ambiguity in the areas of prevention and cure. For instance, a boron deficiency can be prevented by testing the soil before planting. In practice, however, few home gardeners test for and add trace elements until something goes severely wrong. At that point, you're curing the problem, not preventing it. The same ambiguity exists in a number of other situations.

A BASIC PREVENTIVE PLAN

Before vegetables can fall prey to either insects or disease, the plants must be susceptible to them. That is, the right environmental conditions (such as an abundance of moisture or an optimum temperature) and a disease organism or insect ready to pounce must be present in the garden. If any of these elements is *missing,* your plants will remain healthy. So here are the basic preventive measures to use in your own garden to maintain this health.

1. Pick the Right Site

Choose a garden site where the water drains off easily. Either avoid heavy clay soils that hold moisture in the soil or add organic material to create good drainage (see Chapter 3). Excess soil moisture provides just the right conditions for the spread of soil rots and increases the chances that seedlings will rot at the soil line (a condition known as damping off). Standing water or excess moisture also stunts plant growth.

2. Keep That Garden Clean

Clean up piles of trash as they accumulate. It is even more important to remove crop residues when you harvest your vegetables, as dead fruit often provides a perfect environment for an egg depository and a place for some insects to overwinter. In many cases, cleanup alone will drastically reduce the possibility of an insect problem. It will also cut back on diseases transmitted by insects and keep disease infestations from spreading throughout your garden.

3. Prevent the Spread of Disease

Disease spreads easily through a single vegetable. Therefore, it's a good idea to mix crops in any particular row. In addition, since a disease may start with one or several plants and move quickly through the garden when conditions are favorable, destroy infected plants or plant parts as soon as you find them. Also keep in mind that you should avoid working in the garden immediately after a rain or when the plants are wet with dew. Disease organisms that cling to your clothing and hands are more easily transferred to your vegetables at this time.

4. Smokers Take Warning

Wash your hands with soap and water before working in the garden if you smoke. This helps eliminate the spread of tobacco mosaic, which is a problem in some areas.

5. Select Resistant Varieties

Plant vegetable varieties that are resistant to one or more diseases. Some varieties are resistant to several diseases, while others have varying degrees of immunity, ranging from tolerance to partial resistance to complete immunity (see Table 2 – 1). New resistant varieties of vegetables are released each season. Therefore, it is worth your time and effort to look for this kind of information on the seed packet or in the catalog from which you are ordering.

There are two methods of selecting resistant varieties. In the first, identify garden problems from Chapter 9 (fusarium wilt, blight, or other disease), and then select varieties from your nursery seed rack or nursery transplants that are resistant to these diseases. If you have a choice of several resistant varieties, base your decision on size, color, or other qualities generally used in making a seed selection.

In the second case, turn to your county agricultural extension service (listed in the telephone white pages under your specific county). Ask which diseases are a problem locally. Also request a list of recommended vegetable varieties for your state (every state has one, including Hawaii). Select resistant varieties from this list, matching them with the problem diseases. The extension agent should also be able to recommend the best disease-resistant varieties to plant in your area.

6. Start Healthy

Buy certified disease-free seed and healthy transplants, or treat noncertified seed yourself. Disease-free seed is grown in arid parts of the western United States and can be purchased through seed catalogs and at garden centers as "certified disease free." Some growers also treat seed with fungicides, and this is plainly stated in the catalogs and on seed packages.

You can treat your own seed with captan, a powdered fungicide available at garden centers. Tear off one corner of the seed packet. Lift out as much dust from a package of captan as will go on the tip of a blade of a penknife and insert the dust through the hole in the seed package. Fold down the corner and shake thoroughly. Treat large seed in a jar, adding double the amount of captan dust.

Most reputable nurseries sell only healthy transplants, but you should check for yourself. Select vigorous-looking plants without spots on their leaves.

7. Dig Deep, Dig Early

If you deep spade your garden in early Spring, you can destroy the larvae of beetles and the pupae of many caterpillars that overwinter in the soil before they have a chance to emerge and attack your crops.

8. Practice Crop Rotation

Plant individual vegetables in a different spot every year. If you put your garden plan on paper each season, you won't have to worry about remembering where things were. If possible, move the entire garden every three to four years. Cabbage maggots, vegetable weevils, seed corn maggots, and other insects live in the ground adjacent to their host plants and redouble their efforts the next season if their favorite plants are grown nearby. Eggplant, tomatoes, and all members of the cabbage clan are especially susceptible to disease attack if planted in the same spot each year. The length of rotation (the number of years that should elapse before replanting the same spot) is noted for each particular vegetable in Chapter 9.

9. Watch Your Timing

Time your plantings of particular vegetables to avoid peak insect buildups. In some areas, flea beetles destroy radishes, turnips, and similar crops planted in mid-May. If they're planted after June 15, however, they will suffer little damage since the adult (beetle) stage has passed.

In the United States the corn earworm overwinters only in the South and gradually moves north during the growing season. If corn is planted at the earliest possible date, most of it may mature in these areas before the corn earworm becomes severe. Table 2–2, with Figure 2–1, gives peak times in your area for a number of common insects.

Your county agricultural extension agent (found in the telephone-book white pages) can also help. Simply call and ask for advice about when you should plant your vegetables to avoid peak infestations. The agent will be able to tell you of special conditions that exist in your area.

10. Let Other Plants Help

The clever gardener selects plants that attract or repel insect pests. Some, called *trap crops*, attract insects to divert them away from the main crop. Yellow nasturtiums, for instance, attract black aphids away from beans and tomatoes.

Certain other plants repel pests because of inherent chemical compounds that are either obnoxious or toxic to insects. Both the French and African marigold excrete compounds (a-tertihenyl type) that are toxic to nematodes. When grown in soil infested with nematodes, they reduce the nematode population and the severity of any attack.

Some gardeners swear that *companion planting* to control insects works wonders in their gardens. Experiment-station tests, however, still leave the question unresolved. By all means, try this approach in your garden. If it works, you're way ahead; if it doesn't, you have planted some extremely useful herbs and some beautiful flowers. See Table 2–3 for plant insect controls.

11. Give Your Vegetables Elbow Room

Individual vegetables compete with each other for water, nutrients, and growing space. Each vegetable has its own optimum spacing. Cabbages spaced 18 to 24 inches apart produce heads larger than those spaced 12 inches apart. Studies show that cucumbers spaced 12 inches apart produce greater yields than those spaced either 6 or 18 inches apart. Vegetables planted directly in the seedbed (rather than being transplanted) must be thinned out to allow growing room. Unthinned vegetables are frequently small and spindly—carrots twist around each other; radishes won't form bulbs; lettuce won't head—and these weakened plants are more susceptible to insect and disease. Table 2 – 4 provides information about the optimum spacing of all vegetables.

12. Fertilize Regularly

Apply a commercial fertilizer before planting vegetables. Good ones are labeled 10 – 10 – 10 (10 percent nitrogen, 10 percent phosphorus, 10 percent potash), 6 – 10 – 4 (6 percent nitrogen, 10 percent phosphorus, 4 percent potash), or 5 – 10 – 5 (5 percent nitrogen, 10 percent phosphorus, 5 percent potash). Leafy vegetables such as broccoli, cabbage, lettuce, kale, and spinach do well with a high-nitrogen fertilizer. Root crops (beets, carrots, parsnips, turnips, radishes, and potatoes) respond to large quantities of both nitrogen and potash potassium. Beans, melons, onions, celery, and tomatoes require large quantities of nitrogen, phosphorus, and potash.

You can achieve the same effect by spreading horse manure 4 to 6 inches deep on the bed and then spading it into the first 8 to 12 inches of soil. Add bonemeal (4 pounds per 100 square feet) and wood ash or rock phosphate (3 pounds per 100 square feet).

Healthy, well-fertilized plants are less susceptible to disease and insect attack than those growing in soil lacking the required nutrients.

13. Remove Those Weeds

Even if it means a substantial effort, it's worth it to get rid of all weeds in and around the garden. Weeds harbor insects, serve as a host for diseases, and reduce air movement and sunlight, creating conditions conducive to disease development. Weeds also compete directly with vegetables for water, nutrients, light, and space. Studies at Cornell have shown that weeds growing in vegetable plots can cut vegetable production by a whopping 2000 percent.

Control weeds within the garden plot by cultivation (scraping the ground) with a hoe blade nearly parallel to the soil surface and within an inch of the top. This method will keep you from injuring vegetable roots that lie near the soil surface. It isn't necessary to be so careful when removing weeds outside the vegetable beds.

You can also control weeds with a black polyethylene mulch or an organic mulch (see Chapter 4). Organic mulch should be applied 4 to 6 inches deep so that weeds cannot peek through.

Some home gardeners use weed killers, called herbicides. *Nonselective weed killers,* which destroy all vegetation, are useful for clearing weeds off a vacant lot, but should not be used in any area where you intend to grow vegetables within the next year or two.

Selective herbicides will kill weeds without harming particular vegetables. Dacthal W-75, for instance, can be used with about 26 different garden crops (see Table 2 – 5). Unfortunately, no one herbicide can be used safely on all vegetable crops. These herbicides must also be applied at the proper rate and at the right time. Some garden experts recommend selective herbicides for home gardens; others feel they are too difficult to use. I personally never use anything but a hoe to weed my garden. You, however, might like to experiment with Dacthal in your garden to see if it works for you. People at your local nursery will be able to give you more specific advice for your area.

14. Watch That Overhead Watering

Water in the early morning so that the leaves dry quickly, or avoid overhead watering altogether. Late-afternoon and evening watering means that the leaves will remain moist for longer periods of time. Because spores of disease-producing fungi need moisture to germinate, water on the leaves provides favorable conditions for the rapid development of fungus leaf spot, downy and powdery mildew, rust, and other foliage diseases.

15. Plan Ahead

Prevention may take some effort and planning, but in the long run many gardeners find that it is all they need to do to keep their vegetables relatively free of both insects and diseases season after season. What I recommend is planning a yearly prevention program ahead of time. For example, cleanup should take place during the gardening season and immediately following the harvest. Deep spading to control larvae and pupae should be handled in early Spring. Crop rotation should be planned several seasons ahead. Other chores for your garden should be handled at the appropriate time. By marking all preventive chores on a calendar, you will give yourself a visual reminder of exactly what you must do each month and you will be able to spread out the work over the garden year (see Table 2 – 6).

In the next chapter we'll tackle the soil and nutrient problems that can be prevented or cured by a few expeditious steps.

TABLE 2 – 1   SOME RESISTANT VEGETABLE VARIETIES

VEGETABLE	DISEASE	RESISTANT VEGETABLE VARIETIES
Asparagus	Fusarium wilt	Mary Washington
Beans	Blight	The following varieties are resistant to one or more blights: Blue Lake strains, Columbia pinto, Cornell 14, Fullgreen, Furore, Great Northern strains, Kentucky Wonder, Seminole, Starland Wax, USO1140 Tendergreen, Tenderlong
	Anthracnose	Black Seeded Blue Lake, Charlevoix, Gartiot Great Northern strains, Low's Champion, Michelite, Monroe, Montclam, Perry Marrow, Saginaw, Sanilac, Seaway, Seaway 65, Tennessee Green Pod, White Kidney
	Curlytop	Resistant or tolerant varieties: Burtner's Blightless, Columbia Pinto, Earligreen, Earliwax, Golden Gem, Great Northern strains, Idaho Bountiful, Idelight, Improved Golden Wax, Improved Topnotch, Jenkins, Kentucky Wonder Wax, McCaslan, Mountaineer, Pioneer, Puregold, Slendergreen, Slimgreen, Stringless Green Pod, Tendergreen, Yakima Lima beans resistant to mosaic: Burpee Best, Burpee Improved, Carpenteria, Challenger, Detroit Mammoth, Dreer Bush, Dwarf Large White, Early Jersey, Fordhook, King of the Garden, Leviathan, McCrea, New Wonder, Seibert

TABLE 2 – 1   SOME RESISTANT VEGETABLE VARIETIES *(continued)*

VEGETABLE	DISEASE	RESISTANT VEGETABLE VARIETIES
	Powdery mildew	Contender, Dixie Belle, Early Contender, Extender, Flight, Fullgreen, Idaho Refugee, Ideal Market, Kidney Wax, Lady Washington, Provider, Ranger, Round Pod, Seminole, Stringless Green Refugee, Striped Hope, Tenderlong 15, Topcrop, Wade Lima beans: Bridgeton, Thaxter
	Root-knot nematodes	Resistant bean varieties: Alabama Pole No. 1 and 2, Blackeye No. 5, Spartan, State Lima beans: Bixby, Nemagreen, Nemagreen Bush, Westan
	Rust	Bean varieties resistant or tolerant to one or more rust races: Black Wax, Boringquen, Criolla, Dade, Extender, Florigreen, Golden Gate Wax, Golden "No Wilt", Great Northern 1140, Golden Wax, Green Pod, Green Savage, Harvester, Kentucky Wonder strains, Landreth Stringless Lima beans resistant to mosaic: Burpee Best, Burpee Improved, Carpenteria, Challenger, Detroit Mammoth, Dreer's Bush, Dwarf Large White, Early Jersey, Fordhook, King of the Garden, Leviathan, McCrea, New Wonder, Seibert
	Powdery mildew	Contender, Dixie Belle, Early Contender, Extender, Flight, Fullgreen, Idaho Refugee, Ideal Market, Kidney Wax, Lady Washington, Provider, Ranger, Round Pod, Seminole, Stringless Green Refugee, Striped Hope, Tenderlong 15, Topcrop, Wade Lima beans: Bridgeton, Thaxter
Beets	Curlytop	Gardener's Model
	Downy mildew	Detroit Dark Red, Green Top Bunching
Broccoli	Downy mildew	Emperor
	Yellows	Calabrese, DiCicco, Early Green Sprouting, Grand Central, Midway, Waltham 29
Cabbage	Clubroot	Varieties resistant to two or more clubroot varieties: Badger Shipper, Bindsachsener, Bohmerwald

TABLE 2 – 1 **SOME RESISTANT VEGETABLE VARIETIES** *(continued)*

VEGETABLE	DISEASE	RESISTANT VEGETABLE VARIETIES
	Yellows	Allhead Select, Badger Gallhead, Badger Market, Badger Shipper, Badger Blue Boy, Bugner, Charleston Wakefield, Copenhagen Resistant, Early Jersey Wakefield, Empire Danish, Globe 62-M, Glory 61, Golden Acre Y.R., Hybrid 15, Hybrid No. 5 Plus, Improved Wisconsin All Seasons, Little Rock, Polaris, Princess, Prizemaker, Racine Market, Red Hollander, Resistant Golden Acre, TBR Globe 62-M, Titanic, Wisconsin Hollander No. 8, Wisconsin Pride
Cauliflower	Black rot	White Contessa
	Yellows	Early Snowball
	Downy mildew	White Contessa
Celery	Blackheart	Cornell 19, Emerald, Emerson, Florida Golden, Golden Pascal, Golden Phenomenal, Salt Lake, Winter Queen
	Blight	Green Giant, Summer Pascal
	Fusarium wilt	Cornell 16 – 19, Easy Blanching, Emerson Pascal, Florida, Giant Pascal, Golden Michigan State, Green Gold, Golden 99, Golden Pascal, Kilgore's Pride, Masterpiece, Michigan Improved, Pascal 284, Supreme Golden, Tall Golden Plume, Woodruff's Beauty Green celeries are generally resistant
	Mosaic	Green Giant
Corn	Bacterial wilt (Stewart's disease)	Somewhat resistant varieties: Aristogold Bantam, Atlas, Barbecue, Bellringer, Bi Queen, Calumet, Carmelcross, Comet, Country Gentleman, Erie, Evergreen Hybrid, Gold Crest, Gold Rush, Golden Bantam, Golden Beauty, Golden Cross Bantam, Golden Cross W-R, Golden Fancy, Golden Harvest, Golden Jewel, Golden Pirate, Golden Security, Honeycross, Hoosier Gold, Huron, Ioana, Iochief, Iogold, Marcross, Merit, Midway, NK 75, North Star, Northern Cross, Queen Anne, Seneca Chief, Seneca Dawn, Seneca Market, Seneca Scout, Silver Cross Bantam, Spancross, Tendermost, Titan, Whipcross, White Cross Bantam, White Jewel, Wintergarden, Wintergreen
	Helminthosporium leaf blights	Resistant or tolerant varieties: Florida Staysweet, Florigold 107, Gold Cup G, Seneca Wampum, Wintergarden, Wintergreen Popcorn: Ladyfinger
	Rust	Country Gentleman, Crosby

TABLE 2 – 1   SOME RESISTANT VEGETABLE VARIETIES *(continued)*

VEGETABLE	DISEASE	RESISTANT VEGETABLE VARIETIES
	Smut	Partially resistant varieties: Aristogold, Asgrow Golden 60, Bantam Evergreen, Burpee's Honeycross, Country Gentleman, Evertender, Giant Bantam Hybrid, Golden Cross Bantam, Ioana, Iochief, Mellogold, Pennlewis, Prospector, Seneca Brave, Tenderblonde, Victory Golden
Cucumbers	Anthracnose	Resistant or tolerant varieties to one or more races: Addis, Ashe, Calypso, Carolina, Cherokee, Chipper, Dasher, Explorer, Fletcher, Galaxy, Gemini, Gemini 7, Palmetto, Perfecto Verde, Pixie, Poinsett 76, Polaris, Santee, Slicemaster, Southern Cross, Spartan Valor, Stono, Sugar Slice, Sumter, Sweet Slice, Trispear, Wisconsin SMR 18
	Bacterial wilt	Chicago Pickling, Saladin Hybrid Pickler
	Downy mildew	Ashe, Ashley, Barclay, Burpee Hybrid, Challenger, Cherokee 7, Dark Green Slicer, Dasher, Early Marketer, Early Surecrop, Empress Hybrid, Fletcher, Gemini 7, Liberty, Marketmore 76, Medalist, Palmetto, Palomar, Pixie, Polaris, Saticoy, Sensation, Stono, Supermarket, Surecrop, Tasty Green, Total Marketer, Triumph, Victory, Wescan
	Mosaic	Armour, Atlantic Slicer, Burpee Hybrid, Burpee M & M Hybrid, Challenger, Crispy, Dasher, Early Marketer, Early Surecrop, Empress Hybrid, High Mark 11, Hybrid Long Green, Jet, Liberty, Medalist, Nappa 61, Raider, Saladin Hybrid Pickler, Saticoy, Sensation, Shamrock, Spartan Dawn, Spartangreen, Streamliner, Surecrop, Tablegreen, Total Marketer, Triumph, Vaughan's Hybrid, Victory, Wisconsin SMR-12, Yorkstate
	Powdery mildew	Resistant or tolerant varieties: Ashe, Ashley, Cherokee 7, Dasher, Fletcher, Gemini 7, High Mark 11, Marketmore 76, Medalist, Palmetto, Pixie, Poinsett 76, Polaris, Saladin Hybrid Pickler, Stono, Victory, Yates Conqueror, Yates Invader
	Scab	Armour, Ashe, Crispy, Dark Green Slicer, Dasher, Empress Hybrid, Fletcher, Gemini 7, Highmoor, Hybrid Long Green Pickle, Improved Highmoor, Improved Hycrop Pickling, Maine No. 2, Medalist, Poinsett 76, Princess, Raider, Spartan, Spartan Dawn, Spartan Green, 27 Spartan Champion, Victory, Windermoor, Wisconsin SMR-12
Kale	Yellows	Siberian kale
	Black rot	Dwarf Siberian

TABLE 2–1   **SOME RESISTANT VEGETABLE VARIETIES** (*continued*)

VEGETABLE	DISEASE	RESISTANT VEGETABLE VARIETIES
Lettuce	Downy mildew	Artic King, Bath Cos, Big Boston, Calmar, Grand Rapids strains, Imperial strains, Salad Bowl Tania, Valmaine Cos, Valverde
	Bottom rot	Great Lakes 6238, King Crown, White Boston
	Lettuce big vein	Calmar, Caravan, Merit
	Mosaic	Parris Island, Valmaine Cos
	Tip burn	Alaska, Cornell 456, Fairton, Grand Rapids, Great Lakes strains, Great Lakes 6238, Green Lake, Hanson, Ithaca, Kagran Summer, King Crown, Oswego, Premier Great Lakes, White Boston
Melons	Anthracnose	Watermelons: Allsweet, Black Kleckley, Blackstone, Charleston Gray, Chris Cross, Congo, Crimson Sweet, Dunbarton, Early Resistant Queen, Fairfax, Garrison, Garrisonian, Graybelle, Hope Diamond, Improved Tri × 313, Jubilee, Royal Charleston, Spalding, Super Sweet, Top Yield
	Bacterial wilt	Muskmelon: Queen of Colorado
	Fusarium wilt	Muskmelons: Ball 1776, Campo, Canada Gem, Cantaloup Ido, Chaca, Chaca No. 1, Classic Hybrid, Delicious 51, Earli-Dew, Earlisweet Hybrid, Early Dawn, Gold Star, Harper Hybrid, Harvest Queen, Honey Rock, Iroquois, Luscious, Mainrock, Minnesota Honey, Minnesota Hybrid, Resistant Joy, Roadside, Samson, Saticoy, Super Hybrid Muskmelon, Vedrantais Watermelons: Allsweet, Calhoun Gray, Charleston Gray No. 5, Crimson Sweet, Dixie Queen, Family Fun Hybrid, Faribo Black Giant Hybrid, Graybelle, Iopride, Jubilee, Peacock Improved, Peerless, Prince Charles, Redcrisp, Royal Charleston, Special Jubilee, Summit, Super Sweet, Top Yield, Wilhite's Tendergold
	Downy mildew	Muskmelons: Ball 1776, Campo, Dessert Sun, Dixie Jumbo, Early Market, Edisto, Edisto 47, Eureka, Florida No. 1, Floridew, Florigold, Florisum, Georgia 47, Golden Model, Golden Perfection, Granite State, Homegarden, Jacumba, Mainstream, Perlita, Planters Jumbo, Rio Gold, Rio Sweet, Seminole, Super Market, Texas Resistant No. 1, Topmark 27–36SR, Topscore
	Mosaic	Watermelons: Harper, Saticoy

TABLE 2 – 1   SOME RESISTANT VEGETABLE VARIETIES (continued)

VEGETABLE	DISEASE	RESISTANT VEGETABLE VARIETIES
	Powdery mildew	Muskmelons: Ambrosia, Campo, Canada Gem, Chaca, Chaca No. 1, Classic Hybrid, Dessert Sun, Dixie Jumbo, Early Dawn, Edisto, Edisto 47, Eureka, Florida No. 1, Floridew, Florigold, Florisun Four-Fifty, Georgia 47, Gold Cup, Golden Gate 45, Golden Perfection, Homegarden, Honey Ball 306, Imperial 45, Iroquois, Jacumba, Kangold, Luscious, Mainstream, Perlita, Planters Jumbo, Powdery Mildew Resistant No. 45, Rio Gold, Rio Sweet, Roadside, Sampson, Saticoy, Seminole, Short 'N Sweet, Sierra Gold, Smith's Perfect, Sweet 'N Early, Topscore
	Rust	Muskmelons: Rocky Ford Green Flesh
	Scab	Muskmelons: Edisto 47
Mustard greens	Black rot	Florida Broadleaf
	Anthracnose	Southern Curled Giant
Onions	Downy mildew	Red onions have some resistance
	Fusarium root rot (pink root rot)	Asgrow Y2, Beltsville Bunching, Brilliance, Calred, Challenger, Early Crystal 281, Early Supreme, Eclipse, Evergreen Bunching, Excel, Golden, Granex, Henry's Special, Northern Oak, Red Grano, Spano, Texas Early Yellow Grano 302, Texas Hybrid 28, White Granex, White Grano, Yellow Bermuda, Yellow Creole, Yellow Sweet Spanish, Yellow Sweet Spanish Tucker Leeks and chives highly resistant Shallots: Louisiana Pearl, Evergreen
Peas	Fusarium wilt	Ace, Alaska, Alcross, Alderman, Alsweet No. 4683, Apex, Bridger, Bruce, Cascade, Climax, Dark Podded Thomas Laxton, Dark Skinned Perfection, Dwarf Alderman, Dwarf Gray Sugar, Early Perfection, Early Sweet Eureka, Extra Early, Famous, Freezonian, Frosty, Giant Stride, Glacier, Green Giant, Hardy, Horal, Hyalite, Icer, Improved Gradus, Jade, King, Laurel, Laxton 7, Little Marvel Lolo, Mammonth Melting Sugar, Midfreezer, Midway, Morse Market, New Era, New Season, New Wales, Nome, Oracle, Pacemaker, Pacific Market 40, Perfected Freezer, Perfected Wales, Pixie, Pride, Profusion, Progress No. 9, Ranger, Rainier, Resistant Surprise, Shasta, Shoshone, Signal, Signet, Small Late Canner, Small Sieve Freezer, Sprite, Stratagem, Surpass, Teton, Thomas Laxton strains, Victory Freezer, Viking, Wando, Wasatch, Wisconsin Early Sweet, Wisconsin Merit, Wisconsin Perfection, Wyola, Wyoming Wonder, Yukon

TABLE 2 – 1   **SOME RESISTANT VEGETABLE VARIETIES** *(continued)*

VEGETABLE	DISEASE	RESISTANT VEGETABLE VARIETIES
	Root rot	Acquisition, Freezonian, Green Admiral, Horal, Premier, Selkirt, Sutton's Ideal, Wando, World's Record
Pepper	Fusarium wilt	College No. 6, Mexican Chili No. 9
	Root knot	Anaheim Chili, Bush Red, Cayenne, Italian Pickling, Nemaheart, Santaka
	Tobacco mosaic	Allbig, Bell Boy, Big Bertha, Burlington, Calcom, Caldel, California Wonder PS, California Wonder 300, Delaware Bell, Delbell, Early Canada Bell, Early Wonder, Emerald Keystone Resistant Giant, Fresno Chili, Gypsy, Liberty Bell, Long Thin Cayenne, Merced, Midway, Pacific Bell, Paul's World Beater, Resistant Giant No. 4, Titan, Valley Giant Hybrid, Yolo Wonder, Yolo Wonder A, Yolo Wonder B, Yolo Wonder 43, Yolo Wonder L
Potato	Blackleg	Hunter
	Common scab	Anoka, Antigo, Arenac, Avon, Blanca, Catoosa, Cayuga, Cherokee, Chieftan, Early Gem, Emmet, Haig, Huron, Knik, LaRouge, Mayfair, Menominee, Navajo, Netted Gem, Norgold Russet, Norland, Ona, Onaway, Ontario, Osage, Pennchip, Plymouth, Progress, Pungo, Redkote, Redskin, Reliance, Russet Burbank, Russet Rural, Seneca, Soshoni, Superior, Tawa, Viking, Yampa
	Hollow heart	Manota
	Late blight	Ashworth, Avon, Blanca, Boone, Calrose, Canso, Catoosa, Cayuga, Chenago, Cherokee, Cortland, Delus, Empire, Essex, Fillmore, Fundy, Glenmeer, Harford, Hunter, Kennebec, Keswick, Madison, Menominee, Merrimack, Ona, Onaway, Ontario, Placid, Pennchip, Plymouth, Potomac, Pungo, Reliance, Russet Sebago, Saco, Saranac, Sebago, Seneca, Sequoia, Snowdrift, Tawa, Virgil
	Mosaic	Chieftain
Radish	Yellows	Fancy Red, Red Prince
Spinach	Downy mildew	Badger Savoy, Califlay, Chesapeake, Dixie Market, Dixie Savoy, Hybrid 425, Marathon, Resistoflay, Salma, Savoy Supreme, Viking, Viroflay 99, Wisconsin Bloomsdale
	Spinach blight	Badger Savoy, Basra, Chesapeake, Dixie Market, Dixie Savoy, Domino, Old Diminion, Salma, Virginia Blight Resistant, Winter Bloomsdale

TABLE 2–1 SOME RESISTANT VEGETABLE VARIETIES *(continued)*

VEGETABLE	DISEASE	RESISTANT VEGETABLE VARIETIES
Squash	Bacterial wilt	Boston Marrow, Buttercup, Butternut, Delicious, Early Market, Table Queen, Warren
Sweet Potato	Black rot	Norin No. 1, Allgold, Sunnyside
	Fusarium wilt	Allgold, Coppergold, Dahomey, Dooley, Gem, Goldrush, Key West, Nugget, Pumpkin, Red Brazil, Southern Green, Timian, Triumph, White Yam, Yellow Strasburg
	Interal cork	Allgold, Earlyport, Gem, Golden Skin, Jersey Orange, Maryland Golden Sweet, Nancy Gold, Nancy Hall, Nemagold, Nugget, Oklahoma 2, Pelican Processor, Ranger, Red Nancy Hall, Redgold, Yellow Jersey; Tanhoma is tolerant

PEAK INSECT TIMES

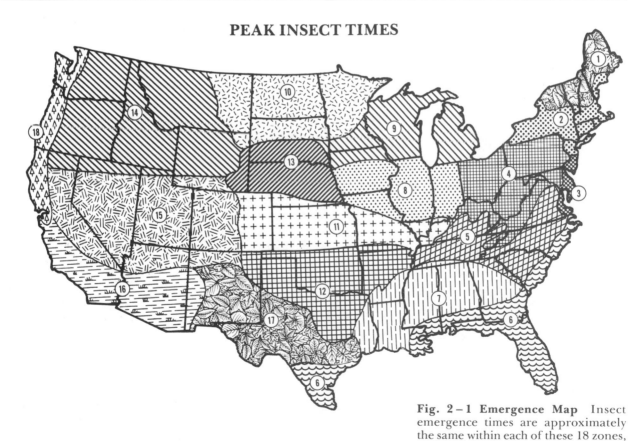

Fig. 2–1 Emergence Map Insect emergence times are approximately the same within each of these 18 zones, although emergence times will vary with the altitude. Find your zone and then consult the insect charts in Table 2–2

TABLE 2 – 2   **PEAK INSECT TIMES**

REGION	ASPARAGUS BEETLE	BEAN APHID	CABBAGE LOOPER	COLORADO POTATO BEETLE
1	Mid-June	NA	July	June
2	May	NA	June – July	May
3	Late April – May	NA	July – September	May
4	Early May	Early June	June	Early May
5	April – May	May – June	Late April – May	May
6	NA	October – May	Entire season	March – May
7	NA	March	Early March	NA
8	May	Spring	Spring	April – May
9	May	June	August	May – June
10	May – June	NA	July	June
11	April – May	NA	Spring	April – May
12	March – April	NA	Year round	NA
13	Mid-June	NA	May	June
14	Late May – June	June – August	June – September	Late June
15	May – June	June – August	May – September	Mid June
16	NA	Spring—Fall	September – October	NA
17	NA	Spring—Fall	August – October	NA
18	April – June	May – July	April – May	April – June

NA = not applicable

TABLE 2 – 2   **PEAK INSECT TIMES**   *(continued)*

REGION	CORN EARWORM	FLEA BEETLE	MEXICAN BEAN BEETLE	SPOTTED CUCUMBER BEETLE
1	July	June	Early June	Mid-June
2	August	May – June	June	Mid-June
3	June – August	April – May	May	May – June
4	July – September	Early May	June	June
5	June	April – July	May	May
6	Spring – Fall	April – August	NA	Entire season
7	June – mid-July	March – April	NA	NA
8	Spring	Late May	March – June	Spring
9	Late July – August	May – June	NA	May – August
10	July – August	NA	NA	June
11	June – September	April – May	NA	May

TABLE 2 – 2   **PEAK INSECT TIMES**   *(continued)*

REGION	CORN EARWORM	FLEA BEETLE	MEXICAN BEAN BEETLE	SPOTTED CUCUMBER BEETLE
12	May – early June	April – August	NA	NA
13	July	June	NA	May
14	Late July	June – July	June – July	NA
15	July	June	May – July	NA
16	NA	NA	NA	NA
17	NA	NA	NA	NA
18	June – July	Late May – June	NA	NA

NA = not applicable

TABLE 2 – 2   **PEAK INSECT TIMES**   *(continued)*

REGION	PEA APHID	SQUASH BUG	SQUASH VINE BORER	STRIPED CUCUMBER BEETLE
1	June	NA	NA	June
2	April	June	June – July	June
3	April	May – June	May – June	Late May – June
4	April	June	June	June
5	May	May	Late June – July	May
6	Entire season	March – August	August – October	NA
7	March	June	June – July	NA
8	May – June	June	Entire season	May
9	April – May	NA	NA	NA
10	May – June	NA	June – July	NA
11	April	June – August	July	NA
12	March – April	May – June	Late May – June	NA
13	May	Late Spring	June	NA
14	May – September	August – September	NA	NA
15	May – September	July – August	NA	NA
16	NA	NA	NA	NA
17	NA	NA	NA	NA
18	May – June	April – May	NA	NA

NA = not applicable

TABLE 2–3   PLANT INSECT PREVENTION

INSECT	REPELLENT PLANT
Ants	Pennyroyal, spearmint, tansy
Aphids	Garlic, nettles, nasturtiums, southernwood, spearmint, stinging nettles
Asparagus beetles	Tomatoes
Cabbage maggots	Hemp, tomatoes
Carrot flies	Leeks, onions, rosemary
Colorado potato beetles	Eggplant, flax, green beans
Cucumber beetles	Radishes, summer savory, tansy
Cutworms	Oak leaf mulch
Flea beetles	Head lettuce, mint, wormwood
Mexican bean beetles	Potatoes, rosemary, summer savory
Nematodes	African and French marigolds
Potato bugs	Horseradish planted at the corners of the potato patch
Squash bugs	Nasturtiums, tansy
White cabbage butterflies	Celery, hyssop, mint, sage, thyme, tomatoes, wormwood, rosemary
Whiteflies	Nasturtiums

TABLE 2–4   VEGETABLE PLANTING GUIDE

VEGETABLE	DEPTH TO PLANT SEED (INCHES)	DISTANCE BETWEEN PLANTS (INCHES)	DISTANCE BETWEEN ROWS (INCHES)
Artichokes	root divisions[a]	60	72
Asparagus	1½[b]	18	36
Beans (snap, bush)	1½–2[c]	2–3	18–30
Beans (snap, pole)	1½–2[c]	4–6	36–48
Beans (lima, bush)	1½–2[c]	3–6	24–30
Beans (lima, pole)	1½–2[c]	6–10	30–36
Beans (fava-broadbean)	2½[c]	3–4	18–24
Beans (garbanzo-chick pea)	1½–2[c]	3–4	24–30
Beans (scarlet runner)	1½–2[c]	4–6	36–48
Beans (soybean)	1½–2[c]	2–3	24–30
Beets	½–1[d]	2	12–18

TABLE 2–4   **VEGETABLE PLANTING GUIDE** *(continued)*

VEGETABLE	DEPTH TO PLANT SEED (INCHES)	DISTANCE BETWEEN PLANTS (INCHES)	DISTANCE BETWEEN ROWS (INCHES)
Black-eye cowpeas (southern peas)	½ – 1[c]	3 – 4	24 – 30
Yardlong beans (asparagus beans)	½ – 1[c]	12 – 24	24 – 36
Broccoli	½[b]	14 – 18	24 – 30
Brussels sprouts	½[b]	12 – 18	24 – 30
Cabbage	½[b]	12 – 20	24 – 30
Cabbage (Chinese)	½[c]	10 – 12	18 – 24
Cardoon	½[b]	18	36
Carrots	¼[d]	1 – 2	14 – 24
Cauliflower	½[b]	18	30 – 36
Celeriac	⅛[b]	8	24 – 30
Celery	⅛[b]	8	24 – 30
Chard (Swiss)	1[d]	4 – 8	18 – 24
Collards	¼[c]	10 – 15	24 – 30
Corn (sweet)	2[c]	10 – 14	30 – 36
Cucumbers	1[c]	12	48 – 72
Eggplant	¼ – ½[b]	18	36
Endive	½[c]	9 – 12	12 – 24
Fennel (Florence)	½[b]	6	18 – 24
Garlic	cloves	2 – 4	12 – 18
Horseradish	root cuttings	10 – 18	24
Kale	½[c]	8 – 12	18 – 24
Kohlrabi	½[c]	3 – 4	18 – 24
Leeks	½ – 1[c]	2 – 4	12 – 18
Lettuce (head)	¼ – ½[c]	12 – 14	18 – 24
(leaf)	¼ – ½[c]	4 – 6	12 – 18
Muskmelons	1[c]	12	48 – 72
Mustard greens	½[c]	2 – 6	12 – 18
Okra	1[d]	15 – 18	28 – 36

[a]Start from root cuttings, slips, crowns or tubers.   [c]Transplant or direct seed.
[b]Transplant seedlings into the garden.   [d]Sow seed directly into the garden.

TABLE 2–4   **VEGETABLE PLANTING GUIDE** *(continued)*

VEGETABLE	DEPTH TO PLANT SEED (INCHES)	DISTANCE BETWEEN PLANTS (INCHES)	DISTANCE BETWEEN ROWS (INCHES)
Onions (sets)	1 – 2	2 – 3	12 – 24
(plants)	2 – 3	2 – 3	12 – 24
(seeds)	½	2 – 3	12 – 24
Parsley	¼ – ½ d	3 – 6	12 – 20
Parsnips	½ d	3 – 4	16 – 24
Peas	2 c	2 – 3	18 – 30
Peppers	¼ b	18 – 24	24 – 36
Potatoes	4 a,d	12	24 – 36
Pumpkins	1 – 1½ c	30	72 – 120
Purslane	½ d	6	12
Radishes	½ d	1 – 2	6 – 12
Rhubarb	root crowns	36	60
Rutabagas	½ d	8 – 12	18 – 24
Salsify	½ d	2 – 3	16 – 18
Shallots	Bulb — 1	2 – 4	12 – 18
Spinach	½ d	2 – 4	12 – 14
(malabar)	½ d	12	12
(New Zealand)	1½ c	18	24
(tampala)	¼ – ½ d	4 – 6	24 – 30
Squash (Summer)	1 c	16 – 24	36 – 60
(Winter)	1 c	24 – 48	72 – 120
Sweet Potatoes	Plants-slips	12 – 18	36 – 48
Tomatoes	½ b	18 – 36	36 – 60
Turnips	½ d	1 – 3	15 – 18
Watermelons	1 c	12 – 16	60

[a]Start from root cuttings, slips, crowns or tubers.   [c]Transplant or direct seed.
[b]Transplant seedlings into the garden.   [d]Sow seed directly into the garden.

TABLE 2–5   DACTHAL W-75 WEED CONTROL CHART

Dacthal W-75 controls weeds as their seeds germinate. Before applying Dacthal W-75, the soil must be raked or cultivated to remove existing weeds and to provide a uniform soil surface. Dacthal W-75 can be used on the vegetables listed below.

VEGETABLES	WHEN TO APPLY
Broccoli, Brussels sprouts, cabbage, cauliflower, collards, garlic, kale, mustard greens, onions, potatoes, turnips	Apply at time of seeding or transplanting
Dry beans, snap beans, southern peas	Apply at time of seeding; do not feed plant refuse to animals
Cucumbers, eggplant, honeydew melons, peppers, squash, tomatoes, watermelons	Apply 4 to 6 weeks after seeding or transplanting and only when plants are well established and growing conditions are favorable for good plant growth; if applied earlier, crop injury may result
Sweet potatoes	Apply at time of transplanting; delayed application can be made up to 6 weeks after planting

TABLE 2–6   PREVENTION CALENDAR

WHEN TO HANDLE	STEPS TO TAKE
Before planting	Choose the right site.
	Cut down or remove weeds outside the garden.
	Deep spade the garden.
	Fertilize before planting.
	Mulch with black plastic.
	Plan for crop rotation.
	Plan planting times to avoid peak insect infestations.
	Buy certified disease-free seed or treat your own seeds with fungicide.
	Buy healthy transplants.
	Select resistant varieties.

TABLE 2–6   **PREVENTION CALENDAR** *(continued)*

WHEN TO HANDLE	STEPS TO TAKE
At planting time	Companion plant.
	Give the vegetables proper spacing.
	Plant several different vegetables in a single row.
	Plant at proper time to avoid peak insect infestation.
	Plant resistant varieties.
	Rotate crops.
	Use selective herbicides as weed killers.
During growing season	Clean up garden trash on a regular basis.
	Immediately destroy infected plants or plant parts.
	Weed regularly.
	Smokers, wash hands.
	Stay out of garden during wet weather.
	Use selective herbicides as weed killers.
	Water early in the morning.
At or after harvest	Clean up garden trash.
	Clean up plant debris, dead fruit.
	Destroy infected plants or plant parts.

CHAPTER THREE

THE CARE AND FEEDING
OF YOUR GARDEN SOIL

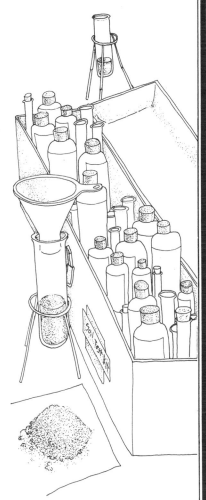

To a nongardener, soil is the subject of TV laundry detergent ads: it's the stuff you sweep out of the house or wash off your face. To a gardener, a real gardener, what those folks are talking about is dirt.

Soil, on the other hand, is the good earth that you plant in and helps create super crops. Bad soil just means problems: stunted plants, yellowing leaves, burned leaf margins, and worse. In this chapter I will discuss first the kind of soil you want and then the soil and nutrition problems you might run into in your garden, how to spot them, and what to do about them.

THE PERFECT SOIL

I haven't yet met a gardener who doesn't dream about having perfect soil—crumbly, well-aerated, sweet-smelling stuff that will grow 10-foot-high corn, elephant-sized watermelons, lip-smacking tomatoes, and other luscious vegetables.

Technically, the perfect garden soil contains 50 percent solid matter and 50 percent pore space. Moisture occupies about half the pore spaces, soil air the other half. Of the solid matter, roughly 45 percent should be mineral matter, 5 percent organic. The water in this soil carries the dissolved nutrients easily to the roots, and the air in the soil provides a constant supply of oxygen while at the same time carrying off carbon dioxide. It also contains all the nutrients necessary to make your plants healthy. More about that later.

BECOME A SOIL DETECTIVE

Most garden soils, however, are far from perfect, and yet many gardeners plant without making any improvements. Then they wonder why their vegetables are far from ideal.

I know someone I call "the something for nothing" gardener. On the first balmy day of Spring when the birds are singing up a storm, he rakes the topsoil a little, plants a few vegetable seeds, and then sits back and waits for the harvest. Six to eight weeks later he calls demanding to know what strange disease has stunted his vegetables and turned the leaves yellow. I always explain that his soil is mostly clay and won't grow much of a crop until he takes the time to improve it.

This advice always goes in one ear and out the other. By next Spring he's back demanding that I look at his garden again. Whatever advice I gave him last year didn't seem to work, he says. The fact is, of course, that most backyard soils are going to need a little help. If you look in your own garden, this is what you're liable to find.

Clay Soil

Clay soil is composed of fine, tiny, flat, waferlike particles that fit together tightly and take in water slowly. Chemically, clay is chiefly silicon and aluminum, with small amounts of sodium, magnesium, iron, calcium, and potassium. When you sprinkle a clay bed, the water runs off instead of sinking in to nourish the roots. If the clay particles do absorb moisture, they hold it so tightly that it's impossible for your plants to use much of it. When it's rubbed between the fingers, wet clay soil feels smooth, soft, and slippery.

When clay dries, it often has the consistency of a brick. The particles are so close together that there isn't any space for air to penetrate, and plant roots have extreme difficulty forcing their way down. Plants grown in untreated clay soil are often stunted and have pale green or yellow leaves.

Sandy Soil

Sandy soil is at the opposite end of the scale. It is lighter than clay but has particles 25 times larger. While sand is easy to dig in, it has almost no capacity to store water, which moves freely through the soil and quickly leaches out the nutrients. Sandy soils warm up faster than clay soils and reflect a considerable amount of heat. Most sandy soils, however, contain enough clay and silt to retain some water and nutrients.

Sandy soil rubbed between the fingers feels grainy and gritty; gravelly soils are self-evident. Plants grown in sandy or gravelly soils frequently have yellow or pale green leaves.

Silt

Silt falls somewhere between clay and sand. It consists of medium-sized gritty particles that pack down hard almost like clay and is usually not very fertile. If a silt topsoil is found over a layer of heavy clay, the plants are often stunted because the clay layer traps and holds water. Silty soil rubbed between the fingers feels a bit slippery and has a grainy texture. Plants grown in silty soils often have pale green or yellow leaves.

Loam

Loam is the kind of soil every gardener wants, and although it isn't exactly the theoretical ideal described earlier, it's close enough to grow really great vegetables. Loam is crumbly granular soil that has close to an even balance of different-sized particles and a good supply of humus (decomposed organic material). A combination of root growth, worms, and bacteria gives the soil grains a good structure, enabling both adequate retention of water for growth and proper drainage. Similarly, air moves freely through this soil and roots find their proper depth. Technically, the U.S. Department of Agriculture considers loam to consist of:

Clay	7 to 27 percent
Silt	28 to 50 percent
Sand	20 to 45 percent

Plants grown in loam are usually vigorous, healthy, and green.

Deciding What You Have

In addition to the touch-and-feel tests for clay, sand, and silt, you can take your own soil sample and then conduct a quart-jar test that will give some pretty sophisticated results.

To take a soil sample, do the following (see Figure 3 – 1):

1   Select 8 to 15 spots throughout the garden area. A zigzag pattern is best.
2   With a soil probe or garden spade, take a sample from each area, 8 inches deep.
3   Discard the top inch of surface.
4   Place the composites in a plastic bag and mix thoroughly.
5   Take one cup of the mixed soil and put it in a small plastic bag if you are shipping it to a lab, or select your soil from this mixture if you are making your own test.

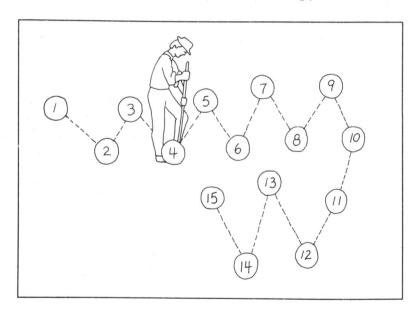

Fig. 3 – 1   Taking a Soil Sample

Here's how to make the soil text (see Figure 3 – 2):

1   Place a soil sample in a quart jar and fill the jar two-thirds full of water.
2   Shake well and let the contents settle for a few hours.
3   Examine the soil layers. Coarse sand and pebbles will be at the bottom, fine sand and silt next, and then clay, with the water at the top.

4   Take a ruler and, from the bottom of the jar, measure to the top of the clay layer. Determine the percentage of materials by dividing the height of each layer (in inches) — clay, silt and fine sand, pebbles and coarse sand — by the total height of the soil column.

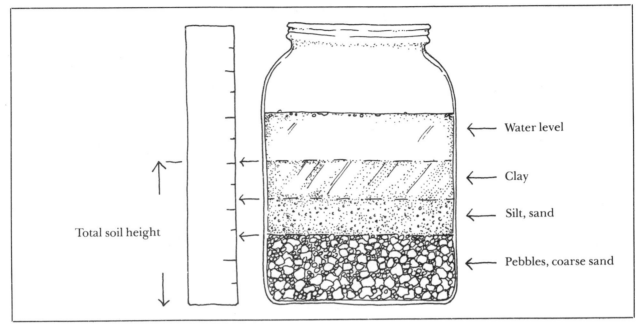

Fig. 3 – 2   Quart-Jar Soil Test

You can estimate the percentage of each material visually, but using a ruler will give more precise amounts. For example, if the total soil column measures 4 inches and there is a 1-inch clay layer, divide 4 into 1 to obtain the percentage of clay (.25, or 25 percent). When you have done this for all the layers, compare the results with the percentages for loam given earlier.

IMPROVING SOIL STRUCTURE

You can improve clay, silt, and sandy soils by adding massive amounts of organic material. I like to shovel a 6-to-8-inch layer of compost, ground bark, sawdust, leaf mold, manure, peat moss, or something similar over the top of the garden area and then spade or rototill it into the soil.

The organic particles in clay soil hold the compacted clay particles apart and act as a kind of glue to help hold the fine clay particles together in crumbs. This opens up the soil and allows air and water to circulate freely to give vegetables a fighting chance.

Adding fine-textured organic material to sandy soil fills the spaces between the grains and helps hold water both by stopping the flow and by absorbing some of it.

Heavy clay soils can also usually be improved by adding 40 to 50 pounds of gypsum (available at most nurseries) per 1000 square feet. The positive calcium ions in the gypsum neutralize the negative sodium ions in the clay and allow the clay particles to group together (flocculate) into bigger soil crumbs that make larger air spaces and permit good water and air penetration.

You may also discover one or two other structural impediments—rocky or shallow soil. I've seen soils so rocky that they can't be penetrated more than an inch or two with the tip of a shovel. If this is your problem, you'll have to bring in a foot or two of topsoil and garden in raised beds or pick out the rocks a few at a time with a spading fork. Neither solution is simple or fun.

Shallow soil is another problem. Sometimes there is an impenetrable layer a foot or so below the soil surface that holds water, creating a kind of swamp in which it's virtually impossible to grow vegetables. This condition can produce stunted plants with pale green or yellow leaves. This problem can sometimes be solved by punching holes in this layer with an auger to let the water drain out.

In order to facilitate the best possible vegetable growth, plenty of space straight down should be provided for the vegetable roots to penetrate into. And, believe me, some of them seem determined to try to reach China.

Tomato roots, for instance, often reach a depth of 10 feet or more; cabbage, 7 to 8 feet; and carrots, 5 feet. To provide for these root systems, you'd have to remove the impenetrable layers (what a job that would be!) and replace them with topsoil. Since most vegetables can get by in a depth of about 1 to 2 feet, however, gardeners with this kind of soil problem are best advised to avoid crops such as tomatoes, cabbage, and the like.

If you decide to go the raised-bed route, plant your garden in an 8-to-12-inch-high raised bed filled with equal parts loam, sand, and organic material (compost, rotted manure, and similar materials). These raised beds provide good drainage, give the roots a good growing medium, and warm up faster in the Spring than regular garden beds. Although raised beds don't allow for full root penetration, they nevertheless generally produce healthy, vigorous vegetable growth. (See my *Growing Vegetables the Big Yield/Small Space Way,* on the Recommended Reading list.)

ALKALINE OR ACID?

Tell gardeners that their soil is too acid or too alkaline and they will nod knowingly. Tell them that their soil has a pH of 5.7 and as often as not you'll get a blank stare. Soil scientists express acid (sour soil) or alkaline (sweet soil) in terms of pH on a scale of 1 to 14. It's actually as simple as ABC: 7 is neutral; below 7 is acid; above 7 is alkaline.

Vegetables, however, are as finicky as people. Each type has its own particular pH requirements (see Table 3 – 1). Potatoes, for instance, do fine in a fairly acid soil (pH range 4.8 to 6.3); tomatoes straddle the fence, growing well in acid to slightly alkaline soil (pH range 5.5 to 7.5); and beets and cabbage dip their toes into both the acid and alkaline range (pH range 6 to 8). Since it's impractical to make one section of your garden one pH and another section a different one, most gardeners compromise on a slightly acid to neutral soil (pH 6.5 to 7).

TABLE 3 – 1   OPTIMUM pH RANGE FOR VEGETABLES

pH	Vegetable
6 to 8	Asparagus, beets, cabbage, muskmelons
6 to 7.5	Peas, spinach, summer squash
6 to 7	Cauliflower, celery, chives, endive, horseradish, lettuce, onions, radishes, rhubarb
5.5 to 7.5	Pumpkins, sweet corn, tomatoes
5.5 to 6.8	Beans, carrots, cucumbers, parsnips, peppers, rutabagas, winter squash
5.5 to 6.5	Eggplant, watermelons
4.8 to 6.3	Potatoes

Technically, soils turn acid because calcium and magnesium ions are leached out of the soil and are replaced by hydrogen ions. This occurs frequently in areas of heavy rainfall.

Soils become more alkaline as calcium, manganese, and sodium ions accumulate and replace hydrogen ions. This often occurs in areas of low rainfall and poor drainage, as well as in areas where there are native limestone deposits. In the Southwest the soil tends to be alkaline; in the Northeast it tends to be slightly acid.

If your soil is too alkaline, your plants will sometimes show yellow leaves, stunted growth, and burning leaf margins. Alkaline soils can sometimes be too salty, and, in extreme cases, heavy brown or white salt deposits are left on the soil surface. Acid soil is not easy to detect visually and will generally require some sort of a pH test.

Testing pH is a simple task. The easiest device to use is a soil-test tape (approximately $3.50). To find the pH of your garden, just press the tape against the soil and compare the color of the tape with the colors on the pH chart. A pH test kit (about $5.00) works on the same principle but uses liquid instead of a tape. A pH meter (about $20) works electrically. When its prongs are placed in the soil, the pH is automatically registered on the scale.

If you need to make a number of pH tests on a continuing basis, a pH meter is the most convenient. If you'll be making only a few tests in a small garden plot, a soil-test tape or pH test kit will do the job perfectly well.

To counteract acid soil, add ground or dolomitic lime at the rate of about 4 pounds per 100 square feet for each unit of pH below 6.5. Some gardeners also use hydrated (burned) lime, but it leaches away rapidly and can burn your hands. To correct alkaline soil, add sulfur at the rate of about 4 pounds per 100 square feet for each unit of pH above 7. Gypsum and soil aluminum sulfate can also be used. Follow directions on the package.

PLANTS GET HUNGRY TOO

Despite the fact that nutrition is just as important to plants as it is to people, many gardeners simply ignore the problem. Then they wonder what's wrong with their vegetables.

Vegetables generally need 15 nutrients for good growth. Three elements—oxygen, carbon, and hydrogen—come from air and water. The other 12 exist in the soil. Nitrogen, phosphorus, and potassium are the major macronutrients needed by vegetables in large amounts.

Magnesium, manganese, copper, zinc, iron, sulfur, calcium, molybdenum, and boron are secondary or micronutrients, and are needed only in extremely small quantities. Now let's look at these elements to see what each does for vegetables and to find out how to tell if any are missing.

Nitrogen

Nitrogen is a major element in plant nutrition. It's the compound that produces leaf growth and a vigorous dark green leaf color. It helps produce a healthy root system, increases the set of fruit, and helps feed soil microorganisms. It is especially important for such leafy vegetables as cabbage, lettuce, spinach, and collards. *Nitrogen deficiency causes yellow leaves and stunted growth. Excess nitrogen delays flowering, produces excessive growth, reduces the quality of the fruits, and renders crops less resistant to disease.*

Phosphorus

All growing plants need phosphorus, which stimulates early root formation, hastens maturity, and is important for the development of fruit, flowers, and seeds; it also helps provide disease resistance and winter-kill protection. *Phosphorus deficiency causes dark or bluish-green leaves followed by bronzing, reddening, or purpling, especially along veins and margins. Lower leaves are sometimes yellow, drying to greenish-brown or black. Plants are often stunted and spindly and mature late. Excess phosphorus produces iron and zinc deficiencies in corn, beans, tomatoes, and other plants.*

Potash

Potash (potassium) is important in the manufacture of sugar and starches. It improves the color of flowers and the length of time the fruit is edible. Potash promotes vigorous root systems and is essential in growing good root crops. It produces strong stems, reduces water loss, increases vigor, helps fight disease, and reduces winter kill. *Potash deficiency causes dry or scorched leaves, and there may be small dead areas along the margins and between the leaf veins. Plants are sometimes stunted and appear rusty. The fruit is often small and thin-skinned. Excess potash produces coarse, poorly colored fruit.* Nitrogen, potassium, and potash are automatically provided by the addition of a standard commercial fertilizer.

Magnesium

Magnesium is important in chlorophyll formation and production. It promotes early and uniform maturity and is important in fruit growth. *Magnesium deficiency causes yellowing of the lower leaves at the margins, tips, and between the veins. The leaves wilt from the bottom up until only the top leaves appear normal.* Magnesium deficiency in corn shows up as yellow leaf stripes. *Excess magnesium may produce a calcium deficiency.* Magnesium deficiency can be corrected with a fertilizer containing magnesium sulfate or Epsom salts—about 1 pound per 1000 square feet of garden space.

Manganese

Manganese is important for normal green plant development. It is essential for both respiration and normal chlorophyll development. *Manganese deficiency causes stunted growth and a mottled yellowing of the lower leaves. Excess manganese may produce small dead areas in the leaves with yellow borders around them.* Manganese deficiency can be corrected with manganese sulfate. Follow instructions on the package.

Copper

Copper is essential for chlorophyll formation, is important in protein formation, and is an enzyme activator. *Copper deficiency produces dark green, grayish-olive, or blue leaf edges that curl upward. Flowering and fruit development is checked. Carrots are poorly colored and bitter. Excess copper causes stunting of roots and prevents the uptake of iron.* Copper deficiency can be corrected by applying about 6 ounces of copper sulfate per 1000 square feet.

Zinc

Zinc is necessary for normal chlorophyll production and cell division. It is also an enzyme activator. *Zinc deficiency causes mottling, yellowing, or scorching of the tissues between the veins.* Zinc deficiency can be corrected by applying 8 ounces of zinc sulfate per 1000 square feet.

Iron

Iron promotes chlorophyll production. *Iron deficiency shows as yellowing leaves and green veins.* It is usually associated with neutral or alkaline high-lime soils. *Excess iron can cause a deficiency of phosphorus or manganese.* Iron deficiency can be corrected by using a soluble organic iron complex, iron sulfate, or chelated iron.

Sulfur

Sulfur helps maintain the dark green color of plants. It is also a constituent of proteins and growth-regulating hormones. *Sulfur deficiency causes young leaves to turn pale green or yellow. The older leaves remain green (yellowing in nitrogen-deficient plants starts with the older leaves). Plants become stunted, dwarfed, and spindly.* Most soils contain adequate sulfur, but if there is a deficiency, ammonium sulfate can be added.

Calcium

Calcium promotes early root formation, improves general vigor, and increases disease resistance. *Calcium deficiency causes distortion in young stems, and stem tips die. Excess calcium can cause a deficiency (reduced intake) of potassium and magnesium.* Calcium deficiency can be corrected by spraying plants with calcium nitrate or adding calcium sulfate (gypsum) to the soil. Follow directions on the package.

Molybdenum

Molybdenum forms chlorophyll and sugar. It is important for seed development and is required in the nitrogen metabolism of all plants, although it is needed only in minute quantities. *Molybdenum deficiency causes stunted, crinkled*

TABLE 3 – 2   THE AVAILABILITY OF PLANT NUTRIENTS IN ACID OR ALKALINE SOIL

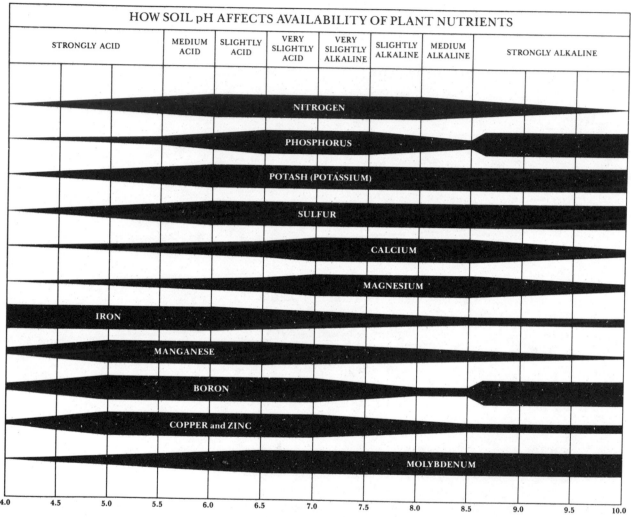

leaves that are pale green or yellow and malformed. Molybdenum deficiency can be corrected by applying sodium or ammonium molybdate (1 pound per acre — about a teaspoonful per 1000 square feet).

Boron

Boron is needed for calcium utilization and normal cell division. Boron influences the conversion of nitrogen and sugars into more complex substances. *Boron deficiency causes scorching of tips and margins of younger leaves (the typical boron scorch). Excess boron causes leaves to turn yellowish-red.* Boron deficiency can be corrected by spraying plants with a borax solution (1 teaspoon per gallon).

The availability of all nutrients for plant growth also depends on the soil pH. In acid soils, iron, manganese, and boron are available in appreciable quantities. In alkaline soils, larger quantities of molybdenum become available for plant use (see Table 3 – 2).

In addition, the amounts given here for correcting secondary and minor nutrient deficiencies are minimum ones. If deficiencies are severe, you will need to apply larger quantities of individual nutrients. To determine the exact amounts, have the soil tested.

Table 3 – 3 provides a quick summary of the preceding information on soil nutrition. Armed with this, you should be able to diagnose and correct many of the problems described in this chapter.

TABLE 3 – 3   SOIL AND NUTRITION PROBLEMS AT A GLANCE

WHAT TO LOOK FOR	POSSIBLE PROBLEMS	POSSIBLE SOLUTIONS
SOIL		
Stunted plants; pale yellow leaves	Heavy clay soil, soil too heavy; use the jar test	Turn a 6-to-8-inch layer of organic material into the soil
Yellow or pale green leaves	Sandy soil, soil too light; use the jar test	Turn a 6-to-8-inch layer of organic material into the soil
Yellow or pale green leaves	Silty soil; use the jar test	Turn a 6-to-8-inch layer of organic material into the soil
pH		
Stunted growth; burned leaf margins; yellowing leaves	Soil too alkaline	Test for pH; add sulfur at the rate of 4 pounds per 100 square feet of pH above 7
pH tests below 6.5	Soil too acid	Test for pH; add lime at the rate of about 4 pounds per 100 square feet
NUTRITION		
Yellow leaves starting with the older leaves; stunted growth	Nitrogen deficiency	Use a commercial fertilizer at the rate of 40 pounds per 1000 square feet

TABLE 3–3   SOIL AND NUTRITION PROBLEMS AT A GLANCE (continued)

WHAT TO LOOK FOR	POSSIBLE PROBLEMS	POSSIBLE SOLUTIONS
Bluish-green leaves followed by bronzing or purpling, drying to a greenish-brown or black	Phosphorus deficiency	Use a commercial fertilizer at the rate of 40 pounds per 1000 square feet or test the soil and follow recommendations
Dry or scorched leaves; dead areas along margins; plants stunted; rusty appearance	Potash (potassium) deficiency	Use a commercial fertilizer at the rate of 40 pounds per 1000 square feet, or test the soil and follow recommendations
Mottling of lower leaves at margins, tips, between veins; leaves wilt from bottom up	Magnesium deficiency	Use 1 pound of Epsom salts per 1000 square feet, or test the soil and follow recommendations
Mottled yellowing of lower leaves; stunted growth	Manganese deficiency	Use manganese sulfate, or test the soil and follow recommendations
Dark green, olive-gray leaf edges; edges curl upward	Copper deficiency	Use 6 ounces of copper sulfate per 1000 square feet, or test the soil and follow recommendations
Mottling, yellowing, or scorching of the tissues between veins	Zinc deficiency	Use 8 ounces of zinc sulfate per 1000 square feet, or test the soil and follow recommendations
Yellow leaves; green veins	Iron deficiency	Use a soluble iron complex, iron sulfate, or chelated iron, or test the soil and follow recommendations
Young leaves turn pale green to yellow; older leaves remain green	Sulfur deficiency	Most soils contain adequate amounts of sulfur; if not, test the soil and follow recommendations
Stem tips die; distortion of young stems	Calcium deficiency	Spray plants with calcium nitrate or add calcium sulfate (gypsum), or test the soil and follow recommendations
Leaves pale green or yellow; leaves crinkled, stunted	Molybdenum deficiency	Use about 1 teaspoon of sodium or ammonium molybdate per 1000 square feet, or test the soil and follow recommendations
Scorching of tips and margins of younger leaves	Boron deficiency	Spray plants with borax solution (1 teaspoon per gallon), or test the soil and follow recommendations

TABLE 3–4 **MAJOR NATURAL SOURCES OF NITROGEN**
(Amounts to Use for Each 2 Percent of Nitrogen Needed)

MATERIAL	NITROGEN (PERCENT)	APPLY PER 100 SQUARE FEET	APPLY PER ACRE
Bloodmeal	15.0	10 oz.	265 lbs.
Felt wastes	14.0	12 oz.	285 lbs.
Hoofmeal and horndust	12.5	13 oz.	320 lbs.
Guano	12.0	14 oz.	335 lbs.
Animal tankage	8.0	1¼ lbs.	500 lbs.
Cottonseed meal	8.0	1¼ lbs.	500 lbs.
Fish scrap	8.0	1¼ lbs.	500 lbs.
Miloganite (activated sludge)	6.0	1⅝ lbs.	665 lbs.
Castor pomace	5.5	1¾ lbs.	725 lbs.
Bonemeal	4.0	2½ lbs.	1000 lbs.
Peanut shells	3.6	2¾ lbs.	1100 lbs.
Tobacco stems or powder	3.3	3 lbs.	1200 lbs.
Cowpea, vetch, or alfalfa hay	3.0	3⅝ lbs.	1450 lbs.
Cocoa shells	2.7	3¾ lbs.	1500 lbs.

TABLE 3–5 **MAJOR NATURAL SOURCES OF PHOSPHORUS**
(Amounts to Use for Each 4 Percent of Phosphorus Needed)

MATERIAL	PHOSPHORUS (PERCENT)	APPLY PER 100 SQUARE FEET	APPLY PER ACRE
Phosphate rock	30.0	¾ lb.	270 lbs.
Bonemeal, steamed	28.0	¾ lb.	280 lbs.
Bonemeal, raw	24.0	⅞ lb.	330 lbs.
Animal tankage	20.0	1 lb.	400 lbs.
Fish scrap, dried	13.0	1¾ lbs.	675 lbs.
Basic slag	8.0	2½ lbs.	½ ton
Sugar wastes, raw	8.0	2½ lbs.	½ ton
Incinerator ash	5.0	4 lbs.	¾ ton
Milorganite (activated sludge)	3.0	7 lbs.	1¼ tons
Cottonseed meal	2.5	8 lbs.	1½ tons

TABLE 3–6   MAJOR NATURAL SOURCES OF POTASH
(Amounts to Apply for Each 2 Percent of Potash Needed)

MATERIAL	POTASH (PERCENT)	APPLY PER 100 SQUARE FEET	APPLY PER ACRE
Flyash	12	14 oz.	335 lbs.
Wood ashes	8	1¼ lbs.	500 lbs.
Greensand	7	1½ lbs.	570 lbs.
Tobacco stems, powder	7	1½ lbs.	570 lbs.
Granite dust	5	2 lbs.	800 lbs.
Seaweed	5	2 lbs.	800 lbs.
Fish scrap, dried	4	2½ lbs.	1000 lbs.

Some of these potash sources also supply varying amounts of nitrogen or phosphorus.

TABLE 3–7   ANIMAL MANURES

MANURE	COMPOSITION			APPLICATION PER 1000 SQUARE FEET
	Nitrogen N	Phosphorus P	Potash K	
Cattle, fresh	0.53	0.20	0.48	Spread manure about 2 inches deep over garden surface; dig in
Chicken, fresh	0.89	0.48	0.83	
Horse, fresh	0.55	0.27	0.57	
Pig, fresh	0.63	0.46	0.41	
Cattle, dried	2.0	1.8	2.2	Spread manure 4 to 6 inches deep over garden surface; dig in
Chicken, dried	2.0 to 4.5	4.6 to 6.0	1.2 to 2.4	
Horse, dried	1.0 to 2.5	0.27	0.45	
Sheep and goat, dried	1.4	1.0	3.0	

TABLE 3–8   BAND FERTILIZING
(Amount of Fertilizer to Use per Row)

INCHES APART PER ROW	OUNCES PER 10 FEET
12	7
18	10
24	13
36	20

Two level tablespoons equal 1 ounce of fertilizer.

PLAYING DOCTOR WITH YOUR SOIL

The symptoms described above are basically a vegetable's way of asking for help. Unfortunately, these general symptoms aren't specific enough in themselves to let you know what to do because some symptoms are evidence of several different nutrient deficiencies. They're the first alert. Before you can cure your plants, however, you must know exactly what the problem is and how severe it has become. That's where soil testing comes in.

In most states, you can take soil samples and have them tested free or for a small fee through the State Cooperative Extension Service agent in your county (see Appendix A). Commercial soil laboratories will also test your soil for a small fee. These are generally listed in the telephone yellow pages under "Laboratories, testing soil." You can also purchase soil-test kits through a nursery or a mail-order firm and test your own soil. When you take a soil sample, select soil from 8 to 15 zigzag spots throughout the garden instead of taking all the soil from one spot (again, see Figure 3–1).

Cooperative Extension Service tests will generally state whether your soil is deficient in nitrogen (N), phosphorus (P), and/or potash (potassium) (K). Typically, the results include specific fertilizer recommendations. They will not usually test for secondary or minor elements unless specifically requested to do so. Some reports tailor the recommendations to the specific crop you intend to grow, so if you're planning to plant whole fields of one specific vegetable, provide this information to whomever conducts the test. A general recommendation is usually good enough for a home garden.

Most do-it-yourself kits test only for nitrogen, phosphorus, and potash (potassium). One popular kit uses a color chart that rates the severity of the nitrogen, phosphorus, and potash (potassium) deficiency by matching the color of the test sample in the tube to the color on the chart. The chart then rates your soil as to the severity of the deficiency (nitrogen is rated from 2 percent to 8 percent deficient).

Instructions tell you how much nitrogen, phosphorus, and potash are needed. You can also purchase more sophisticated test kits (in the $300-plus range) that test for secondary and minor elements. See Tables 3–4 through 3–7 for organic nutrient sources.

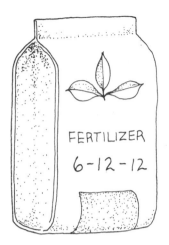

Fig. 3–3   Fertilizing by the Numbers

Fertilizer numbers refer to the percentage of nitrogen, phosphorus, and potash (potassium) contained in the bag. This particular bag contains 6 percent nitrogen, 12 percent phosphorus, 12 percent potash (by weight).

FERTILIZING BY THE NUMBERS

The composition of the fertilizer to use in your garden will depend on the test results. Commercial fertilizers are marked with the numbers 6–12–12, 5–10–5, or something similar. These numbers are simply fertilizer talk for the percentage of nitrogen, phosphorus, and potash (potassium) in that particular fertilizer. A hundred pounds of 6–12–12 has 6 pounds (6 percent) nitrogen, 12 pounds (12 percent) of available phosphorus, and 12 pounds (12 percent) soluble potash. (See Figure 3–3.)

Many vegetable experts say that unless the soil is really depleted you don't need a soil test. Simply fertilize it each season with an all-purpose commercial fertilizer such as 10–10–10 (10 percent nitrogen, 10 percent phosphorus, 10 percent potash), 6–12–12 (6 percent nitrogen, 12 percent phosphorus, 12 percent potash), or 5–10–15 (5 percent nitrogen, 10 percent phosphorus, 15 percent potash).

Leafy vegetables such as broccoli, cabbage, lettuce, kale, and spinach do well with a high-nitrogen fertilizer. Root crops (beets, carrots, parsnips, turnips, radishes, sweet potatoes, potatoes) respond to large quantities of both nitrogen and potassium. Beans, melons, onions, celery, and tomatoes require large quantities of nitrogen, phosphorus, and potash. You can also provide a balance of nutrients organically by following the instructions below.

Types of Fertilizer

There are several different kinds of fertilizer for use in home gardens. *Dry powdered fertilizers* quickly move nutrients to the vegetables. *Fertilizer compressed into pellets* (a variation of powdered fertilizers) releases nutrients more slowly than nonpellet types. Most gardeners use dry fertilizers on gardens that are more than 200 to 300 square feet in size because they are less expensive.

Apply dry commercial fertilizers such as 5–10–10 or 10–10–10 at the rate of about 50 pounds (25 quarts) per 1000 square feet (5 pounds per 100 square feet). There are three major methods of application.

1   Broadcast the fertilizer over the entire garden area and mix it in to a depth of about 3 inches.

2   Place the fertilizer in bands on each side of the row. (a) Line up a string for your row before the plants go in. (b) With a hoe, dig a trench 3 inches on either side of the string 2 to 3 inches deep. (c) Place the fertilizer in the trench and cover with soil. (See Table 3–8 for amounts to use.)

3   A combination of both the above methods. Spread half the total dry fertilizer over the entire bed and apply the other half in bands set 3 inches on either side of the row and slightly below the seed.

When leafy crops and root crops are half grown and when tomatoes, peppers, beans, cucumbers, and similar crops begin to form fruit, using a side-dressing, apply 15 pounds of a complete commercial fertilizer (containing 5 percent nitrogen) per 1000 square feet.

There are many other types of commercial fertilizers that can be used in home gardens. For complete information for your area, request a pamphlet on home-garden fertilization from your State Cooperative Extension Service (see Appendix A).

Time-release fertilizer pellets are coated with resin or other similar substance and slowly diffuse the nutrients through the coating. Use this type for very small plots and for plants in containers. One application is enough for the entire season. Use according to instructions on the package.

Liquid fertilizers are sprayed on the vegetables and are absorbed through leaves, stems, and branches. Use them for very small plots or containers. Liquid fertilizers frequently contain secondary and minor (trace) elements.

Organic fertilizers are preferred by strictly organic gardeners, who want to supply their nitrogen, phosphorus, and potash requirements with organic materials. Tables 3–4, 3–5, and 3–6 give the nitrogen, phosphorus, and potash (potassium) content of various organic materials that can be used in conjunction with home test kits. A good general method for providing all needed organic nutrients is to work about 6 inches of rotted horse manure into the bed and then sprinkle it with about 4 pounds of bonemeal and 3 pounds of wood ash per 100 square feet. See Table 3–7 for other recommendations.

COMPOST: BECOMING PART OF THE CYCLE

Everybody swears by compost, and well they should. Compost is a part of the natural cycle of turning growing materials back into the soil to help sustain it. Since compost improves soil texture and adds nutrients, every gardener should compost and turn it into the soil each Spring. A compost consists of one or more organic materials that have been piled together and allowed to decompose to a point where it breaks readily into elements that plants can absorb. It contains decaying materials such as leaves, sawdust, manures, grass clippings, food scraps, and similar items. You can build your compost pile on open ground, in a bin, or even in a garbage can. The books *Vegetable Gardening Know-How* and *Growing Vegetables the Big Yield/Small Space Way* provide comprehensive information on composting (see Recommended Reading for details).

THE GREEN MACHINE

Some gardeners grow plants to be plowed or tilled under as "green manure" for soil improvement. Green manure improves soil texture by increasing the humus content and building up the available nutrients in the topsoil. Many green-manure crops reach deep into the subsoil, absorbing valuable nutrients and bringing them into the plant tissues. When the crop is turned under, these nutrients help revitalize the topsoil. Common green manures include alfalfa, clover, buckwheat, millet, rye, and grass.

Experiment-station tests show that many crops are an extremely good source of nitrogen, especially the legumes (peas, beans, and similar crops), which have the ability to turn nitrogen from the air into soil forms that plants can use. Experiments with green manures show tremendous increases in the yields of potatoes, corn, and beans. For most gardeners, green manuring can reduce fertilizer needs by 50 percent.

EARTHWORMS: MOTHER NATURE'S SOIL ARRANGERS

Organic gardeners have long known that the earthworm is the best thing that can happen to a garden. Earthworms physically improve the soil by burrowing and by swallowing the soil and excreting it in the form of castings. This provides better air space and root access, and improves water absorption.

We've known for some time that earthworms grind the soil, mix it with calcium carbonate, and send it on through to be digested by enzymes. These final earthworm castings contain nitrogen, phosphorus, and potash. But until recently, soil-test results were inconclusive as to whether or not worms actually added nutrients to the soil.

During the last few years, however, University of Georgia scientists have been growing vegetables side by side in pure worm castings and pure potting soil. In every case, the vegetables grown in the worm castings won hands down, growing bigger and better crops than the potting soil.

Gray-pink earthworms (*Helodrilus caliginosus* and *Helodrilus foetida*) do the best work in garden soils. They can't be put in hard clay soils because they'll leave, but they'll help make a fairly good soil better. The fishworm (*Eisenia foetida*) is a good addition to compost piles. See earthworm sources in Appendix B.

As we have seen, even the most severe structural or nutritional soil problems can be corrected if you're willing to do the necessary work. In the chapter on watering that follows, the emphasis will be on prevention rather than correction, because most watering dilemmas can be avoided by taking appropriate steps before problems occur.

CHAPTER FOUR

WATER—THE
HAZARDOUS NECESSITY

Water might well be called the essential ingredient in all plant growth, as almost every plant process takes place in its presence. Water is necessary in the plant's food-manufacturing processes (photosynthesis), is the main constituent of living cells, and is abundant in growing young plant tissues. It keeps plant stems and leaves stiff. And water is the main ingredient in most of the vegetables we eat — for example, 91 percent of asparagus, 87 percent of beets, 95 percent of cucumbers, and 94 percent of tomatoes.

All this might suggest that all you have to do in order to grow sumptuous vegetables is pour on the water. Unfortunately, Mother Nature simply doesn't work that way. Watering a vegetable garden is, in reality, a balancing act. Too much is just as harmful as too little.

THE IDEAL SOIL/WATER RELATIONSHIP

Water in the soil carries dissolved nutrients that are taken up by the roots. Soil air provides a constant supply of oxygen, and it also carries off carbon dioxide. An ideal soil for plant growth generally contains 50 percent solid matter and 50 percent pore space (the passageways between the particles). Moisture should occupy about half of the pore space.

Too Much Water

When you completely fill the soil air spaces (that's called field capacity), you cut off the oxygen supply and stop root growth. The longer the air is cut off, the greater the damage. Once the roots are damaged, rot-causing organisms enter and root rot frequently sets in. The symptoms

When you water so much and/or so often that you keep the soil air spaces constantly filled above 50 percent but don't keep them quite full enough to cut off the plant's oxygen, you generally create lush leaf growth at the expense of fruit development. This is often the case with tomatoes, eggplant, and peppers that are only slightly overwatered. The symptoms: The plant produces lots of green leaves but little fruit.

Too Little Water

When the water in the soil air spaces falls below 50 percent, the plant must work harder to grow. A plant that doesn't get a full quota of H_2O, say agronomists, is under *water stress*. Water stress affects different vegetables in various ways. A cucumber under stress stops growing; a tomato ripens all its fruit; muskmelons lose their sweetness during the ripening period. Once a vegetable experiences water stress, it can't really be salvaged, no matter how much it is watered. The first symptom is the wilting of leaves. See Table 4–1 for the critical stress periods of different vegetables. Stress problems for individual vegetables will be covered in Chapter 9.

Uneven Water Supply

When the soil dries out completely, is watered, dries out again, and is then watered once more, a number of problems are created. In fact, plants can suffer if this happens only once. Carrots can crack, cabbage heads can split, potatoes can become knobby. Uneven moisture problems for specific vegetables will also be covered in Chapter 9.

HOW MUCH WATER?

To keep vegetables growing at their maximum rate, water until your particular soil type is filled to field capacity in the main plant root zone (about 1 foot deep for most vegetables; about 2 feet deep for corn, tomatoes, and a few other larger vegetables), and then don't water again until most of the available water has been used. This prevents overwatering and yet maintains enough water for good growth.

   The amount of water your plants use depends on temperature, wind, rainfall, and individual plant needs. The amount of water your soil holds depends on the soil texture. Sandy soil holds less water than clay; clay holds water so tightly that not all of it is available for plant use; loam makes adequate amounts of water readily available for your vegetables. (See Chapter 3.)

   If you know what kind of soil you have, you can roughly estimate when your soil is saturated, or has reached field capacity (see Table 4–2). If you have loam soil you will need approximately one inch of water to saturate the first foot. Place a large transparent measuring cup in the garden. When an inch of water has accumulated in the cup, you have applied all the water the top foot of your garden can hold.

TABLE 4–1   CRITICAL WATERING PERIODS

Vegetables need a constant water supply for best growth. A lack of adequate water, however, affects vegetable quality most during the following periods.

VEGETABLE	CRITICAL PERIOD
Asparagus	Spear development
Beans	Pollination/pod development
Broccoli	Head development
Cabbage	Head development
Carrots	Root enlargement
Cauliflower	Head development
Corn	Tasseling/ear development
Cucumbers	Flowering/fruit development
Eggplant	Flowering/fruit development
Lettuce	Head development
Melons	Flowering/fruit development
Onions	Bulb enlargement
Pumpkins	Flowering/fruit development
Squash	Flowering/fruit development
Tomatoes	Flowering/fruit development

   Table 4–3 gives a general guide to average daily water use. Now, let's take an example. You have loam soil and live

of soil waterlogging are stunted, yellow plants and plants that are wilted and collapsed.

in an area where the summers are warm. Loam holds one inch of water, so you turn on the sprinkler until the measuring cup holds an inch. It will take about two hours to saturate that first foot of soil. If you're raising tomatoes or corn, you'll want to water twice as long.

If, from Table 4–3, you decide your plants are using a quarter inch (.25) of water a day, the available water in the first foot of soil will be depleted about four days after being saturated. Therefore, you would water most vegetables about two hours every four days. This is only a general guide, since — because of weather conditions — vegetables will often use twice the normal amount of water from one day to the next.

Here is a general fail-safe watering method to make sure that soil moisture stays within a safe level: Water deeply for two to four hours, and then don't water again until the soil dries out to a depth of 4 to 8 inches. Check this with a trowel.

TABLE 4–2   SOIL WATER HOLDING CAPACITY
(Inches of Water Needed per Foot of Soil Depth)

SOIL TYPE	APPROXIMATE WATER HOLDING CAPACITY
Sandy	.8
Clay	1.5
Loam	1.0

TABLE 4–3   PLANT WATER USE GUIDE
(Inches of Soil Water Used per Day in a Vegetable Garden)

SEASON	WARM SUMMER (80 degrees F. and above)	COOL SUMMER (Below 80 degrees F.)
Summer	.25 to .35	.15 to .2
Spring/Fall	.1 to .2	.1 to .15

HOW TO WATER

Home gardeners generally water overhead (Figure 4–1) or use some sort of a drip system (Figure 4–2). Following is a description of the principal types.

Overhead Watering

There are five types of overhead watering devices.

1   *Pulsating sprinklers.* Water striking an arm moves the pulsating, or rainbird, type of sprinkler in a 50-to-75-foot circle. These are available in brass or less expensive plastic and can be used with an underground pipe system or a portable spike or sled base. One pulsating sprinkler will water a medium-sized garden and can be adjusted to operate in a full or partial circle. These sprinklers have almost no disadvantages.

2   *Oscillating sprinklers.* The arm of the oscillating sprinkler moves back and forth to water a square or rectangular area of about 50 to 60 feet. They can also be adjusted to water a portion of this space. Oscillating sprinklers, like the pulsating type, have few disadvantages.

3   *Rotating sprinklers.* Rotating sprinklers consist of rotating arms or blades propelled by a spray of water. They water in a 5-to-50-foot circle. Some of the larger rotating sprinklers can travel down a hose laid across the garden and will water an area of up to 1500 square feet. Some water is wasted by a rotating sprinkler, since it cannot be adjusted. It must also be moved several times to water most vegetable gardens.

4   *Nonmovable sprinklers.* Nonmovable sprinklers have holes that sprinkle water in circles, squares, or rectangles up to 100 square feet. There are no moving parts. These sprinklers must be moved several times to water an average-size garden.

5   *Sprinkler spray heads.* Spray heads are made from plastic or brass and are usually connected with an underground pipe system. The head offers varying patterns, including quarter, half, three-quarters, and full circles. The underground pipe used in this system makes cultivating the garden difficult.

Fig. 4–1 Overhead Watering

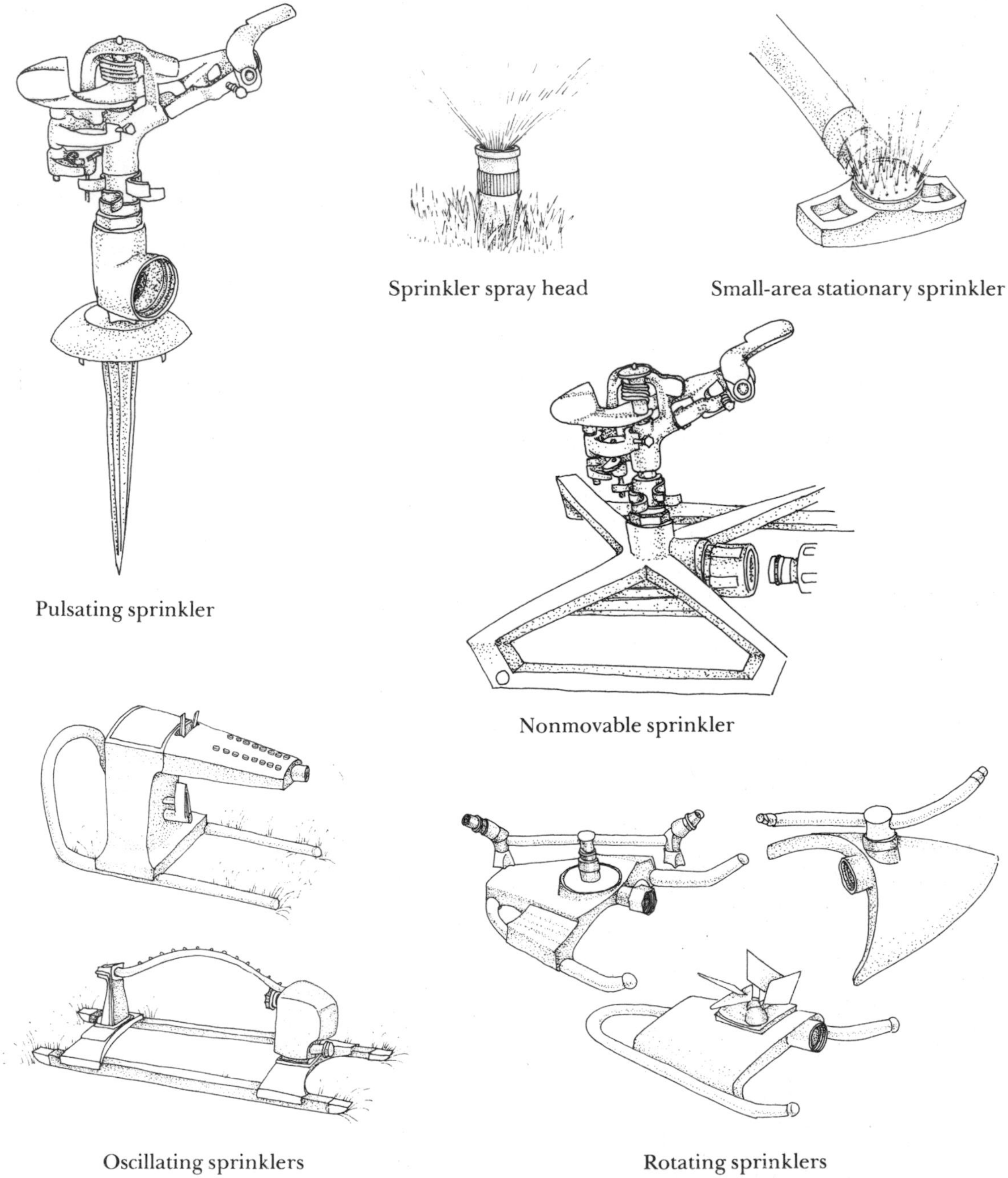

Sprinkler spray head   Small-area stationary sprinkler

Pulsating sprinkler

Nonmovable sprinkler

Oscillating sprinklers   Rotating sprinklers

Besides sprinkler watering, some gardeners like to hand water overhead. There are a variety of hose nozzles, including hand-held nozzles, fan sprays, and ground bubblers. Wands ranging from 24 to 52 inches permit watering underneath the leaves. Hand watering is fine for small gardens but can become tedious for gardens of more than 100 square feet.

When you overhead water, you should:
1   Water early in the morning, which enables the leaves to dry out quickly; moisture left on leaves frequently creates a mildew problem (see Chapter 2). In addition, some plant leaves such as squash can burn if the plants are watered during the hot part of the day.
2   Overhead water tomatoes only until the fruit begins to ripen, and then, to keep the fruit from cracking, water on the ground until the fruit has been harvested.

Overhead watering is used today by a majority of home vegetable gardeners. The chief advantage is that it's an easy way to water. The principal disadvantage is that a great deal of water is lost by evaporation.

Drip Irrigation

Drip irrigation is the frequent, slow application of water to the soil through small mechanical devices called emitters that release water at a very low rate. The system consists of three main parts: basic controls, a main line or lines, and emitters with small extension tubes.

The *basic controls* include a shutoff valve, a pressure regulator, and a filter. The shutoff valve turns the system on and off. The pressure regulator reduces water pressure from 50 to 80 pounds per square inch in the household water line to the low rate of 5 to 25 pounds per square inch needed by most drip systems. The filter screens out sediment and other particles that could plug the small emitter openings.

The *main line* consists of ⅜- to ½-inch black polyethylene hose to carry water from a garden hose or water outlet either across the top portion of the garden (the *main header*) or up and down the rows (the *laterals*).

Fig. 4 – 2   Composite of drip irrigation systems

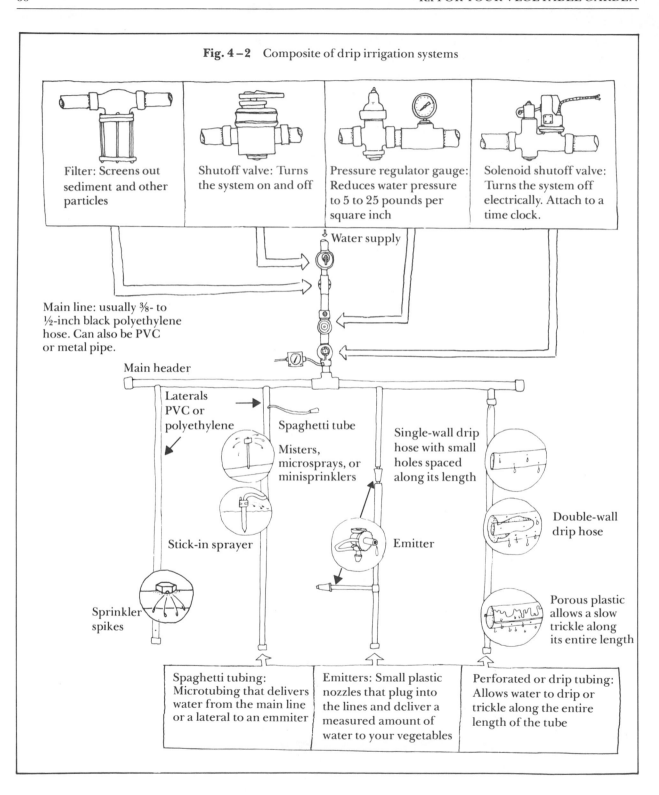

Filter: Screens out sediment and other particles

Shutoff valve: Turns the system on and off

Pressure regulator gauge: Reduces water pressure to 5 to 25 pounds per square inch

Solenoid shutoff valve: Turns the system off electrically. Attach to a time clock.

Water supply

Main line: usually ⅜- to ½-inch black polyethylene hose. Can also be PVC or metal pipe.

Main header

Laterals PVC or polyethylene

Spaghetti tube

Misters, microsprays, or minisprinklers

Single-wall drip hose with small holes spaced along its length

Stick-in sprayer

Emitter

Double-wall drip hose

Sprinkler spikes

Porous plastic allows a slow trickle along its entire length

Spaghetti tubing: Microtubing that delivers water from the main line or a lateral to an emmiter

Emitters: Small plastic nozzles that plug into the lines and deliver a measured amount of water to your vegetables

Perforated or drip tubing: Allows water to drip or trickle along the entire length of the tube

Emitters are small plastic nozzles that plug into the main lines and deliver a measured ½, 1, 2, 3, or 4 gallons of water per hour directly to the vegetables. An emitter can be connected to the main line by small ⅛-inch microtubing (called spaghetti tubing) or it can be plugged into the main line, with spaghetti tubing used to deliver water to individual plants.

There are at least 50 kinds of emitters on the market today. Drippers are small plastic devices with a barb at one end that snaps into the main-line hose; the other end dispenses water. Misters, microsprays, and minisprinklers are essentially low-volume versions of regular sprinklers. Misters, for instance, emit a fine spray of water. Standard drippers are best for delivering water directly to large plants such as tomatoes and eggplant that are spaced 1 to 3 feet apart.

Perforated or drip tubing (a form of emitter) is 10-to-30-foot-long plastic tubing with holes spaced 12, 18, or 24 inches apart along its length. One kind of drip tubing dispenses water along the entire length of the tube after the perforated tubing has been plugged into a main line placed across the top of the garden. Each perforated tube is laid down an individual garden row. Most kinds of perforated tubing deliver 2 to 6 gallons of water per hour for every 10 feet of tubing. Drip tubing is especially adapted for watering closely spaced row crops such as carrots, beets, and radishes.

You should follow the same general guidelines when drip watering as for other kinds of watering. Turn your system on for about 30 minutes and then check with a trowel to make sure the water has penetrated the first foot of soil. If it hasn't, continue watering until it does. After that, check daily with a trowel, and don't water again until the soil has dried out to a depth of between 4 and 8 inches.

Drip systems are available in kit form (from $19 up) or as individual components at plumbing-supply stores. You can put your own system together, and it is generally easy to install in an average-size garden.

Drip irrigation is by far the most efficient method for watering vegetable gardens. Only a small key area of soil is watered around your vegetables, little or no water is lost to evaporation and surface runoff, and there is no sprinkler overshoot. Drip irrigation is an important step forward in water conservation. As water becomes more expensive in the future and water conservation considerably more important, many vegetable gardeners will use this method exclusively.

FOOLPROOF WATERING

You can take a lot of the guesswork out of watering by hooking your system (either overhead or drip) into an electric timer (Figure 4–3) or by using a moisture sensor (Figure 4–4).

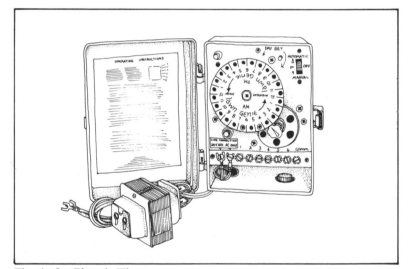

Fig. 4–3   Electric Timer

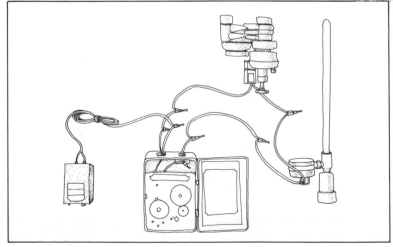

Fig. 4–4   Moisture Sensor

Simple timers, consisting of a clock that turns on the water for a given number of minutes a day, start at about $30. Sophisticated timing devices that allow you to set the program ahead for several days at a time or to deliver different amounts of water to separate parts of your garden cost up to several hundred dollars.

Moisture sensors (which sell for under $200) automatically keep soil water at a safe level. The sensing device is buried in the garden 8 to 10 inches deep, and water is turned on when the sensor dries out. Or the needed moisture content can be dialed and the sensor will turn on the water when the soil reaches that level. The major drawback to a moisture sensor is its cost, but it is nevertheless the ultimate answer to making sure that vegetables get exactly the amount of moisture they need at all times.

MULCHING MEANS MOISTURE

Mulch can also be used to ensure adequate soil moisture for vegetables. A mulch is simply a layer of material spread on the vegetable bed that shades the ground completely, reduces soil evaporation, and helps retain soil moisture. Many organic materials make a good mulch, such as wood chips, sawdust, grass clippings, horse manure, or compost.

Place organic mulches around the stems of your plants and cover the ground completely. Since organic material cools the soil, mulch in late Spring after the soil temperature has warmed to at least 65 degrees F. The best time to spread an organic mulch is right after a rain, as it keeps the moisture in the soil for an extended period of time.

You can also use clear or black polyethylene film and aluminum foil as a soil mulch, as all three cut down water evaporation. Both clear and black plastic increase the soil temperatures under the plastic, while aluminum foil reduces soil temperatures. Warm-weather crops such as tomatoes and peppers do well under black plastic; leafy and root crops do well under aluminum foil.

To use a plastic mulch, soak the soil first and then lay down a plastic strip the length of the row, securing it with soil on the ends and sides. Cut out planting holes with a tin can and cut X-shaped slits about 3 inches long so that water can soak in (see Figure 4–5). If you're watering with a drip system, lay it directly on the soil, under the plastic.

Water is a powerful enough force in the garden that it is worth repeating the fail-safe approach: Water deeply for two to four hours, and then don't water again until the soil dries out to a depth of 4 to 8 inches. If you follow this rule and garden in well-drained soil, you will probably be able to deal with conditions ranging from drought to several days of rain. Simply test with a trowel. In Chapter 9 you will find watering instructions about specific vegetables.

In the next chapter we will look at a number of the other natural factors that affect the quantity and quality of your home harvest.

Fig. 4–5 Planting with a Plastic Mulch

Lay a plastic strip over a tilled row and anchor edges with soil. Use a tin can to cut holes for the plants.

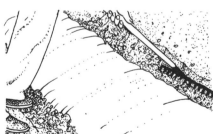

Secure edges of plastic covering with soil in a trench.

Cut X-shaped slits to allow water to enter.

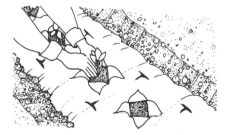

Pull back edges to transplant as usual.

For slower runoff and better water penetration, let the plastic form shallow basins around each plant.

CHAPTER FIVE

WEATHERING THE ELEMENTS

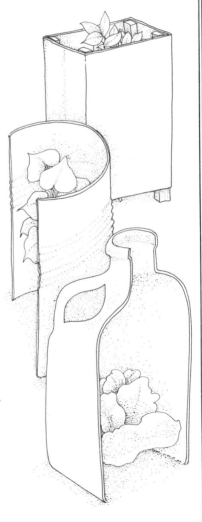

This chapter will explore such peculiarities of nature that can affect the growth and quality of homegrown vegetables as temperatures that are too high or too low, summer hail, and too much or too little sun. While we can't control Mother Nature, we can learn to cooperate or compensate so that our gardens have more than an even chance.

SOME GERMINATION GEMS OF WISDOM

Surprisingly, most vegetables germinate seed, grow, and set (form) fruit within a very narrow temperature range. Each vegetable seed has an individual soil-temperature-tolerance range. Some seed, such as lettuce and onion, tolerate soil temperatures as low as 32 degrees F.; germination at these temperatures is slow, but the seed will live and will germinate as the soil temperature warms up. Other seeds, such as bean and sweet corn, will rot if left in the ground more than a few days at temperatures below 55 to 60 degrees F.

Vegetable seeds also stop germinating at temperatures of between 86 and 104 degrees F., depending on the vegetable. During hot weather, surface soil temperatures often rise much higher than this. Thus even if the seed has germinated, the seedlings (especially carrots and beets) can die of heat injury at the soil surface. Germination and seedling survival during hot weather can be helped by placing a 2-inch layer of organic material such as compost (see the section on mulch in the previous chapter) over the soil after the seeds have been planted. This reduces soil temperature and holds in moisture.

To ensure good germination of seed, plant vegetables within the proper temperature range as shown in Table 5–1. You can check the soil temperature with a special soil thermometer, available at most nurseries.

WARM- AND COOL-SEASON CROPS

Vegetables are generally divided into warm-season and cool-season crops. Plants harvested for their fruit, such as tomatoes, melons, eggplant, peppers, and squash, need a lot of heat and long days to grow well and form fruit. Leafy and root vegetables, such as carrots, beets, spinach, and cabbage, do well when the weather is on the cool side.

Within these general categories, each vegetable has its own growing-temperature range. Radishes will grow between 40 and 75 degrees F., for example, and corn between 50 and 95 degrees F. (See Table 5–2.)

HARDY AND TENDER CROPS

Vegetables might also be categorized by the time span between the time they are planted and the last Spring frost. There are three major designations: *very hardy* (planted four to six weeks before the last frost), *hardy* (planted two to four weeks before the last frost), and *cold tender,* planted on, or a week or two after, the last frost (see Table 5–3).

You can extend the season and protect all plants from frost and wind by covering them with hotkaps, cut-off plastic jugs, or other plastic protective devices (see Figure 5–1). For a complete discussion of season extension, read my *Growing Vegetables the Big Yield/Small Space Way* (see Recommended Reading).

In addition, individual vegetable varieties have their own temperature ranges. Early varieties require less total summer heat to mature than mid-season varieties. Most midget vegetables need less total heat than most other vegetables.

If you live in an area of cool Summers (below 70 degrees) or short Summers (under 140 days), you can grow crops that require a longer or hotter season (such as melons) by planting the earliest available varieties. Those with the shortest days to maturity (listed in all seed catalogs) have the lowest heat requirements.

Fig. 5–1 Protective Devices

Hotkap and Hotent

Hotkaps, heavy-wax-paper cones, protect plants against the elements and birds.

Hotents are effective for growing seedlings of large plants, such as squash or tomatoes. Approximate size: 11 inches wide, 14 inches long, 8½ inches high.

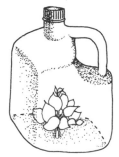

Plastic jug. Remove bottom to convert to a minigreenhouse.

Tunnel Protectors

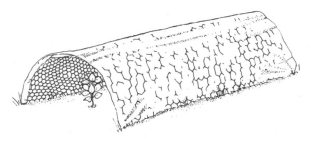

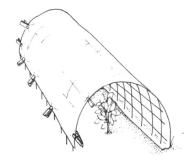

This tunnel cloche is made of chicken wire.

A half cylinder of fence wire. Draped plastic can be held with clothespins, folded back when it's warm.

Root crops are also affected by high or low soil temperatures. This will be covered under individual vegetables in Chapter 9.

TABLE 5–1   **SOIL TEMPERATURES FOR VEGETABLE SEED GERMINATION**

VEGETABLE	MINIMUM	TEMPERATURE (DEGREES F.) OPTIMUM	MAXIMUM
Asparagus	50	75	95
Beans (lima)	60	80	85
Beans (snap)	60	85	95
Beets	40	85	95
Broccoli	40	85	95
Cabbage	40	85	95
Carrots	40	80	95
Cauliflower	40	80	95
Celery	40	80	95
Cucumbers	60	95	105
Eggplant	60	85	95
Endive	32	75	75
Lettuce	32	75	75
Melons	60	95	105
Okra	60	95	105
Onions	32	80	95
Parsnips	32	70	85
Peas	40	75	85
Peppers	60	85	95
Pumpkins	60	95	105
Parsley	40	80	95
Radishes	40	85	95
Spinach	32	70	75
Squash	60	95	105
Sweet corn	50	85	105
Swiss chard	40	85	95
Tomatoes	50	85	95
Turnips	40	85	105

TABLE 5–2 **APPROXIMATE MONTHLY TEMPERATURES FOR BEST GROWTH AND QUALITY OF VEGETABLE CROPS**

TEMPERATURE (DEGREES F.)			
OPTIMUM	MINIMUM	MAXIMUM	VEGETABLE
55–75	45	85	Chicory, chives, garlic, leeks, onions, salsify, scolymus, scorzonera shallots
60–65	40	75	Beets, broad beans, broccoli, Brussels sprouts, cabbage, chard, collards, horseradish, kale, kohlrabi, parsnips, radishes, rutabagas, sorrel, spinach, turnips
60–65	45	75	Artichokes, cardoon, carrots, cauliflower, celeriac, celery, Chinese cabbage, endive, Florence fennel, lettuce, mustard greens, parsley, peas, potatoes
60–70	50	80	Lima beans, snap beans
60–75	50	95	Sweet corn, southern peas, New Zealand spinach
65–75	50	90	Chayote, pumpkins, squash
65–75	60	90	Cucumbers, muskmelons
70–75	65	80	Sweet peppers, tomatoes
70–85	65	95	Eggplant, hot peppers, martynia, okra, roselle, sweet potatoes, watermelons

FRUIT SET

Eggplant, peppers, tomatoes, beans, and peas start to form fruit (called fruit set) when the female parts of a vegetable flower are successfully pollinated by the male parts. The success or failure of this pollination depends a great deal on the temperature. The determining factor for such vegetables as peppers and tomatoes is the nighttime, not the daytime, temperature. Most tomatoes require temperatures above 55 degrees F. for at least part of the night to set fruit. Night temperatures above 75 degrees F. inhibit fruit set and cause blossom drop.

Low or high temperatures can cause misshapen tomato fruit and puffiness because these temperature extremes interfere with the growth of pollen tubes and normal fertilization of the ovary (female parts). In addition, catfacing (puckering of the blossom end of the fruit with scarring between the lumps) can occur when cool weather at the time of flowering causes the blossom to stick to the small fruit.

Many of these problems can be corrected by placing clear poly-ethylene plastic covers over the plant cages when temperatures fall below 60 degrees F.

THE LONG-DAY/SHORT-DAY FACTOR

As a general rule, vegetables need a minimum of six to eight hours of direct sunlight a day. The total length of daylight received (called day length) also makes a difference. In fact, vegetables are categorized according to the amount of day length they need to produce flowers and fruit. Some, such as spinach, Chinese cabbage, and corn, start to flower in late Spring as they begin to receive more than 12 hours of daylight. These are called long-day plants. Gardeners want corn to flower (tassel and produce ears), but it drives them crazy when the lengthening days of late Spring trigger the flowering of Chinese cabbage or spinach long before the plants are ready to harvest.

Other vegetables, called short-day plants, produce flowers only when they receive less than 12 hours of daylight. Still other vegetables like tomatoes are day-neutral or intermediate-day plants and will flower and fruit under a wide variety of day lengths.

Day length can also influence the bulbing of onions. Some varieties need a long day (over 12 hours of daylight) to induce bulbing while others bulb only when days are short (less than 12 hours of daylight). This is also discussed under individual vegetables in Chapter 9.

TOO MUCH SUN

Cool-weather crops often do poorly when the Summer sun is intense and hot, as the exposed parts of the fruits of warm-weather crops can become 20 degrees hotter than the shaded parts. This contributes to uneven ripening and blotchy fruit. If the sun is hot enough (over 90 degrees F.), the exposed parts of plants frequently become sunscalded—that is, a yellow or white patch appears on the side of the fruit toward the sun. This spot may remain yellow or it may shrink and form a large flattened grayish-white spot. Sunscalding of peppers and tomatoes is especially prevalent in varieties that have little foliage.

TABLE 5–3   CLASSIFICATION OF VEGETABLE CROPS ACCORDING TO THE EFFECTS OF FROST OR LIGHT FREEZES

COOL-SEASON CROPS		
HARDY		HALF HARDY
Asparagus	Kohlrabi*	Beets*
Broad beans	Leeks*	Carrots*
Broccoli	Mustard greens	Cauliflower
Brussels sprouts	Onions*	Celery*
Cabbage*	Parsley*	Chard*
Chives	Peas	Chicory
Collards	Radishes*	Chinese cabbage*
Garlic	Rhubarb	Globe artichokes
Horseradish	Spinach	Endive
Kale*	Turnips*	Lettuce
		Parsnips*
		Potatoes
		Salsify

*Seed stalks develop after prolonged exposure to low temperatures.

WARM-SEASON CROPS		
TENDER		VERY TENDER
Cowpeas		Cucumbers
New Zealand spinach		Eggplant
Snap beans		Lima beans
Soybeans		Muskmelons
Sweet corn		Okra
Tomatoes		Peppers, hot
		Peppers, sweet
		Pumpkins
		Squash
		Sweet potatoes
		Watermelons

Protect cool-weather vegetables such as lettuce by providing partial shade. A lath frame supported on 2-foot-high posts works fine. Shadecloth (a plastic screening that cuts sun intensity) is a fairly recent development now being used by many gardeners. It is available in many garden centers for $15 to $20 for a 6-by-10-foot piece and can be installed over the beds on a plastic pipe-frame support.

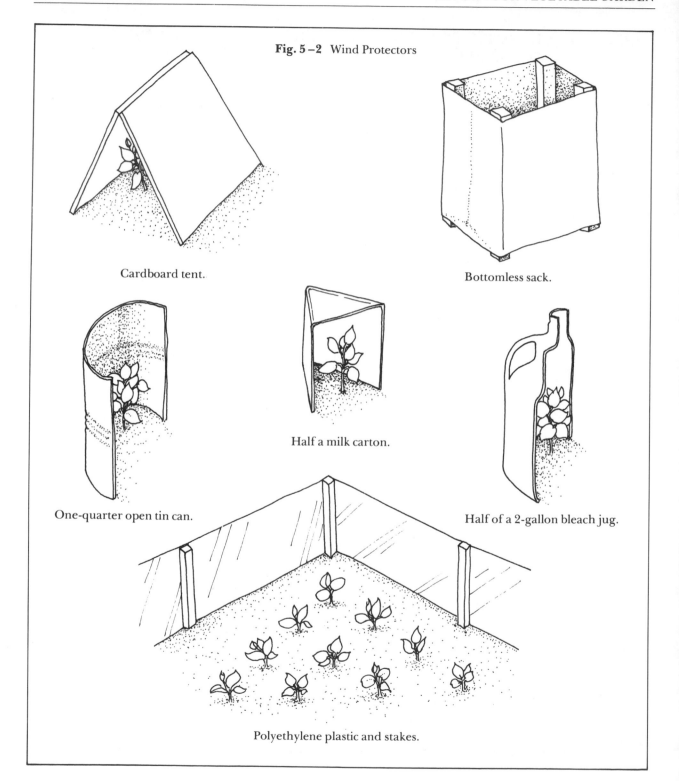

Fig. 5–2 Wind Protectors

Cardboard tent.

Bottomless sack.

Half a milk carton.

One-quarter open tin can.

Half of a 2-gallon bleach jug.

Polyethylene plastic and stakes.

Shadecloth that casts 30 percent shade is preferable when temperatures are below 85 degrees F. (in late Spring in many areas). When temperatures rise above 85 degrees and the sun is intense, use 47 percent shadecloth. During summer in desert climates, 55 percent shadecloth gives best results. Cool-season vegetables do not need shading in areas subject to general overcast.

You can also reduce the chances of sunscalding of tomatoes, peppers, and similar crops by growing varieties that have heavy foliage (see Chapter 9).

TOO LITTLE SUN

Plants that receive much less than six hours of sun a day (as distinct from day length) often become spindly, unproductive, and taller than normal. If certain sections of your garden receive less than six hours of light, you can supplement the natural light with a reflector panel. Make these panels by stapling or gluing kitchen aluminum foil to a large piece of cardboard or plywood—4 by 4 feet, 4 by 6 feet, and 5 by 8 feet are good sizes—mounted on a wood frame. Light reflectors should be set up on the east, west, or north side of your garden, or on all three. You'll have to experiment to determine the size and placement that work best for you.

WIND AND HAIL

Plants subjected to strong winds divert energy from setting and bearing fruit to self-protection, and harvests under wind-stressed conditions are usually poor. Protect your plants from wind with portions of milk cartons anchored by wire, bottomless sacks, or a 2-foot-high plastic wall run along the windward side (see Figure 5–1). Frost-protection devices (Figure 5–2) also make good wind protectors.

Hail, which frequently occurs along with summer thunderstorms, can destroy cucumbers, squash, and beans. Lettuce will be reduced to a pulpy mass but will come back. Although shredded, corn will produce a crop as if nothing happened. Carrots and asparagus will not be affected.

You can protect susceptible plants for short periods by placing a clear plastic polyethylene sheet over a few plants or over an entire garden.

In some gardens, the problems created by soil, water, and Mother Nature's other peculiarities account for a good 50 percent or more of all garden troubles. Other home growers find insects and diseases to be a far greater hazard. Whatever the situation in your garden, both insects and diseases destroy millions of dollars' worth of crops annually. The next two chapters will help you understand, prevent, and control both of these very serious garden problems.

CHAPTER SIX

WHAT'S BUGGING YOUR GARDEN?

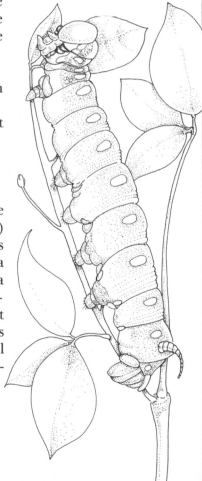

In this chapter, we're going to get really tough, take the gloves off, and start fighting back against those insects that won't be stopped by the prevention tactics discussed in Chapter 2.

To do this, let's begin by taking a close look at those pests that do the most damage to your vegetables. These unwanted marauders divide neatly into four categories (see Table 6–1):

1. Beetles, caterpillars, and other pests that chew holes in the leaves of vegetables.
2. Insects such as aphids, true bugs, and whiteflies that suck plant juices.
3. Insects that bore into leaves and fruit.
4. Soil insects that carry on the attack from below.

Most of these insects go through a series of stages. The beetle, fly, or moth (called the "adult" in insect language) lays eggs which hatch a worm (called the *larva*) that eats everything in sight. The larva of a beetle is a *grub;* the larva of a fly is called a *maggot;* the larva of a moth or butterfly is a *caterpillar.* When the larva reaches its maximum size, it enters a nonfeeding dormant stage (the *pupa*); the adult insect emerges from this pupa. Both the adult and the larva stages can be extremely destructive. The control of each insect will be discussed individually under each vegetable in Chapter 9.

TABLE 6–1   VEGETABLE INSECTS AT A GLANCE

TYPE/ INSECT	WHAT TO LOOK FOR	DESCRIPTION	PREVENTION	NATURAL CONTROLS	CHEMICAL CONTROLS
Leaf Chewers					
Beetles	Irregular holes in leaves	1½- to 2-inch-long insects with biting mouth parts, hard front wings	Keep the garden area free of refuse; spade deeply in the Spring to kill larvae; plant marigolds throughout the garden to discourage beetles	Pick beetles off by hand	Spray with Sevin or malathion or use a botanical spray— pyrethrum, rotenone, or ryania
Caterpillars	Chunks chewed out of leaves	1- to 3-inch-long brown to green "worms"	Clean up and dispose of crop refuse; remove weeds	Pick caterpillars off by hand; use Bacillus thuringiensis	Spray with malathion or Sevin or use the botanical spray rotenone
Earwigs	Holes in leaves	Ugly night-feeding insects with big pincers	Keep garden refuse cleaned up	Trap in rolled-up newspapers	Use diazinon or commercial earwig bait
Grasshoppers	Large holes chewed in leaves; plants stripped	Big (1- to 2½-inch long) insect with large rear legs	Turn soil under in Fall to bury eggs deeply	Trap in quart jars filled with 1 part molasses, 7 parts water	Spray or dust with Sevin, malathion or diazinon or use the botanical spray rotenone
Slugs/Snails	Leaves eaten; trails of silvery slime	Slimy, legless soft-bodied creatures, with or without shells	Reduce hiding places by keeping garden free of debris	Drown in a shallow saucer of beer; trap by scattering cabbage or lettuce leaves at night, and then pick up in morning	Use a commercial slug poison or a dehydrating agent
Weevils (beetles with a snout)	Chunks out of leaves or roots eaten by grubs or adults	Weevils are beetles with long beaks	Keep the garden area free of refuse; spade deeply in the Spring to kill larvae; plant marigolds throughout the garden to discourage beetles (weevils)	Pick adult weevils off by hand	Use diazinon, malathion, or Sevin or the botanical spray rotenone

TABLE 6–1   **VEGETABLE INSECTS AT A GLANCE** *(continued)*

TYPE/ INSECT	WHAT TO LOOK FOR	DESCRIPTION	PREVENTION	NATURAL CONTROLS	CHEMICAL CONTROLS
Juice Suckers					
Aphids	Colonies of sucking insects on leaves	Tiny (⅛-to ¼-inch long), black, yellow, green insects	Spearmint and garlic help repel aphids	Remove with blast from a garden hose; use soap solution; mulch with aluminum foil; control with lacewing flies, praying mantises, or ladybugs	Control with malathion or use botanical sprays pyrethrum, rototone, ryania
Leafhoppers	Leaves appear scorched or wilted	Wedge-shaped, brown or green insects			Spray with Sevin or malathion
Spider mites	Affected leaves turn pale green; dusty webs between leaves (tap leaf over a sheet of paper; moving specks are mites)	Minute spiderlike insects	Avoid working among infected plants to keep from spreading mites	Use a strong spray from a hose to wash mites away	Spray with diazinon or Kelthane
Thrips	Scars on foliage; leaves may be brown-edged, spotted, or streaked; damage on onions appears as white blotches	Thin 1/25-inch-long needlelike black or straw-colored insects	Keep weeds out of garden; keep garden clean	Control with ladybugs	Treat with two or three applications of diazinon or malathion
Whiteflies	A cloud of white wings fly from plant when disturbed	Small (1/10-inch-long) white-winged sucking insects	Plant marigolds (marigolds excrete substances that are absorbed by vegetable roots to repel whiteflies)	Use wasps to destroy whiteflies; hose off with a stream of water	Spray with malathion or use the botanical spray rotenone
Stem borers	Sudden wilting of leaves or holes in stems	"Worm" that bores inside stems	Clear debris and weeds from garden	Slit stem with a knife, take out borer	Dust with Sevin or malathion

TABLE 6–1   **VEGETABLE INSECTS AT A GLANCE** *(continued)*

TYPE/ INSECT	WHAT TO LOOK FOR	DESCRIPTION	PREVENTION	NATURAL CONTROLS	CHEMICAL CONTROLS
True bugs	White or yellow blotches appear where bugs have fed; if attack is severe, leaves wilt, turn brown, and die	Small 1/10- to 5/8-inch-long insects with sucking beaks	Fertilize plants to keep growing vigorously	Destroy bugs that collect under leaves at night; use sabadilla (Doom); search for and crush egg masses	Spray vines with Sevin or malathion or use a botanical spray— pyrethrum, rotenone, or ryania
Corn earworm	Kernels at the tip of the corn ear are brown and eaten away; bores into fruit of other plants	2-inch green to brown caterpillars	Plant corn varieties with long, tight husks: Dixie 18, Country Gentleman, Golden Security, Silver Cross Bantam	Apply a few drops of mineral oil inside the ears when the silks first appear	Dust with Sevin
Leaf miners Fly maggots	Small tunnels within the leaves	Small (¼-inch-long) thin maggot	Deep spade before planting to help control maggots; cover plants with cheesecloth		Control adult flies with diazinon or malathion
Soil Insects					
Maggots	Tunnels in bulbs; yellowing leaves	Soft legless wormlike larvae of flies	Delay planting until late Spring or Summer		Treat soil with diazinon
Beetle or moth larvae (wireworms, cutworms, white grubs)	Plant growth stunted; "worms" bore into roots; young plants cut off at soil line	Wormlike insects in soil	Keep the garden free of refuse; put cardboard collars around plants (push 1 inch into soil to keep cutworms away from plants); deep spade in Spring to destroy some larvae		Use diazinon or treat soil with diazinon before planting

CHEWING INSECTS

Both beetles and caterpillars are plant gobblers that chew holes in the leaves and fruit of your vegetables (see Figure 6–1). These holes may be tiny pinpoints or irregular larger holes. You may even discover that whole leaves have been devoured and entire areas of fruits have been chewed away. Following are descriptions of the major chewers in your garden.

The Beetles

Beetles, as every experienced gardener knows, are obnoxious insects with biting mouth parts and hard front wings that can make short work of your vegetables. There are a number that would like to call your vegetable garden home for at least part of the year.

Asparagus beetles are slender, a quarter of an inch long, and brownish in color. Both adults and larvae feed on the new shoots and leaves of asparagus. As soon as asparagus appears, the beetle lays eggs on the tips. Within a week the eggs hatch and start to feed. After 10 to 14 days, these larvae burrow into the ground to become yellow pupae. The asparagus beetle is found wherever asparagus is grown.

Bean leaf beetles are reddish to yellowish, about a quarter of an inch long, and have black spots on their backs and black margins around their front wings. The adult beetles, which are found throughout the United States, eat irregular-shaped holes in the leaves of all kinds of beans and cowpeas.

Blister beetles are slender gray, black, or striped insects about three-quarters of an inch long. Only adult beetles injure plants, but swarms of them feed ravenously on the foliage and blossoms of almost any kind of vegetable. The heavy-jawed larvae do not harm vegetables; instead, they burrow through the soil to find and eat grasshopper larvae. These beetles reach the destructive stage in early summer, when they emerge to feed in swarms and lay eggs in the soil. They can raise blisters on the skin if crushed. Blister beetles are found primarily east of the Rocky Mountains.

Colorado potato beetles are half-inch-long hemispherically shaped insects with black spots on the front parts of their bodies and five black stripes on each wing sheath. They look like Volkswagens. The larva of the Colorado beetle is brick-red and has rows of black spots along its sides. This beetle overwinters in the soil as an adult and then emerges in the Spring to lay eggs on the underside of the leaves. The eggs hatch in four to nine days; the larvae mature in two or three weeks. This pest is found everywhere in the United States and southern Canada except in parts of Nevada, Florida, and California.

Cowpea curculios are blackish, chunky beetles about a fifth of an inch long. The grub is whitish, legless, and has a

Fig. 6–1   Chewing Insects—Beetles

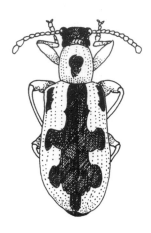

Asparagus beetle

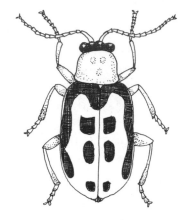

Bean leaf beetle

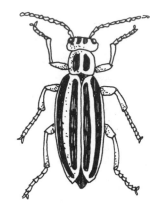

Striped blister beetle

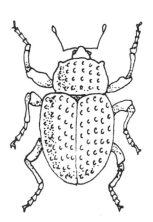

Cowpea curculio

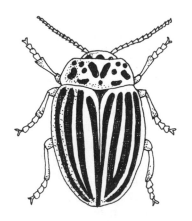

Colorado potato beetle

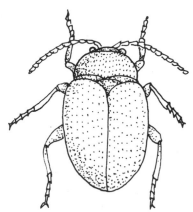

Flea beetle

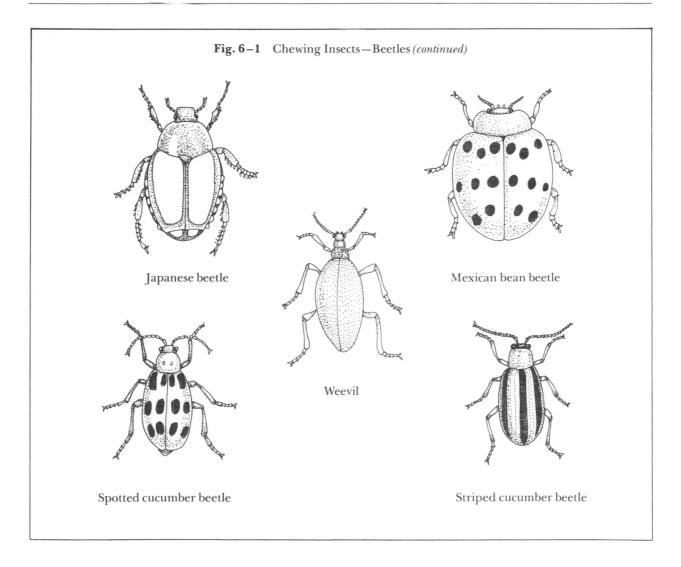

Fig. 6–1 Chewing Insects—Beetles *(continued)*

Japanese beetle

Mexican bean beetle

Weevil

Spotted cucumber beetle

Striped cucumber beetle

yellow head; it feeds within the growing pods of cowpeas. The adult feeds on green snap peas and deposits eggs in holes eaten through the pods. It is found mostly in the South.

Flea beetles are tiny bronze or black beetles about a sixteenth of an inch long. The adult beetles jump like fleas when disturbed and eat what looks like tiny shotholes in the leaves of vegetables. The white quarter-inch larvae feed on the roots or seeds of germinating plants. They do the most damage when germination is delayed by cool temperature, giving them time to eat more seeds. They are found throughout the United States.

Japanese beetles are half an inch long, shiny coppery-brown, and have a row of white hair tufts along their bodies. The section behind the head is metallic green. The larvae are small white grubs that feed on the roots of grasses. Although the Japanese beetle attacks 300 different kinds of plants, it damages only a few vegetables. This pest is found in every state east of the Mississippi River.

Mexican bean beetles are about a quarter of an inch long, coppery-yellow, and have 16 black spots on their wing covers. They resemble their relative, the ladybug. The larva is oval and yellow with a long black-tipped spine. Both larvae and adults feed on the undersides of the leaves of beans, cowpeas, and soybeans, skeletonizing the leaves. When an infestation is severe, this pest will attack the leaves, pods, and stems. It lays eggs in masses on the underside of the leaves and produces one generation a year in the North, two in the central states, and three or more in the South. It is found east of the Rocky Mountains.

Spotted cucumber beetles (Dabrotica) are about a quarter of an inch long, yellow, and have black spots on their backs. The adult chews large, irregular holes in foliage. The larva, known as the southern corn rootworm, tunnels through the roots of cabbages, corn, cucumbers, melons, peas, and other vegetables. Both adults and larvae spread bacteria that cause cucumber and corn wilts. When the temperature rises above 70 degrees F., the beetles start to feed and lay eggs at the bases of stems. The newly hatched larvae feed underground. The spotted cucumber beetle and its close relative, the western cucumber beetle, is found almost everywhere. Infestations are especially severe in the South.

Striped cucumber beetles are about a quarter of an inch long, yellow or black, and have three stripes on their wing covers. The larvae are slender and white, becoming brownish at the ends. The adults eat leaves, stems, and fruits of tender young plants. The beetles pass the winter on the ground under leaves or plants. After feeding on the foliage for several weeks, they lay their eggs in the soil. The larvae then bore into roots and stems below the soil line. This pest also spreads cucumber wilt bacteria and cucumber mosaic.

Vegetable weevils (beetles) are grayish-brown with a light-colored "V" on their wing covers. The larvae are light green with light yellow heads. Both adults and larvae feed on the leaves and roots of many vegetables. The vegetable weevil is found everywhere in the United States.

The Caterpillars (Moths or Butterflies)

These really destructive garden pests are the larvae of moths or butterflies. Generally, they go through four stages — egg, larva, pupa, and adult moth or butterfly. The larva, or caterpillar, stage is the most troublesome for gardeners. After hatching from eggs, caterpillars feed almost continuously on vegetables until they enter a dormant pupal state. All adults have wings. Figure 6 – 2 shows the most destructive ones that you might find in your garden.

Cabbage loopers are pale green 1½-inch-long caterpillars that are sometimes called measuring worms because they fold into a loop and then stretch to full length as they crawl. They chew irregular holes in the leaves of many vegetables. The adult, an inch-long, brown-gray moth, emerges in the Spring and lays single eggs on the upper surface of leaves. The eggs hatch in about two weeks on the vegetables, and four or more generations may appear in a single year. It is found throughout the United States and Canada.

Corn earworms (also called *tomato fruitworms*) are without a doubt a corn lover's nightmare. This 2-inch-long green to brown caterpillar seems to insist on boring into the plumpest corn ears, where it feeds on the kernels. After feeding for about a month, it drops to the ground and tunnels several inches into the earth to pupate. Adults emerge in about two weeks as green to brown moths. Unfortunately, each female moth can lay as many as 3000 eggs. Besides corn, this pest also attacks beans, lettuce, potatoes, tomatoes, and other vegetables. The earworm is found everywhere in the United States and Canada, but infestations are especially severe in the South.

The *Imported Cabbage Worm* attacks all members of the cabbage family, including Brussels sprouts, cabbage, cauliflower, collards, kale, and radishes as well as lettuce. This one-inch long green caterpillar chews the outer leaves and tunnels inside cabbage and cauliflower heads. They pupate in cocoons suspended from plants and in garden refuse. The white cabbage butterfly with black spotted wings then emerges in early Spring. The females lay several hundred eggs underneath the leaves, which hatch in less than a week into caterpillars. The imported cabbage worm is found throughout the United States and Canada.

Cutworms (and their close relatives, *army worms*) are 1½ to 2 inches long, smooth, dull gray to black in color, and are

Fig. 6 – 2   Chewing Insects — Caterpillars

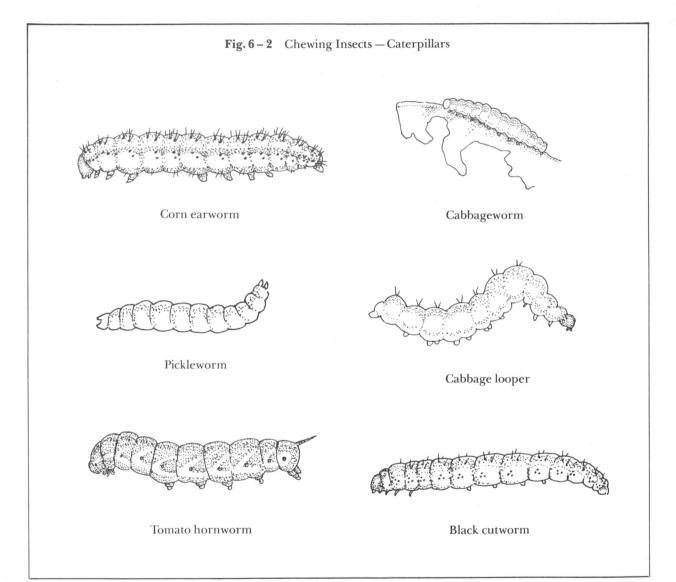

Corn earworm

Cabbageworm

Pickleworm

Cabbage looper

Tomato hornworm

Black cutworm

usually found just under the surface of the soil during the day. At night they feed on the plants near the soil surface or crawl up the plant to feed on foliage. You know cutworms are working in your garden when you find stems of your favorite vegetables cut off at ground level. This pest spends the winter as a naked pupa in the soil, and the adult emerges in the early Spring. The female lays 60 or more eggs in patches on leaves, tree trunks, and brush. In a few days, the eggs hatch into worms ready to go on the attack. The cutworm is found worldwide.

Garden webworms, working under the protection of their own silken coverings, chomp on the stems, leaves, and fruits of beans, corn, cowpeas, peas, soybeans, and other plants. This pale green caterpillar grows to about an inch long and then spends the Winter in the pupal stage in the soil. In the Spring the small buff-colored females lay clusters of eggs on the leaves. Caterpillars hatch in a week, spin a web shelter, and feed for a month. The garden webworm is found throughout the United States and Canada.

The ferocious-looking *tomato hornworm* always looks as if it's ready to attack any gardener who dares come too close. Even though this 3-to-4-inch green caterpillar has a horn projecting from its hind end, it is harmless; it cannot sting or bite. It does, however, chew big hunks out of the foliage of tomatoes, eggplant, peppers, potatoes, and related vegetables. If left alone, it will sometimes strip the plant bare of leaves. This pest spends the Winter underground in a brown hard-shelled spindle-shaped case. Large moths with 5-inch wingspans emerge in early Summer and lay single yellow-green eggs on the underside of leaves. They are found throughout the United States and Canada.

Miscellaneous Chewing Insects

These are neither beetles nor caterpillars, but they can sometimes be just as destructive (see Figure 6 – 3). Here are the major ones to watch for.

Earwigs are ugly night-feeding insects with a pair of pincers (forceps) at the rear end of their abdomens. They feed on leaves at night and then hide in the soil and other dark places during the day.

Grasshoppers don't usually attack vegetable gardens, but when they do they can be especially destructive. Those found in gardens are 1 to 2½ inches long and are usually dark gray, green, brown, or black. The female buries her eggs about an inch below the soil line. Grasshoppers are found throughout the United States and Canada.

Slugs and *snails* can be a terrible nuisance in the home garden by devouring young shoots and seedlings and chewing large round holes in leaves near the ground. These pests feed at night and on cool, overcast days, but they tend to hide on warm, sunny days. You can always tell when they are invading your garden by the telltale trail of silvery slime

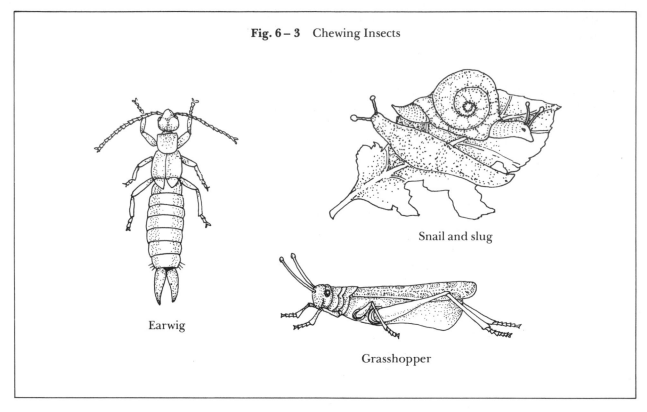

Fig. 6 – 3   Chewing Insects

Snail and slug

Earwig

Grasshopper

they leave everywhere they go. Slugs and snails attack many kinds of vegetables and are found almost everywhere.

SUCKING INSECTS

A number of insects, such as aphids, whiteflies, leafhoppers, spider mites, and others (see Figure 6 – 4), suck out plant juices, causing a spotty or yellow discoloration of the leaves and shoots. This damage may be difficult to spot in the beginning, but a severe infestation may result in wilting and curling of leaves and shoots. All sucking insects except leafhoppers congregate in large groups. Here are the major ones to watch for.

Aphids are obnoxious pests, the bane of every gardener. They are tiny (1/16 to 1/8 inch long), pear-shaped sucking insects in numerous colors — green, yellow, orange, black, gray, pink, brown, and even white. The saliva of some species stunts growth and causes leaves to wilt and curl. All aphids secrete honeydew (plant sap enriched with sugars and amino acids), which attracts ants.

Aphids have a strange life cycle. Wingless females emerge from eggs as nymphs. They mature and give birth to living young without being fertilized. These young reproduce in the same way for several generations until some develop wings and fly off to other plants. In the Fall, winged males as well as females are born. Aphids generally produce 20 or more generations each season and are found almost everywhere.

Whiteflies are minute (1/30 inch long) sucking insects that pierce the leaves or stems of vegetables and draw out the sap. They have two pairs of wings covered with a waxy powder. Whiteflies are often present in large numbers on the undersides of leaves but go unnoticed until the plant is disturbed, when they fly out in a cloudlike swarm. Whiteflies secrete a sticky honeydew that becomes a growing surface for sooty black fungus. The female whitefly lays 20 to 25 eggs that hatch into nymphs. After feeding for some time, the nymphs enter a pupal stage from which they emerge as adult whiteflies. Like aphids, they are found almost everywhere.

Leafhoppers—strange-looking, slender, wedge-shaped insects up to a half-inch long—damage plants by piercing them and sucking sap. Vegetables attacked by leafhoppers often have discolored, crinkled, curled leaves and exhibit wilting or browning leaftips and margins, often called hopperburn. Eggplant, celery, lettuce, potatoes, and rhubarb are especially susceptible. Adult leafhoppers migrate south in the Winter and return north in the Spring. More than 2000 species are found all over North America.

Thrips are active, needle-thin insects that look like black or straw-colored slivers. They have two pairs of slender wings edged with long hairs. Thrip species are named for the plants they attack, and thus there are onion thrips and bean thrips. Thrips also damage carrots, cabbage, cauliflower, celery, cucumbers, melons, squash, tomatoes, turnips, and other vegetables by sucking plant juices. Female thrips insert eggs in leaves and stems, and pale nymphs hatch in about a week and start to feed. There are several generations a year, but they are most numerous in late Spring and mid-Summer. Thrips are found worldwide.

There are several species of *spider mites* that attack vegetables, but the one most often found in home gardens is the two-spotted or red spider mite. This tiny pest is about as big

Fig. 6 – 4   Sucking Insects

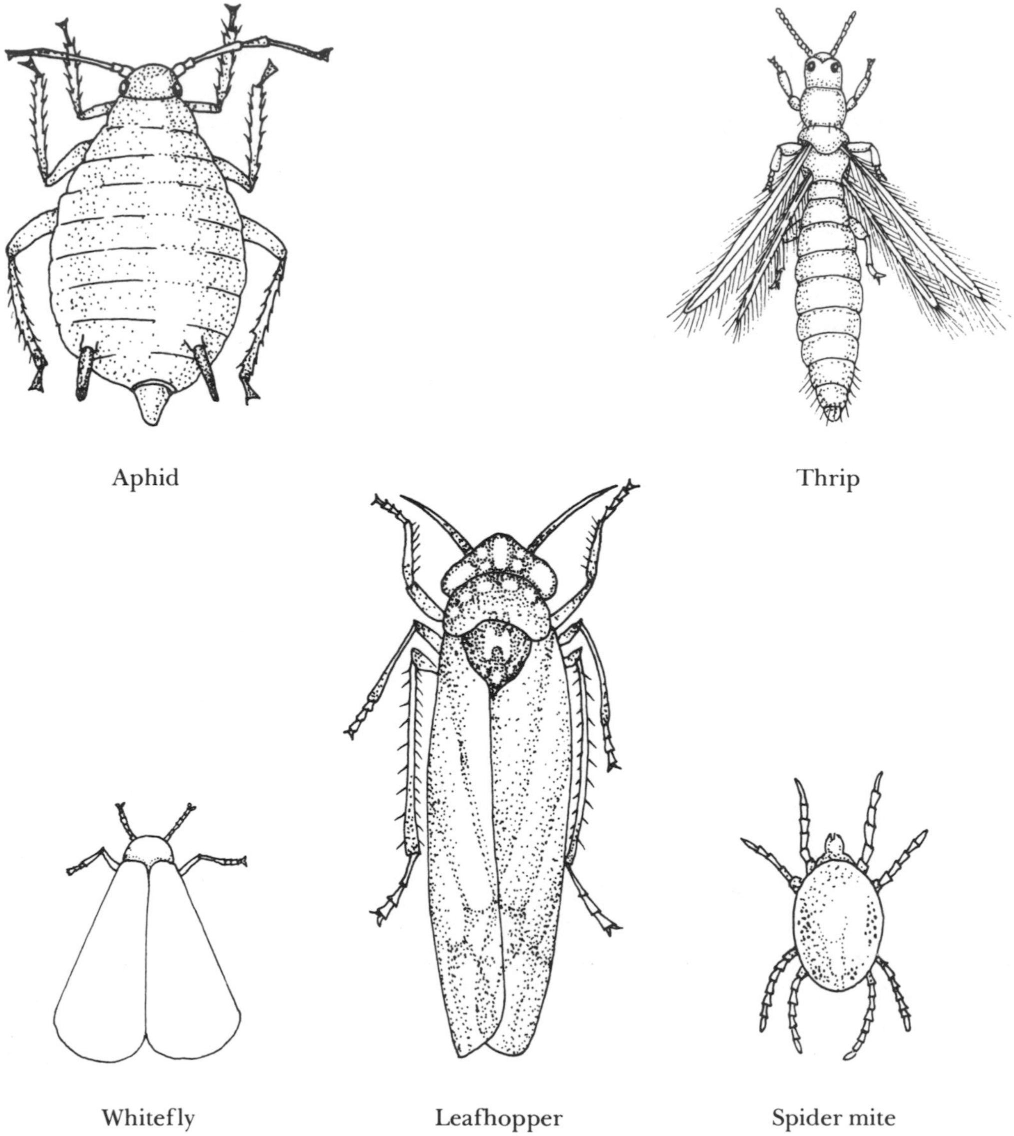

Aphid

Thrip

Whitefly

Leafhopper

Spider mite

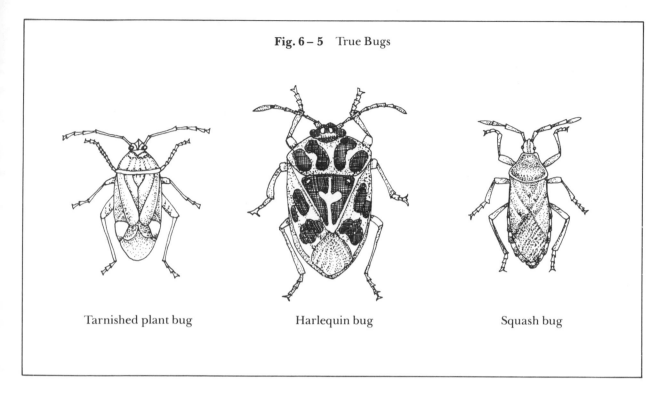

Fig. 6 – 5 True Bugs

Tarnished plant bug   Harlequin bug   Squash bug

as a speck of pepper, and although it is called the red spider mite, it is more often green, yellow, or brown. To tell whether your plants are under siege, place a piece of white paper under a small plant and shake the plant; if mites are present, some will fall on the paper and you'll see small specks moving. Mites lower the vitality of plants by destroying leaf tissue and by sucking nutrients. The affected leaves turn pale green and may show blisters on the upper sides.

Mites construct silver webs over flower buds or leaves and between stalks. They attack a number of garden vegetables, including tomatoes. Female mites lay 100 or more eggs attached to webs on the undersides of leaves. Mites have a one- to two-week life cycle, and as many as 17 generations develop each year. Spider mites are found everywhere in North America.

Many people refer to all insects as "bugs," but in actuality entomologists (insect experts) put *true bugs* in a class by themselves as distinct from beetles, caterpillars, and other insects (see Figure 6 – 5). They are relatively small creatures (1/10 to about 5/8 inch long) with forewings that are thickened toward the base and long slender beaks that suck sap out of vegetables. Young true bugs resemble the adults except that they are even smaller. Here are the most mischievous.

Garden flea hoppers are black, long-legged jumping "bugs" up to 1/10 inch long that attack plants by sucking out the sap. In the Spring, females pierce leaves or stems and insert eggs. There may be five generations in a season. They are found mostly east of the Rocky Mountains.

Harlequin bugs—flat, broad, shield-shaped, 3/8 inch long—can be spotted by their unusual coloring: black with red, orange, or yellow bands and stripes. The green nymphs (young bugs) suck out so much sap that white or yellow blotches appear where they have fed. If the bugs attack in sufficient numbers, leaves wilt, turn brown, and die. They are found throughout the southern half of the United States.

Squash bugs are 5/8 inch long and are black or brown on top, yellow underneath. Leaves attacked by squash bugs wilt rapidly, becoming black and crisp. They attack all vine crops, particularly squash and pumpkins. Squash bugs spend the winter under dead leaves, boards, and similar material. In the Spring the females lay yellow eggs on the undersides of leaves. The nymphs are bright green when they emerge and molt several times before becoming winged adults. There is generally only one generation a year. Squash bugs are found throughout the United States.

Tarnished plant bugs are quarter-inch-long flat oval bugs that are streaked with brownish to yellow or yellow-black blotches. This insect also has a clear yellow triangle marked with a black dot on the lower third of each side. The nymphs are yellow-green with black dots. By injecting fluid into the plant, the bug causes deformed leaves on beets and chard, wilted and discolored stems on celery, and blackened shoot tips, dwarfing, and pitting on beans. It also attacks many other vegetables. It is found throughout the United States.

BORERS

Borers are either grubs (that become beetles) or caterpillars (the larvae of moths) that feed inside stems (see Figure 6–6). Some borers eat the tissues of swelling buds and fruits;

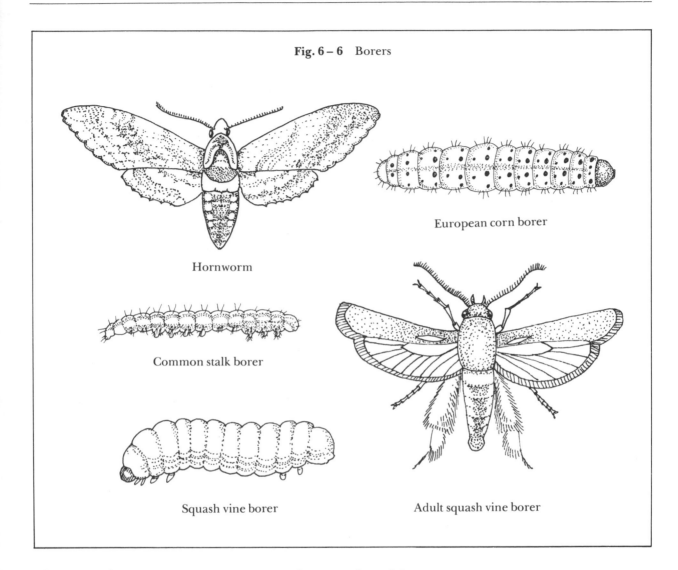

Fig. 6 – 6 Borers

Hornworm

European corn borer

Common stalk borer

Squash vine borer

Adult squash vine borer

others attack roots or stems. Here are the ones found in most home gardens.

European corn borers are flesh-colored caterpillars up to an inch long with rows of round brown spots. The adult moth has a one-inch wingspan and is yellow-brown with wavy dark bands. Caterpillars first eat holes into the leaves and then bore into the stalks and ears. Bent stalks and castings outside of tiny holes in the stalk indicate that borers are at work. The corn borer is the most destructive corn pest known. The female moth lays about 400 eggs on the underside of corn leaves; the caterpillars hatch in about a week and winter in old stalks left in the garden. It is found almost everywhere in the United States.

Potato tuberworms are three-quarter-inch pink or pinkish-white worms with brown heads. They destroy potatoes and also attack eggplant and tomatoes. The adult is a narrow-winged gray-brown moth. The larvae mine the leaves and stems, causing shoots to wilt and die. They also migrate down the stems to the potatoes and burrow in many directions through the flesh. The adult moths lay their eggs one at a time on the underside of the leaves or in the eyes of the potato. After the emerging larvae feed, they pupate in dirt-covered cocoons on the ground. The potato tuberworm is found across the southern part of the United States and as far north as Washington and Colorado.

Squash vine borers are inch-long wrinkled white caterpillars with brown heads. The adult resembles a wasp, with clear copper-green forewings (1½ inches across) and an orange-and-black abdomen. The larvae (caterpillars) eat holes in the stems of vine crops. The insect winters in the soil in a black cocoon. When vines start to produce runners, the moth emerges. The female "pastes" eggs on the stems and leaf stalks near the ground. The larvae hatch in about a week and bore into the stems. This pest is especially damaging east of the Rocky Mountains.

Stalk borers are cream-colored 1-to-1½-inch-long caterpillars with dark brown or purple bands that lighten on the full-grown caterpillar. The adult is a gray moth with a one-inch wingspan. The caterpillars enter the stems of vegetables and eat out to the inside, while the outer leaves remain green. If they enter near the top and eat downward, the plant wilts. They hatch in early Spring, return to the ground in two to four weeks, and change into moths just below the surface of the soil. The female lays more than 2000 eggs on grasses and a few other plants. The stalk borer is fairly widespread east of the Rocky Mountains.

Spinach leaf miners are pale green maggots that tunnel inside plant leaves, giving them a blistered appearance, and also attack beets and chard. The adult is a thin, gray quarter-inch-long fly. The adult lays up to five oval white eggs on the underside of a leaf. The maggots eat for one to three weeks before dropping from the plant to spin cocoons in the soil. The adult fly emerges two to four weeks later. The spinach leaf miner is found throughout the United States and Canada.

SOIL PESTS

Those marauding plant destroyers (see Figure 6 – 7) that attack from below the soil line are root maggots, the larvae of flies, grubs, root-feeding beetle larvae, wireworms, the larvae of "click" beetles, and cutworms (the last of which was covered under caterpillars). Most destroy vegetables by boring into bulbs, large roots, and stems.

Maggots are the larvae of flies (resembling the common housefly). They are white or yellow, legless, soft wormlike creatures that leave irregular pits in the bulbs and roots of many vegetables.

Cabbage maggots are the 1/3-inch-long wedge-shaped larvae of the cabbage-root fly. Plants attacked by the cabbage maggot may be stunted and pale, and the roots are often honeycombed with slimy, curving tunnels. The female fly deposits tiny white eggs on the stems of plants near the soil. In a few weeks, the maggots emerge and attack the plants. This pest is found throughout North America and does especially well in cool (below 65 degree F.) weather.

Carrot rust flies are strange-looking 1/5-inch-long shiny green flies with black eyes and yellow heads. Their ugly, yellowish, legless maggots do all the damage by feeding on carrots, celery, fennel, and parsnips. After hatching on the leaves, they work their way down to feed on the roots, causing the leaves of the plants to wilt and turn yellow. If the attack is severe, entire roots can be destroyed. They are commonly found in eastern Canada and the northern United States.

Onion maggots are the yellow larvae of the onion fly and resemble ordinary houseflies. The leaves of plants attacked by this insect become flabby and faded. The maggot itself tunnels through bulbs and stems, destroying plant tissue. The adult fly lays eggs either in the soil or inside the bulb at the base of the leaves. There are two to three generations per year. The third generation attacks at about harvest time, helping to cause onion-storage rot. The onion maggot affects onions grown in the northern part of the United States.

White grubs and wireworms, both of which can be a nuisance in the garden, are the larvae of the June beetle.

White grubs are 1-to-1½-inch-long "C"-shaped insects with hard brown or black heads. The adults are 1/2-to-3/4-inch-long brown beetles. The grubs are most frequently

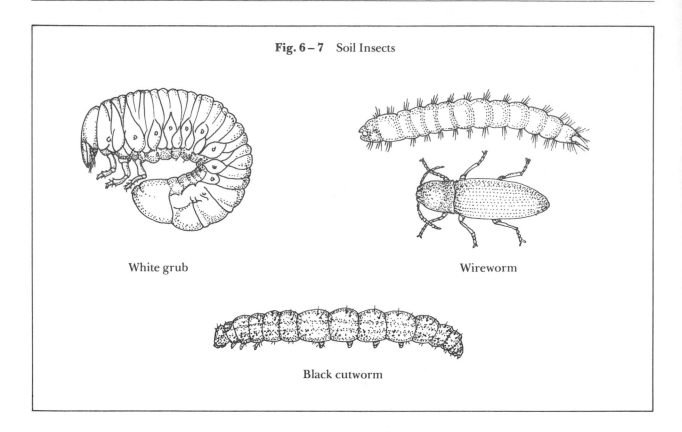

Fig. 6 – 7   Soil Insects

White grub

Wireworm

Black cutworm

found in soil containing an abundance of humus (organic material). They feed on the roots and underground stems of a number of vegetables. Their life cycle takes three to four years and begins when the female beetle lays eggs in grassy areas. The grubs hatch in three to four weeks and then feed until early Fall, when they burrow deep in the soil. For the next two years they feed during the growing season. The third year they remain in the soil as adult beetles, emerging during the fourth Summer to begin the cycle all over again. The white grub is particularly troublesome in the South and Midwest.

Wireworms are the larvae of *click beetles*. They are shiny, yellow to brown insects that are up to 5/8 inch long. They bore into seeds, potato seed pieces, potatoes, and other root crops. Adult click beetles are about a half-inch long, black, and slender. They got their name because when placed on their backs they snap onto their feet with a clicking sound. If wireworms bore into a plant, it comes up but becomes thin and patchy. These pests do great damage to corn as well as potatoes. Each generation requires two to three years to mature. Wireworms are found throughout North America.

HANDLING THE INSECT PROBLEM

There are a number of ways to deal with insect pests in your garden. Here's a rundown on the most effective methods available.

Get Physical with Those Insects

The easiest way to get rid of beetles or caterpillars is to pick them off your vegetables and squash them underfoot or drop them in a jar of water. Let the jar stand for a few hours and then pour the contents into a hole and cover with dirt. This method works well unless you're confronted with an all-out attack.

Spray sucking insects such as aphids with a garden hose. They can come back, of course, but many times this simple water treatment stops them in their tracks.

Use Mechanical Methods

Many insects are night feeders and will hide during daylight hours. You can trap them by placing rolled-up newspapers or a few boards around the garden, and then burn the papers or boards or squash the trapped insects. In addition, sticky squares of paper placed among the rows often trap maggots and a few other pests. Use either Tanglefoot (a commercial product available at most nurseries) or molasses to make them stick. Snails and slugs can be trapped and drowned in a saucer of beer.

Aluminum foil unrolled on the ground around your plants with the shiny side up repels aphids, leafhoppers, Mexican bean beetles, and thrips. The key to aphid protection is bright reflected sun; plant your seedlings far enough apart so that the leaves don't shade the soil. The reflected heat also causes many crops to mature earlier.

Twelve-inch-square boards painted orange or bright yellow, coated with mineral oil or Tanglefoot, and placed near infested plants attract whiteflies in great numbers. Other methods will be covered under individual vegetables.

Try Soapy Water or Mineral Oil

Two common nontoxic substances control many insects. The first, called *mineral oil* (it's not really mineral oil but a safe, nonpoisonous light oil spray), works by smothering slow-moving insects. It is quite effective in controlling the corn earworm. You can purchase this oil spray at all garden centers.

The second is *soapy water,* which often works wonders on such persistent hangers-on as aphids. Mix about 20 tablespoons of soap flakes in 6 gallons of water and spray your plants with a spray gun or tank. It can't hurt the plants.

Use Aromatic Sprays

Many gardeners use a wide variety of foul-smelling homemade plant sprays they swear do the trick. Here are three to try.

1   Gather plants with the most disagreeable odors you can find, such as chives, garlic, and marigolds. Put the cloves, petals, and leaves in a pot or pan and add water to cover the ingredients. Bring the mixture to a boil, strain off the solid particles, and dilute the liquid with five parts water. As soon as this brew cools, you're ready to spray.

2   Boil tomato stems and leaves in water. Cool and then strain off the solid particles. Spray the liquid on your vegetables. This mixture is said to repel a number of pests.

3   Mix a simple rhubarb spray by cutting up a pound of rhubarb leaves. Boil them in one quart of water for 30 minutes and then strain out the leaves and store the liquid in a bottle. To help the solution stick to the leaves, add a dab of liquid soap when it has cooled. The oxalic acid in this mixture is very effective for controlling aphids.

Turn the Good Guys Loose

There are a number of *predator insects* (see Figure 6–8) just ready and waiting to go to work gobbling up the pests in your garden. You can order them by mail (see Appendix B).

Fig. 6-8 Good-Guy Bugs

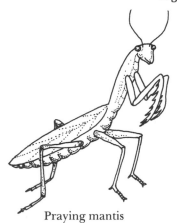

Praying mantis

Praying mantises consume quantities of beetles, caterpillars, and grasshoppers. The young eat aphids and other insects.

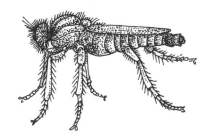

Robber fly

Robber flies eat everything from grasshoppers to beetles.

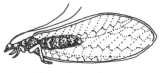

Green lacewing

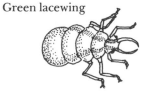

Lacewing larvae

The larvae of the lacewing (the aphidlion) devours many insects.

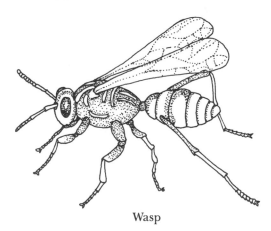

Wasp

Wasps help destroy more than 200 insect pests.

Convergent lady beetle

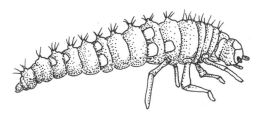

Ladybug larva

Ladybugs help rid the garden of aphids.

The *ladybug,* age-old symbol of good luck, is familiar to most gardeners with its spotted bright orange-red hemispherical shell. It eats two and a half times its own weight each day in aphids, mealybugs, moth eggs, and spider mites. The ladybug larva is a blackish spiny-bodied little beast with six short legs and red, blue, or yellow spots. It also consumes a number of insects before it becomes an adult.

The *praying mantis* (a funny-looking walking-stick-like insect) consumes huge quantities of beetles, caterpillars, and grasshoppers. The young eat aphids, flies, and other small insects.

Lacewings (sometimes known as stinkbugs) are those fragile-looking light-green insects most gardeners see from time to time. The lacewing adult is mainly a nectar lover. The larvae (known as aphidlions) have a gluttonous appetite for aphids, mealybugs, mites, leafhoppers, thrips, and other insects.

Syrhip flies, which look something like bees, are also nectar lovers, but their larvae will gobble up aphids, scale insects, and soft-bodied bugs.

Robber flies have long whiskered faces, long abdomens, and look like bumblebees, and they eat everything from grasshoppers to flies and bees.

There are a number of *wasps* (including the trichogramma wasp) raised commercially for pest control. These wasps lay their eggs inside more than 200 insect pests, including cutworms.

If you plan to use predators, you'll have to order a large number of good insects. Many gardeners recommend a combination of ladybugs, lacewings, and praying mantises. Don't be surprised if they immediately take off to the garden nextdoor. You'll be more likely to keep them if you (1) provide water; (2) plant a variety of flowering plants along with your vegetables; and (3) keep something growing in the garden the entire season.

Bring Out the Biological Weapons

You can conduct germ warfare against several types of insects in your garden by using bacteria. Here are the major ones to try.

Bacillus thuringiensis (sold under the names Dipel, Thuricide, Biotrol, and Agritrol) produces a toxin that is especially effective in controlling leaf-munching worms (caterpillars) such as the cabbage looper, the imported cabbageworm, the European corn borer, and the tomato hornworm. This insecticide doesn't store too well because the live bacteria spores may die within several months to two years. Mark the date on the package and try to use within a few months.

Bacillus popilliae (sold as Doom and Milky Spore Disease) is one of the most effective controls available for the Japanese beetle grub.

Grasshopper spore is a new product containing the spore of a natural parasite that attacks grasshoppers. Dust it among your plants. When insects eat the spore they lose interest in feeding and become lethargic. Other grasshoppers often attack and eat the weakened insects, thus spreading the disease further. The effect is slow at the beginning, but will reduce the grasshopper population noticeably over a couple of seasons.

Use Chemical Botanical Sprays

These botanical sprays are deadly to insects. Fortunately, they are harmless to birds, animals, and humans. They are generally considered to be "organic."

Pyrethrum is a material derived from dried-flower extracts of chrysanthemum cineraefolium. That's a fancy name for a cousin of the garden chrysanthemum from Kenya and Ecuador. Proper doses will kill insects on contact and are especially effective against aphids, leafhoppers, caterpillars, thrips, and leaf miners.

Rotenone is an insecticide derived from the roots (and sometimes the stems) of tropical shrubs and vines of the genera Derris and Lonchocarpus. Rotenone not only acts on contact but is a stomach poison, so it can control many sucking and chewing insects, including beetles, caterpillars, thrips, aphids, and leafhoppers.

Ryania is a naturally occurring insecticide derived from the stems and roots of Ryania speciosa, a South American shrub found in Trinidad and the Amazon basin. Like rotenone, ryania is both a contact insecticide and a stomach poison. It is especially effective against the European corn borer, but also controls a wide variety of other insects.

Sabadilla is made from the seeds of a lilylike Mexican plant *(Schoencaulon officinale)*. Again, it is both a contact and stomach poison and is especially effective against squash bugs.

Use Chemical Insecticides

Three chemical pesticides commonly used today are completely safe in the home garden: *carbaryl* (sold under the name Sevin); *diazinon* (sold as Spectracide and Gardentox); and *malathion*. There are others recommended by some authorities for home gardens (such as methoxychlor), but I feel it's best to stick to these three plus Kelthane for spider mites.

The Medfly situation in California has created some controversy about the safety and use of malathion and other chemical insecticides. Agriculturists claim that these chemicals are perfectly safe, but environmentalists insist

TABLE 6–2   DAYS FROM LAST INSECTICIDE APPLICATION TO HARVEST

CHEMICAL	VEGETABLE	TIME LAPSE (DAYS)
Diazinon	Beans, cabbage, cucumber, squash	7
	Broccoli, cauliflower, peppers	5
	Carrots, collards, kale, lettuce, onions, radishes, spinach, turnips	10
	Peas	No time limitation
	Potatoes	35
	Tomatoes	1
	Watermelons	3
Malathion	Beans, cucumbers, squash, tomatoes	1
	Beets, cabbage, carrots, cauliflower, kale, mustard greens, radishes, spinach	7
	Broccoli, cowpeas, eggplant, onions, peas, peppers, turnips	3
	Lettuce	7 for head lettuce / 14 for leaf lettuce
	Okra	Do not apply after pods form
	Potatoes, sweet potatoes	No time limitation
Sevin (carbaryl)	Beans, carrots, corn, cowpeas, cucumbers, eggplant, okra, peas, peppers, potatoes (foliage only), squash, tomatoes, watermelons	No time limitation
	Beets, broccoli, cabbage, cauliflower, head lettuce, radishes, turnips	3 for root crops / 14 for leaf crops
	Collards, kale, leaf lettuce, mustard greens, spinach	14

people shouldn't be exposed to them. Studies to date, however, have shown diazinon, malathion, and Sevin to be safe for home-garden use. All three are toxic to bees as well as to most garden pests. As a precaution, it is recommended that you stop spraying several days before harvesting your crop (see Table 6–2).

You can buy these chemicals as:

1   A concentrated liquid, called emulsifiable concentrates (EC) by gardening experts. Shake the container thoroughly and then measure out the amount you need and mix it with the recommended amount of water.
2   A powder that you mix with water, called a wettable powder (WP). Stir this powder in a small amount of water to make a smooth paste. Then add it to the required amount of water and stir until it is completely mixed. Shake frequently to keep the powder from settling to the bottom.
3   A dust to be used straight from the package. The various types are described under individual insecticides. For best results when applying dusts and sprays, thoroughly cover the surfaces of all infested plants.

Whether you use emulsifiable concentrates, wettable powders, or dust will depend on your own preference except in certain specific situations; see Chapter 9 for instructions.

Diazinon (sold as Spectracide and Gardentox) is an organic phosphate that is especially useful in the soil to control cutworms, grubs, and wireworms. It is also used to control numerous other insects (see Chapter 9 for recommendations under individual vegetables). Turn over the soil with a shovel or rototiller and then apply diazinon and work thoroughly into the top 3 to 5 inches of soil before planting. For every 1000 square feet of soil use:

1   Twelve tablespoons of 25 percent emulsifiable concentrate (EC) in three gallons of water.
2   One cup of 50 percent wettable powder (WP) in three gallons of water.
3   Two quarts of dry sand added to 10 ounces of diazinon 14 percent granules. Mix thoroughly to ensure even distribution of the small quantities of dry diazinon.

Malathion (sometimes sold as Cythion) is a contact phosphate compound that is useful for controlling all sucking insects such as aphids, leafhoppers, mites, and the like. Spray or dust all plant surfaces thoroughly. For every 1000 square feet of soil use:

1   Two teaspoons of 57 percent emulsifiable concentrate (EC) in one gallon of water.
2   Two tablespoons of wettable powder (WP) in one gallon of water.
3   Five percent dust; see instructions on package.

Carbaryl (Sevin) is a contact phosphate that is useful in controlling over 170 chewing insects. It is widely used by home gardeners. For every 1000 square feet of soil use:

1   Two tablespoons of 50 percent wettable powder (WP) in one gallon of water.
2   Ten percent dust or 5 percent bait; see instructions on package.

EVERYTHING YOU NEED TO KNOW ABOUT SPRAYERS AND DUSTERS

Every gardener needs a sprayer or duster to deal with insect pests, to apply fungicides and fertilizers, and for many other purposes (see Figure 6 – 9). The problem is that there is an incredible variety of types on the market today. Which ones should you buy for your own garden use? Here's a quick look to help you decide.

Small handsprayers come in two types: the Windex-bottle variety that you pump with your fingers, and the hand-pump type. The Windex-bottle type is fine for spraying vegetables growing in a few containers, but if you're growing much more than this, the work will be too much of a chore. The pump variety will handle up to about a 1000-square-foot garden without too much effort. The pump is mounted on top of a metal or glass container. You can buy inexpensive (about $3) single-action sprayers that stop spraying at the end of each stroke or continuous-action sprayers (about $6) that keep spraying as long as you keep pumping. Some come with adjustable nozzles to handle a

Fig. 6-9 Sprayers and Dusters

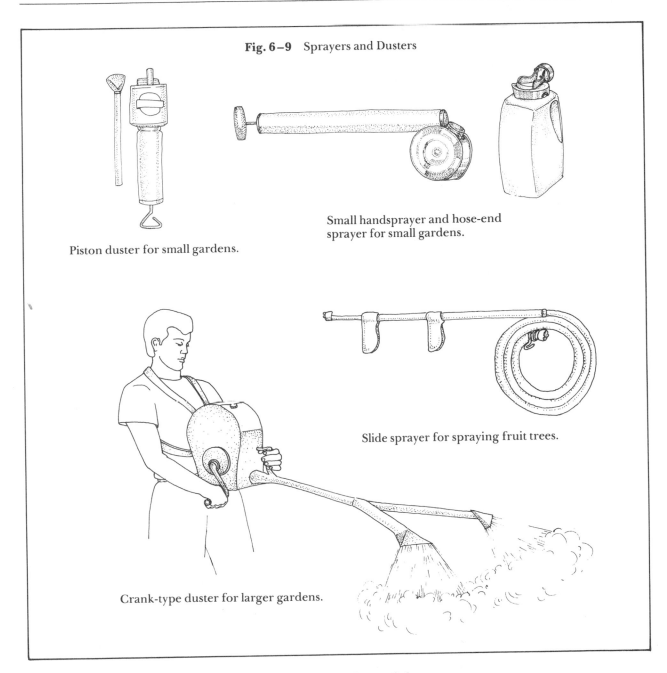

Piston duster for small gardens.

Small handsprayer and hose-end sprayer for small gardens.

Slide sprayer for spraying fruit trees.

Crank-type duster for larger gardens.

wide variety of spraying chores. They are especially useful for spraying under leaves.

Hose-end sprayers ($5 to $15) use a holding jar that attaches directly to a garden hose. Just add the chemicals according to the directions; they will be mixed to the right

Fig. 6–9   Sprayers and Dusters *(continued)*

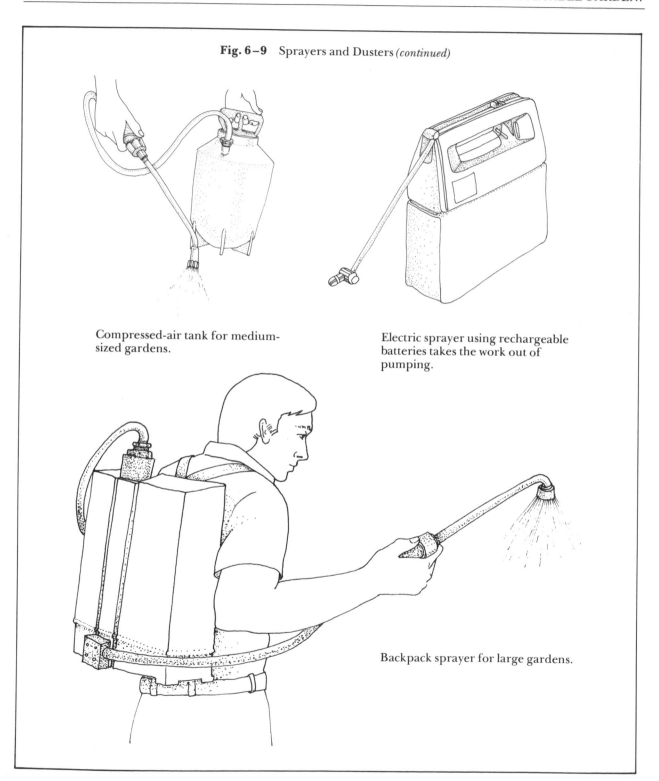

Compressed-air tank for medium-sized gardens.

Electric sprayer using rechargeable batteries takes the work out of pumping.

Backpack sprayer for large gardens.

proportions in the jar by the action of the hose. Many come with a variety of adjustable nozzles. Hose-end sprayers are useful for applying chemicals to small gardens of up to about 1000 square feet. Since the water pressure from the hose applies the spray automatically, hose-end sprayers are less work than the hand-pump types. Their major drawback is that they are not as easy to use underneath the leaves.

Slide sprayers, often called trombone sprayers (about $10), use a round brass slide pump. To spray, pump the slide back and forth. This sprayer uses an open bucket, not a tank. It is excellent for spraying fruit trees, but it is not as good for vegetable gardens since it was designed to shoot a long-distance spray. Also keep in mind that you must carry an open bucket throughout the garden.

Compressed-air tanks ($20 to $50) are made of galvanized steel or plastic and are pumped by hand to create air pressure. They are available in sizes of one to 15 gallons or more. Most have adjustable nozzles that put out a mist, spray, or stream. A long hand wand allows you to reach easily under the leaves. The best size for home gardens is two or three gallons, carried by a shoulder strap. These are excellent for medium to small gardens because they have enough capacity to cover the entire garden in one mixing and are extremely easy to handle. A variation of this is the *electric sprayer,* which uses a rechargeable battery for compressor power instead of a hand pump.

Dusters come in two basic types. The first, the *piston duster* for small to medium gardens, stores dust in a chamber. The dust is forced out by pushing in on the piston. These small devices hold up to two quarts of dust. The second, the *crank duster,* operates with a hand crank that forces the insecticide into a fan where it is blown out over the vegetables. Crank dusters probably aren't practical unless you're cultivating a large acreage.

There are also large *backpack sprayers,* which hold about four gallons of liquid, and *power-driven sprayers on wheels,* which hold 10 gallons or more. Using this kind of capacity on a small garden is a classic example of overkill, but a backpack sprayer can be useful for larger home orchards.

Today's chemical insecticides are a lot safer than the ones used a few years ago, but it's still wise to take a few precautions. Here are the ones I advise:

1   Keep insecticides in a safe place away from children and pets.
2   Read the label instructions carefully and follow them exactly when preparing and applying insecticides.
3   Make sure you stick with the dosage specified on the label.
4   Use pesticides only on a calm day. This is especially important when using dusts, as even a light wind can scatter them everywhere in your garden. If it rains right after dusting or spraying, make another application.
5   Wash with soapy water immediately if you spill any insecticide on your body. Wash all exposed skin after dusting or spraying, even if you haven't spilled anything.
6   Wrap the empty container in a newspaper and then put it in the trash.
7   Refer to Table 6 – 2 so that you'll know when to stop application in preparation for the harvest.
8   Wash all vegetables thoroughly before eating.

What I have attempted to provide is a general guide you can use to become better acquainted with those pests that try to make a meal out of your garden along with a survey of the botanical, biological, and chemical tools you can use to avoid or cure problems. In Chapter 9 you will find more specific instructions for getting rid of the insects that attack individual vegetables.

CHAPTER SEVEN

DEALING WITH VEGETABLE DISEASES

Plant doctors (plant pathologists, that is) consider a vegetable to be sick (diseased) when it doesn't develop or produce normally because it is being attacked by some living organism. Technically, environmental plant problems such as sunscald and blossom drop can also be considered diseases, but they have already been covered.

A typical leaf or stem infection has the following appearance: a sunken, brown center is bordered by a tan or yellow area that is surrounded by a pale green border into which the disease is growing (see Figure 7–1). Infected fruit also shows similar color zones. Although leaf and fruit discoloration may occur with insect damage, the discoloration does not appear in definite zones.

CHECKING OUT THE VEGETABLE DESTROYERS

Here's a rundown on the most common diseases that can attack your plants (see Table 7–1). Specific diseases that infect individual vegetables and their control will be covered in detail in Chapter 9.

Bacteria

Bacteria are typically one-celled plants that swarm through every inch of your soil (see Figure 7–2). By estimate, one pound of garden soil contains over 2 million bacteria. The thought is staggering. Fortunately, most bacteria are harmless and many are beneficial in helping to break down organic matter in the soil. Some, however, kill vegetables or make them inedible. The most visible characteristic of a bacterial infection in vegetables is an oozing gelatinous fluid flowing from the infected area.

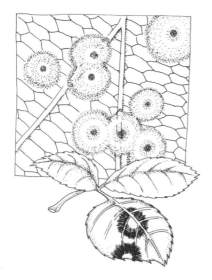

Fig. 7–1 Disease

Typical leaf and stem infection shows concentric color zones. Often the center is sunken.

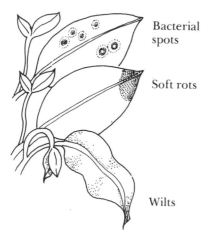

Bacterial spots

Soft rots

Wilts

Fig. 7–2 Bacterial Damage

You might find any of the following three kinds of bacterial damage in your garden: bacterial spots, soft rots, and wilts.

Bacterial spots, or *blight,* may start as dark green spots or streaks on the leaves and stems, later turn gray, brown, or reddish-brown, and ooze a gelatinous fluid. The spots may even drop out, leaving ragged holes, and the leaves may wither and die. Scabby or sunken brown spots or blotches caused by bacteria are generally called blights.

Soft bacterial rot may infect the leaves, branches, and fruit of plants. The infected area is generally bordered by a lighter yellow or tan area. Advanced infection causes large sunken dark areas on the fruit that frequently ooze a gelatinous fluid.

Bacterial wilt occurs when the bacteria invade and plug up the water-conducting tubes of the plant. If you slice the stem of an infected plant, it will ooze a gelatinous fluid. To the gardener's dismay, often seemingly healthy, vigorous plants simply dry up and wilt overnight.

There is no chemical control for bacterial diseases except through the treatment of vegetable seeds before planting. Certain insects such as the flea beetle and cucumber beetle carry bacterial disease in their digestive tracts. When these beetles have lunch in your garden, they spread the disease.

Fungi

Fungi are minute nongreen plants that exist everywhere in the garden soil (see Figure 7–3). One pound of soil contains up to 225 million of them. Like bacteria, some fungi break down organic matter into nutrients that can be used by vegetables. In contrast, other fungi attack live plants. With the exception of rots, fungal diseases tend to start with a sunken dark area that is later bordered by yellow, tan, or light green.

You will find eight general types of fungal infections in your garden: mildews, rusts, rots, cankers, scab, spots, wilts, and smuts.

Mildews fall into two groups—powdery and down mildew. *Powdery mildew* shows up as superficial white to light grayish patches on the upper surfaces of leaves and on buds. Plants infected with *downy mildews* have pale green or yellow areas on the upper leaf surfaces, with light gray or purplish patches below. The leaves wilt, wither, and die. Seedlings may wilt and collapse. Both mildews affect a wide number of vegetables. Mildew attacks are most severe in cool, humid, or wet weather and are common in areas with cool nights and warm days.

Rust sometimes appears as bright yellow, orange, red, reddish-brown, or black powder pustules (blisters) on the underside of the leaves. This is a complicated disease, since the forms that attack vegetables require two different plants (called alternate hosts) to complete the life cycle. The rust that attacks corn completes its alternate life cycle on oxalis. In extreme cases, plants attacked by rust wither and die.

Rot is not one general disease but several. Plants with *root rot* may gradually or suddenly lose vigor and their leaves will become pale or yellow. The actual root decay may be mushy and spongy, caused by both fungi and bacteria. In many cases, nematodes (microscopic worms) provide the wound by which root rotting fungi and bacteria enter. When seedlings rot, wilt, collapse, and die before or after emergence, it is called *damping off*. *Fruit rot* often starts as one or more spots that enlarge to include a portion or all of the fruit. Rots can attack practically all the vegetables in your garden.

Cankers are dead areas on the stem. They are oval or irregular in shape, often sunken or swollen, and typically discolored. Some completely girdle the stem. The plants are often stunted. Blackleg of cabbage falls within this category and is probably one of the most serious vegetable diseases.

Scab, as the name suggests, usually appears as roughened crustlike raised or sunken areas on the surface of leaves, stems, fruit, roots, or tubers. The leaves may wither and drop early. Scab is caused by a few bacteria and a wide range of fungi.

Fungal leaf spots vary in size, shape, and color. The centers of the spots may fall out, and they may also enlarge to form big blotches. Wet seasons, high humidity, and water splashed on foliage increase the incidence of leaf spots. Certain leaf spots have special names such as *black spot, tar spot,* and *anthracnose.*

Wilt may seem like one disease, but it is basically three. Each type invades and plugs up the water- and food-con-

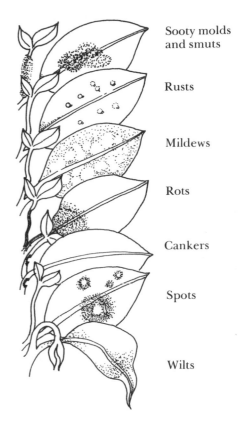

Sooty molds and smuts

Rusts

Mildews

Rots

Cankers

Spots

Wilts

Fig. 7–3 Fungal Damage

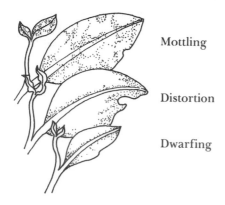

Mottling

Distortion

Dwarfing

Fig. 7–4   Types of Viral Damage
Ring spots
Mosaics
Yellows

ducting vessels inside the plants. These wilts are sometimes confused with root rot.

Bacterial wilt was discussed earlier in this chapter. *Fusarium* and *verticillium wilt* are fungi. Don't let these names bother you; just wilt will do. Plants attacked by both verticillium and fusarium wilt are usually stunted and yellow. The wilting starts at the base of the stem and proceeds upward.

Smuts and *sooty molds* produce massive amounts of black sooty spores. Smut is a fungus disease that produces dark brown to black sooty-looking spore masses inside swollen whitish blisters. Sooty mold shows up as unsightly superficial dark brown or black blotches on leaves, fruit, and stems. It can be removed easily by rubbing, and causes little damage to most plants.

Viruses

Viruses are complex single molecules that act like living organisms. There are more than 200,000 of these marauding molecules to an inch. To identify viruses, plant pathologists usually group them together by what they do to the plant. Viral diseases often show up as a distortion (puckering or curling) of leaves, flowers, or fruits; stunted plants; yellow streaking; or mottled leaves (see Figure 7–4).

A few of the viruses that affect vegetables are *aster yellows* (plants stunted and yellow), *curlytop* (dwarfed plants with bunched, curled leaves), *mosaic* (leaves have mottled yellow or light green areas), *ringspot* (yellow or brown concentric rings), and *yellows* (plants uniformly yellow, may wilt and die). Viruses will be covered in more detail under individual vegetables in Chapter 9.

There is no chemical control for a virus. Good cultural practices and use of virus-resistant vegetables provide the best protection (see Chapter 2). Since many viruses are spread by sucking insects such as aphids and leafhoppers, you can also limit the viral diseases in your garden by controlling insects that spread the diseases (see Chapter 6).

Parasitic Nematodes

Parasitic nematodes that attack plants are vigorous, slender, tiny roundworms. They are generally included under diseases because the symptoms they cause are similar.

Most nematodes are harmless because they feed on decomposing organic material and other soil organisms. Nematodes that attack living vegetables suck the green color and cause stunting of vegetables, wilting, dieback, and similar signs.

The *root-knot nematode* causes galls to form on the roots of many vegetables. The first indication of nematode injury in a garden or field is often the appearance of small circular or irregular areas of stunted plants with yellow or bronzed foliage. This area gradually enlarges. There are a number of chemical and nonchemical ways to protect your vegetables from nematodes.

TABLE 7–1 VEGETABLE DISEASES AT A GLANCE

TYPE/DISEASE	WHAT TO LOOK FOR	PREVENTION AND/OR NATURAL CONTROLS	CHEMICAL CONTROLS
BACTERIA Bacterial spot	Dark green spots or streaks that later turn gray, brown, reddish; can ooze gelatinous fluid	Rotate crops; keep plants vigorous by fertilizing	Fixed copper sprays help control rot and blight
Soft bacterial rot	Infected areas on leaves, branches, or fruit bordered by yellow or tan area; advanced infection causes large sunken dark areas, frequently oozing gelatinous fluid	Avoid planting in undrained soil; rotate crops on long rotation	Treat soil with diazinon before planting to control insects that spread rot
Bacterial wilt (spread by insects)	Plants wilt and die; symptoms identical to fusarium and verticillium wilt	Destroy infected plants; grow resistant varieties (see Chapter 2)	Use Sevin plus malathion to destroy insects that spread bacterial wilt
FUNGI Mildew	Grayish patches on upper surface of leaves (powdery mildew); pale green or yellow areas on upper surface, light gray or purple below	Rotate crops; avoid overhead sprinkling; plant resistant varieties	Downy mildew—use maneb, zineb, or fixed copper; powdery mildew—apply sulfur spray when mildew first appears
Rust	Yellow, orange, red, or brown pustules on underside of leaves and stems	Destroy nearby weeds that show rust; collect and destroy infected plants when first seen	Use maneb, zineb, or folpet

TABLE 7–1   VEGETABLE DISEASES AT A GLANCE (continued)

TYPE/DISEASE	WHAT TO LOOK FOR	PREVENTION AND/OR NATURAL CONTROLS	CHEMICAL CONTROLS
ROTS	Stems, leaves, roots, and/or fruit become mushy and spongy	Plant in well-drained soil; collect and destroy infected material and plant debris; keep fruit off soil	Treat seed with captan; use captan in seedbed before planting
Canker	Sunken or swollen discolored dead areas on stem that sometimes girdle stem	Destroy infected plants; use four-year rotation; purchase healthy-looking plants	
Scab	Roughened crustlike raised or sunken area on surface of leaves, stem, fruit, roots, and tubers	Practice long crop rotation; plant resistant varieties; remove weeds	Spray nonroot crops with captan, maneb, zineb, ziram
Fungal leaf spots/Blight	Spots on leaves; centers may fall out; spots may enlarge to form blotches	When severe, collect and burn infected material	Control insects with Sevin or malathion (many spread disease); spray with captan, maneb, zineb
Wilt	Leaves turn pale green to yellow; plants wilt and die	Use resistant varieties; practice long rotation; collect and destroy infected plants	
Smut/Sooty mold	Dark brown to black sooty-looking masses inside swollen white blisters	Pick off and burn infected parts before blisters open; grow resistant varieties	
VIRUSES	Distortion of leaves, flowers, fruit; stunted plants; yellow streaking or mottling	Destroy diseased material; keep down weeds	Many viruses are transmitted by insects; control insects with Sevin or malathion
NEMATODES	Yellowing, stunting, wilting, dieback; knots on roots	Destroy infected plants; plant resistant varieties; rotate plantings	Use telone in the soil

PREVENTING VEGETABLE DISEASES

Many of the measures covered in Chapter 2 are extremely effective in preventing these diseases from getting out of hand in your garden. You will find them in summary form in Table 7–2.

TABLE 7–2 CONTROL PRACTICES FOR DISEASES

	CROP ROTATION	DISEASE FREE SEED	GARDEN CLEANLINESS	HEALTHY TRANSPLANTS	RESISTANT VARIETIES	SEED TREATMENT	SITE SELECTION	WEED CONTROL
Bacterial spots/Blight	X	XX	X	XXX	X	X		
Bacterial wilt	X			XXX			X	
Soft bacterial rot								
Cankers	XXX		X					
Mildew				XXX	X			
Rot	X	X	X	XXX			X	
Rust				XXX	X			
Scab	X		X		XX			
Smut			X		XX			
Spots, fungal		XX	X		XX			
Wilt	X			XXX	XXX			
Viruses		XXX		XXX	XX			X

XXX   Excellent method of control
XX   Good method of control
X   Some control may be obtained

Resorting to Fungicides

A fungicide is any chemical that kills or inhibits a fungus that lands on or attacks vegetables. There are really two kinds: *protective fungicides,* which prevent the disease from entering the plant, and *killer* (erradicant) *fungicides,* which kill or inhibit fungi after they penetrate the plants (see Table 7–3) for a rundown of popular fungicides.

Fungicides are sold at nurseries and garden stores under a wide variety of trade names such as Captan Garden Spray, Ortho 50W, Ortho Rose and Garden Fungicide, Karthane W. D., and others. Many are often mixed together to provide a multipurpose spray that controls a wide variety of diseases. Fungicides are also sometimes mixed with insecticides to provide both insect and disease control in the same application.

TABLE 7–3   **COMMONLY USED FUNGICIDES**

COMMON NAME	ACTIVE INGREDIENT	SELECTED NAMES	DISEASES
Captan	N (trichloromethylthio) tetrahydrophthalimide	Captan 50-W, Captan Garden Spray, Orthocide 50 or 80 Wettable, Orthocide 75 Seed Protectant, Chipman Captan Dust	Damping off, seedling blight in plant beds, leaf spots, blights, fruit rots. Used also as a seed protector. Does not control powdery mildews or rusts.
Chloranil	Tetrachloro-p-benzoauinone	Spergon, Spergon Seed Protectant, Geigy SP	Foliage diseases. Use as a soil and bulb treatment.
Dexon	p-(dimethylamino)		Damping off, root rots of many vegetables. Use as a seed and soil fungicide.
Dichlone	2-3-Dichloro-1,4-naphthoquinnone	Phygon, Niagara Phygon, Cross Phygon-XL	Blights and fruit rots of vegetables. Damping off, seed treatment.
Difolatan	N-(1,1,22 tetrachloroethyl-sulfenyl)-cis-4-cyclohexene-1,2-dicarboximide		Downy mildews, anthracnose, leaf spots, and blight. May be used as a seed or soil treatment. Chemically related to captan and folpet.
Dinocap	2-(1-methylheptyl)-4-6-dinitrophenyl cronate	Karathane Liquid Concentrate, Karathane Dust	Powdery mildews. Used in combination with other fungicides and insecticides.
Bordeaux mixture	Copper sulfate, hydrated lime	Copper Hydro Bordo, Ortho Bordo Mixture	Fungus leaf spots, blights, anthracnose.
Copper fungicides (fixed or neutral)	Metallic copper	Tri-Basic Copper, Basic Copper Fungicide, Micro Nu-Cop	Leaf spots, blights.

TABLE 7–3   **COMMONLY USED FUNGICIDES** *(continued)*

COMMON NAME	ACTIVE INGREDIENT	SELECTED NAMES	DISEASES
Ferbam	Ferric dimethyldithiocarbamate	Fermate Ferbam Fungicide, Ortho Ferbam 76, Ferbam W-76	Damping off, seedling blights.
Folpet (a close relative of captan)	(Phaltan) N-trichloromethyltiopthalimide	Corona Folebt 50 Ortho Phaltan Rose and Garden fungicide	Powdery mildews.
Lanstan	1-chloro-2-nitropane		Damping off, crown and root rots, clubroot in cabbage, some wilts.
Maneb	Manganese ethylenebis (dithiocarbamate)	Manzate Maneb Fungicide, Dithane M-22	Rust, foliage, fruit diseases. Especially useful for tomatoes, potatoes, and other vine crops; does not control powdery mildew.
Metiram (Polyram)	Zinc polyethylene thiuram disulfide complex		Rusts, downy mildews, leaf spots, and blights. Seed protector.
PCNB	Tetrachloroiso-phthalonitrile		Many root, stem, and crown rots, e.g., clubroot, potato scab, pink rot of celery. Damping off.
Streptomycin	Streptomycin sulfate, basic copper sulfate terramycin	Agrimycin 17, Phytomycin, Ortho Streptomycin, Agri-strep	Bacterial spot on peppers, tomato baterial wilts, blights, blackleg of potato.
Sulfur products	Sulfur		Powdery mildew on many plants, some leaf rusts, leaf blights, fruit rots.
Zineb	Zinc ethylenebis (dithiocarbamate)	Dithane Z-78, Parzate Zineb, Ortho Zineb	Rusts, leaf spots, blights, fruit rots.
Ziram	Zinc Dimethyldithiocarbamate	Zerlate Ziram Fungicide, Z-C Spray or Dust	Wide variety of diseases. Especially useful on the tender seedlings of most vegetables.

Fungicides are available as either dust or liquid, and both are equally effective. Dusts are easy to apply without messy mixing or measuring and are also less likely to burn the foliage. If you dust, apply a thin film to all aboveground plant surfaces. Dust in the early morning or evening when the plants are damp and the air is calm.

Sprays are messier than dusts but usually remain on the plants longer. All parts of the plant must be coated with a fine, misty spray that wets the surface evenly. Many fungi and bacteria penetrate only the underleaf surface, so cover that area especially well. Spray from the top of the plant down, the bottom up, and the inside out.

It is important to wait from one to several days after using a fungicide before harvesting your vegetables. In addition, it is important to follow the following rules when using any fungicide.

1   Read the label on each fungicide container and heed all warnings.
2   Use only on the crops specified.
3   Store fungicides in their original, labeled containers.
4   Keep out of reach of children and away from pets.
5   Wash with soap and water after handling fungicides.

Chapter 9 explains exactly which fungicides and/or preventive controls to use on particular vegetables and for what diseases.

With care and the use of the proper controls when appropriate, disease should really be only a minor problem. In my own garden I seldom have disease problems. When I do, I can usually control them easily by switching (the next season) to resistant vegetable varieties, by rotating crops, and by applying the right fungicides when I really need them.

CHAPTER EIGHT

KEEPING THE CRITTERS OUT

Somewhere during the first year most gardeners lose their starry-eyed belief that all critters are cute and friendly. They begin to realize that a number of those cuddly-looking creatures can be downright destructive.

When I gardened in the city, the neighbors' cats and dogs tore up whole rows of radishes and carrots, and the birds had a feast on my young cucumbers. Later, in the country, I had to battle tenacious gophers, marauding deer, and my own ducks for the right to harvest vegetables.

Faced with this summer-long siege, some gardeners decide that all critters are personally out to get their garden. As a result, they defend their vegetable plots with shotguns, traps, poison bombs, and anything else they can lay their hands on.

Fortunately, successful gardening doesn't really require such drastic tactics. In some cases just the expedience of planting a row of garlic will do the trick. However, what works for one gardener doesn't always work for another. Some gardeners, for instance, find that ground red pepper scattered around the garden drives gophers up the wall. Others swear by the efficiency of buried wine bottles, and some have good luck with gopher windmills. A few, however, find that none of these methods work and resort to more drastic devices such as traps or gopher gas to get the job done.

There are five kinds of deterrents you can try. The following general discussion covers aromatics, physical barriers, traps, poison baits or gas, and miscellaneous devices. For specific devices, see Tables 8–1 through 8–7.

Aromatics give off an odor that make some animals hold their noses and stalk from your garden. Effective aromatic deterrents vary from mothballs and garlic to lion dung (this will probably involve a visit to your local zoo) and almost anything inbetween. Aromatics are generally inexpensive and easy to use. However, they are only partially effective and vary from garden to garden.

Physical barriers (see Figure 8–1) consist of fences, cages to protect entire beds, or individual seed protectors made of paper caps, hotkaps, and window screens. Deer-proof fences also fall within this category and should be at least 8 feet high, although they need be only 4 feet high if you use the outrigger extensions and single strands of wire. Fences designed to keep out rabbits should be constructed of wire or special fence wire that becomes smaller (to about 2 inches) toward the bottom and should be buried 6 inches underground to keep rabbits from digging underneath. Barriers are the most effective of all methods. Unfortunately, they are also the most expensive.

TABLE 8–1 BIRDS

CONTROL	HOW TO USE	ADVANTAGES	DISADVANTAGES
Barriers			
Hotkaps	Place over individual seedlings	Easy to use	Expensive if many are needed
Dixie cups	Cut the tops out and place over individual seedlings; especially useful for young cucumbers, squash	Easy to use; inexpensive	None
Screen caps	Cut out an 8-inch-by-8-inch (or larger) square from window screen cloth; staple together to form a cone	Protects small groups of seedlings	Not large enough for an entire seedbed of one crop
Netting (mosquito netting or commercial bird netting)	Place netting on stakes over entire seedbed	Good for larger beds of lettuce and other leafy vegetables	Must be removed to weed or harvest
Other			
Scarecrow	Make of crossed stakes and old clothes	Durable	Only partially effective

TABLE 8-2 DOGS AND CATS

CONTROL	HOW TO USE	ADVANTAGES	DISADVANTAGES
Aromatics			
Black Leaf 40 home brew (U.S. Department of Agricultural mixture)	2 tablespoons Black Leaf 40 (nicotine sulfate) in a gallon of water; spray around garden every two weeks	Easy to apply	Must be renewed every two weeks
Chili powder/ground garlic	Mix together in equal proportions; sprinkle around garden; replenish weekly	Easy to prepare	Washes away easily; more effective for cats than dogs
Commercial repellent stakes	Place in ground around garden	Long-lasting; does not wash away	Only partially effective
Commercial sprays or aerosol repellents	Spray around garden area; replenish every few days	Easy to use	Washes away easily
Stale cigars	Scatter tobacco around garden; replenish as needed	Inexpensive; easy to use	Washes away easily; only partially effective
Barriers			
Chicken-wire cages	Install 2- to 3-foot-high chicken-wire cages over individual beds of carrots, radishes, and similar crops	Completely effective against both dogs and cats	Requires special construction; protects only limited area
Fence	Install 4-foot chicken-wire or mesh fence around garden	Positive control over dogs	Fences do not stop cats; relatively expensive

TABLE 8-3 DEER

CONTROL	HOW TO USE	ADVANTAGES	DISADVANTAGES
Aromatics			
Commercial liquid repellents	Spray in garden area or around perimeter	Fairly inexpensive	Must be renewed every two months
Commercial deer-repellent bags	Hang on stakes around garden; keep watered	Easy to use	Only partially effective
Lion dung	Scatter around garden	Extremely effective; some gardeners swear by it	Must make effort to obtain from a zoo

TABLE 8–3   DEER (continued)

CONTROL	HOW TO USE	ADVANTAGES	DISADVANTAGES
Kitty litter	Scatter around garden	Inexpensive	Only partially effective
Dried blood, fish heads, bloodmeal	Scatter around garden	Easy to apply	Only partially effective
Human or dog hair	Scatter around garden or hang in sack pouches around garden	Inexpensive; easy to use; old-time gardeners insist this method works best	Large quantities needed
Barriers			
Aluminum strips, pie pans	Hang from twine around edge of garden	Easy to install; inexpensive	Only partially effective; deer sometimes ignore them
Mesh-metal fencing 3 to 4 feet wide	Lay flat on ground around perimeter of garden	Easy to install; deer don't like to walk across hard-to-see, unfamiliar surface	No positive control; deer can still cross if extremely hungry
4-foot vertical fence	Place single-strand wire on outriggers to extend 5 feet beyond fence	Least expensive of vertical deer fencing	Not as effective as full 8-foot fencing
8-foot fence	Install with gate completely around garden	Complete control of deer problem	Expensive
Portable chicken-wire cages	Place over certain parts of garden to keep deer away from selected vegetables	Portable; not as expensive as fencing	Can protect only a few vegetables

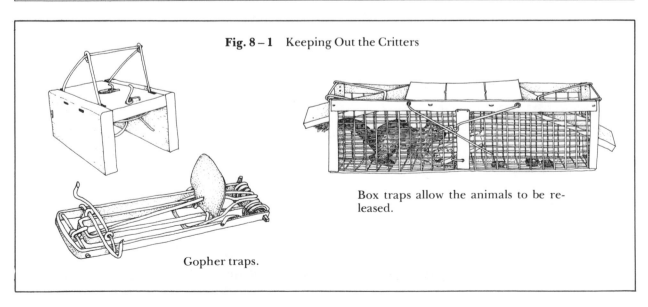

Fig. 8–1   Keeping Out the Critters

Box traps allow the animals to be released.

Gopher traps.

Fig. 8–1 Keeping Out the Critters *(continued)*

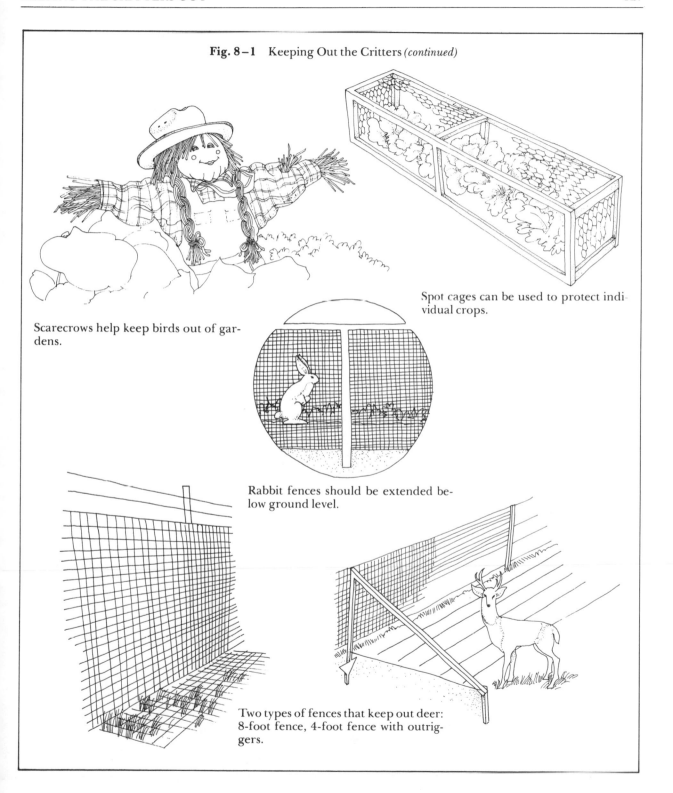

Spot cages can be used to protect individual crops.

Scarecrows help keep birds out of gardens.

Rabbit fences should be extended below ground level.

Two types of fences that keep out deer: 8-foot fence, 4-foot fence with outriggers.

TABLE 8–4 **RABBITS**

CONTROL	HOW TO USE	ADVANTAGES	DISADVANTAGES
Aromatics			
Animal lard	Rub on plants	Inexpensive; easy to use	Only partially effective
Chili powder/ground garlic	Mix together in equal proportions; sprinkle around garden; replenish weekly	Easy to prepare	Washes away easily
Commercial liquid repellent	Spray around garden area; replenish every few days	Easy to apply	Washes away easily
Mineral repellent (ground limestone, talcum, powdered-rock phosphate)	Sprinkle around garden	Easy to apply	Ingredients sometimes hard to find in small quantities
Wood ashes	Scatter around garden; replenish as needed	Fairly effective	Washes away easily
Aromatic Plants			
Mint leaves	Scatter around garden; replenish weekly	Easy to use	Only partially effective
Barriers			
2-foot-high mesh fence or chicken-wire (mesh must be less than 2 inches apart at bottom)	Fence garden area	Completely effective	Relatively expensive
Traps			
Commercial box traps	Place around garden; bait with lettuce leaves, carrots	Safe for animals; rabbits are trapped alive and released elsewhere	Relatively expensive

TABLE 8–5 **RACCOONS, WOODCHUCKS, SKUNKS**

CONTROL	HOW TO USE	ADVANTAGES	DISADVANTAGES
Aromatics			
Animal lard	Rub on plants	Inexpensive; easy to use	Only partially effective

TABLE 8–5   **RACCOONS, WOODCHUCKS, SKUNKS** *(continued)*

CONTROL	HOW TO USE	ADVANTAGES	DISADVANTAGES
Chili powder/ground garlic	Mix together in equal proportions; sprinkle around garden; replenish weekly	Easy to prepare	Washes away quickly
Mothballs, naphthalene flakes	Scatter around garden	Easy to use	Only partially effective
Aromatic Plants			
Garlic	Plant around perimeter	Long-lasting	Only partially effective

TABLE 8–6   **MICE**

CONTROL	HOW TO USE	ADVANTAGES	DISADVANTAGES
Aromatics			
Mothballs, naphthalene flakes	Scatter around garden	Easy to use	Only partially effective
Aromatic Plants			
Mint leaves	Scatter around garden; replenish weekly	Easy to use	Only partially effective
Poisons			
Commercial baits (grains)	Scatter around garden	Extremely effective	Harmful to pets and children

TABLE 8–7   **GOPHERS AND MOLES**

CONTROL	HOW TO USE	ADVANTAGES	DISADVANTAGES
Aromatics			
Chili powder/ground garlic	Mix together in equal proportions and sprinkle in main tunnel; replenish weekly	Inexpensive	Only partially effective

TABLE 8–7 **GOPHERS AND MOLES** *(continued)*

CONTROL	HOW TO USE	ADVANTAGES	DISADVANTAGES
Human hair	Sprinkle liberal amounts in the main runways	Inexpensive	Large-enough quantities not always available (try a beauty or barber shop)
Mothballs, naphthalene flakes	Place in main tunnels	Easy to use; inexpensive; an old-time gopher control	Gophers and moles often toss the mothballs out of the tunnels; naphthalene flakes are difficult to get into tunnels
Stink scat	Mix 1 teaspoon castor oil and 1 teaspoon liquid detergent in a gallon of water; spray on plants	Ingredients easily available; easy to use	Only partially effective
Aromatic Plants			
Castor beans	Plant around edge of garden	Easy to plant	Highly poisonous; harmful to pets and humans
Scilla bulbs (member of lily family)	Plant throughout garden	Easy to plant and grow	Only partially effective
Elderberry cuttings	Place cuttings in holes and runs	Easy to use	Must be replaced frequently
Mole plant	Plant here and there in garden	Easy to grow	Limited effect on gophers
Poisons/gas			
Commercial poison baits (wheat, peas, oats)	Place in main tunnels	Extremely effective if placed in main tunnels	Harmful to pets and humans
Draino	Pour generously in main tunnels	Extremely effective	Harmful to pets and humans
Carbon monoxide	Run hose from car exhaust to tunnels; block all exits	Easy to use	Only partially effective
Commercial gopher gas (aerosol can)	Place probe in tunnel and press handle	Easy to use; effective if gophers or moles are close by	Harmful to pets and humans
Highway flares (like those kept in cars for emergencies)	Place lighted end in main runway; plug up holes	Easy to obtain and use; safe for humans	Difficult to keep limited amount of gas in tunnel

TABLE 8–7 **GOPHERS AND MOLES** *(continued)*

CONTROL	HOW TO USE	ADVANTAGES	DISADVANTAGES
Traps			
Macbee trap (a sort of super mousetrap)	Dig down from burrow to main tunnel (about 7 inches); place two traps on either side of hole in main tunnel; place a board across and fill the digging hole	Most old-time gardeners say this is the only sure-fire method	Requires a lot of work
Commercial box traps	Dig down as for Macbee trap; place in main tunnel	Gophers are trapped alive and released elsewhere	Requires a lot of work
Commercial rat traps	Place just outside gopher's hole; bait with green onions, pieces of broccoli	Easy to use	Hazardous to other animals
Barriers			
Metal sheets (one-foot square)	Drive into ground to blockade main tunnel every 10 feet	Can be done easily from aboveground	Metal sheets hard to find; only partially effective
Other			
Wine or pop bottles	Bury bottles in a row up to their necks around the perimeter of the garden; the wind whistling over the necks create a vibration that scares the animals	Inexpensive	Requires a lot of work
Gopher windmill (a small windmill that sets up vibrations in the ground)	Place in the ground in the garden about 20 feet apart	Seems to work well— many gardeners report excellent results	Initial cost of about $8 each

Traps used today are either a Macbee type of spring steel trap (like a big mousetrap) that kills animals instantly or a box trap that catches them alive. Animals caught in box traps are released away from your garden. Traps are probably the best method available for removing gophers, but they are relatively expensive.

Poisonous baits and *poisonous gas* are still used by many gardeners. Poisonous grains, peanuts, and oats are available for use against moles, gophers, and mice. Gas canisters are used in the war on moles and gophers. These methods are easy to use and fairly inexpensive, but they present danger to children and pets.

Miscellaneous devices include a number of things that gardeners have discovered worked for them; these are covered extensively in Tables 8–1 through 8–7.

Gophers and moles require special treatment. Gophers create a system of tunnels consisting of a main tunnel and a number of lateral tunnels that may cover an area up to 2000 square feet. Acting like miniature bulldozers, gophers push soil out of their burrows and deposit it at the ends of the lateral tunnels. Moles make a similar tunnel system. Mole holes, however, are left open at the center of the mound; gophers always plug theirs with dirt.

Before you can eliminate either of these nuisances, you have to find the main runway. Take a shovel and level all the gopher mounds flat. The next day look for fresh mounds and dig down about 8 inches. If you find a tunnel that runs straight through, you have found the main run.

If there is only a single tunnel that angles off in another direction, you have found a lateral. Probe the lateral (follow it) with a stick or metal rod until you come to the main run. Then dig down to the main tunnel and set your traps on either side of the hole. Place a board over the hole and cover it with dirt to shut out the light.

The method you choose to ward off garden critters will depend on your pocketbook and how much effort you wish to expend. Start with something simple. If that works, fine. If it doesn't try another approach, and then another, until you have the problem licked. In most cases it won't take that much effort to outwit your intruders, especially if you approach this problem with the same vigilance and emphasis on prevention that you use to protect your garden from pests and disease.

In the final chapter, we will be looking at the whole range of problems affecting individual vegetables and the solutions favored by expert gardeners.

CHAPTER NINE

Rx FOR INDIVIDUAL VEGETABLES

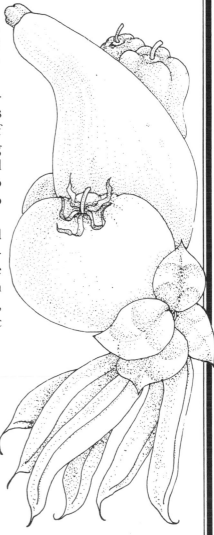

If you are having trouble with bitter cucumbers, forked, misshapen carrots, tip-burned lettuce, or something similar, this chapter will help you make a quick diagnosis and offer one or several solutions.

We begin with a quick identification chart for the general environmental troubles that befall many vegetables (Mother Nature's Puzzlers). This is followed by a series of charts, each devoted to an individual vegetable offering similar information about the potential environmental problems that could affect that vegetable as well as "what to look for" guides to insects and diseases. These charts also offer both natural and chemical methods of control.

Because this book covers the entire United States and southern Canada, you will find more environmental problems, insects, and diseases listed here than you will ever see in your own garden. If you come across vocabulary with which you are unfamiliar or if you need more information, see the preceding chapters which deal with the specific problem.

TABLE 9–1 GENERAL GARDENING PROBLEMS AFFECTING ALL VEGETABLES

Mother Nature's Puzzlers

WHAT TO LOOK FOR	POSSIBLE CAUSES	POSSIBLE CURES
Darkened areas on stems and leaves. Young plants turn brown, die.	Fertilizer burn. Fertilizer placed directly on plants or leaves or too much fertilizer in soil.	Keep fertilizer off plants. Mix thoroughly in the soil to a depth of 3 inches or apply in bands (See Chapter 3). Apply a "complete" commercial fertilizer (one with nitrogen, phosphorus, and potassium) at the rate of 4 pounds per 100 square feet or mix animal manures into the soil.
Plants stunted in growth. Sickly yellow color.	1 Soil may have deficiency.	1 Apply a "complete" commercial fertilizer rich in nitrogen (10-10-10 will do) at the rate of 4 pounds per 100 square feet. Or work 4 to 6 inches of animal manure into soil. Test for trace element deficiency if problem does not clear up.
	2 Soil is compacted or isn't draining properly.	2 Add 5 to 6 inches of organic matter to soil. Turn in thoroughly to a depth of 8 to 12 inches.
	3 Overwatering.	3 Do not keep soil soggy. Water for 2 to 3 hours then do not water again until soil is dry from 4 to 8 inches deep. Check with trowel. (See individual vegetables.)
	4 Low soil pH.	4 Soil test for lime. Identify and use control measures.
	5 Insects or diseases.	5 See insect and disease charts.
Weak, spindly plants.	1 Too much shade.	1 Change garden or plants to a location that has at least 6 to 8 hours of sunlight a day.
	2 Plants spaced too close to each other.	2 Thin to the spacings suggested on seed packages for particular vegetable.
	3 Too much nitrogen.	3 Avoid excess fertilization.
Downward curvature of young leaves. Prominent light colored veins, rolled edges, distorted leaf surfaces.	Weed killer damage.	Do not use 2-4 D weed killers in your garden.
Plants have dark or bluish green leaves followed by bronzing, reddening, purpling. Stunted.	1 Phosphorus deficiency.	1 Apply a "complete" commercial fertilizer rich in phosphorus (6-12-12 will do) at the rate of 4 pounds per 100 square feet. Or add rock phosphate or bone meal at the rate of 2 to 4 pounds per 100 square feet.
	2 Low temperatures.	2 Plant at recommended times or protect plants with hot kaps, plastic jugs with bottoms cut off, or other protective devices.

TABLE 9–1 GENERAL GARDENING PROBLEMS
AFFECTING ALL VEGETABLES *(continued)*

Mother Nature's Puzzlers

WHAT TO LOOK FOR	POSSIBLE CAUSES	POSSIBLE CURES
Scorching, browning, or bronzing of leaf margins. Older leaves affected first. Plants appear rusty.	Potassium deficiency.	Apply a "complete" commercial fertilizer rich in potassium (5-10-15 will do). Or add wood ash or green sand at the rate of 2 to 4 pounds per 100 square feet.
Plants wilt.	1 Poor drainage, excess water in soil.	1 Improve soil structure by turning 5 to 6 inches of organic matter into the soil to a depth of 8 to 12 inches.
	2 Lack of moisture in soil.	2 Cover the soil with 2 to 3 inches of organic material.
		3 Water two to three hours at a time. Don't water again until the soil is dry to a depth of 4 to 5 inches. Check this with a trowel. This keeps the moisture content within a safe range.
Many blossoms drop off before fruit forms. Failure to set fruit.	1 Low moisture supply in soil. Blossoms drop when exposed to hot dry winds.	1 Use a 2 to 3 inch organic mulch around plants to conserve soil moisture.
	2 Low night temperatures.	2 Problems discussed under individual vegetable.
	3 High temperatures.	3 Problems discussed under individual vegetable.

ARTICHOKES

Artichokes grow best in areas of long mild Winters and cool Summers. They grow mightily in the California coastal fog belt south of San Francisco and in the Louisiana coastal regions. Artichokes can be grown in hot Summer areas, but where the ground freezes in Winter they will have to be replanted yearly. Some gardeners in cold areas cut back the tops to 12 inches and cover the root crown with a mulch of leaves or compost. Surprisingly, artichokes have very few problems, but here are the ones to watch for.

TABLE 9–2 **ARTICHOKES**

Mother Nature's Puzzlers

WHAT TO LOOK FOR	POSSIBLE CAUSES	POSSIBLE CURES
The edible part of the artichoke, the leaf bract, becomes tough and leathery.	This happens when Summer heat opens the buds.	Harvest buds when they are closed "tight" and before they have started to open.

Insects

WHAT TO LOOK FOR	PEST	PREVENTION AND/OR NATURAL CONTROLS	CHEMICAL CONTROLS	GEOGRAPHICAL LOCATION
Colonies of sucking insects on buds and leaves. Curled and distorted leaves, sticky substance on stems, leaves.	aphids	Companion plant with spearmint and garlic. Mulch with aluminum foil. Remove with blast from garden hose. Use soap solution on leaves.	Malathion or diazinon or use botanical sprays such as pyrethrum, rotenone, or ryania.	Widespread throughout the U.S. and Canada.
Trails of silver slime. Aphids, earwigs, and worms between the bracts that can't be washed out after picking.	slugs snails aphids earwigs worms	Control with lacewing flies, praying mantises, or ladybugs. Reduce hiding places by keeping garden free of debris. Use a shallow dish of beer with lip at ground level. After picking, immerse the artichoke for 10 minutes in warm salt water. Shake buds upside down. This removes aphids, earwigs, and worms between brachts.	Control with a slug and snail bait (Slug-Geta) or try dehydrating agent (Snail Snare).	Widespread.

TABLE 9–2   ARTICHOKES (continued)

Diseases

WHAT TO LOOK FOR	DISEASE	PREVENTION AND/OR NATURAL CONTROLS	CHEMICAL CONTROLS	GEOGRAPHICAL LOCATION
Heads and crown parts become slimy and foul smelling.	head/crown rot	Keep down weeds.	Apply a mixture of captan and PCNB (sold as Terracap, Soil Treater "X," PCNB-Captan).	Widespread.

ASPARAGUS

The Romans grew and enjoyed asparagus as early as 200 B.C. From there it spread rapidly throughout Europe. Fortunately, asparagus is easy to grow with a minimum of effort and few problems. Here's a rundown on what to expect.

TABLE 9–3   ASPARAGUS

Mother Nature's Puzzlers

WHAT TO LOOK FOR	POSSIBLE CAUSES	POSSIBLE CURES
Yellowing of plants and leaves.	1 Consistent overwatering.	1 Water very carefully. A good rule of thumb: Water 2 to 3 hours then not again until soil has dried out to a depth of 4 to 8 inches. Check with a trowel.
	2 Soil pH is below 6.5.	2 Test the soil for pH level and add lime (see Chapter 3).
Brown or discolored spears, soft consistency.	Crop comes up too early in the spring and some spears become frozen. Becomes more obvious as the temperature warms up.	Discard early spears. Or protect with hot kaps or plastic jugs with bottoms cut out.
Crooked, curved, or misshapen spears.	1 Wind-driven sand injures spears.	1 Protect spears from blowing sand (see Chapter 5).
	2 Too close cultivation nicks spears.	2 Be careful not to damage spears when weeding asparagus beds.

TABLE 9–3 ASPARAGUS (continued)

Insects

WHAT TO LOOK FOR	PEST	PREVENTION AND/OR NATURAL CONTROLS	CHEMICAL CONTROLS	GEOGRAPHICAL LOCATION
Tips gnawed, shoots channeled, plants frequently marred by black stains.	asparagus beetle	Garden cleanliness. Beetles spend the winter in cracks in wood and wood structures. Companion plant with tomatoes. Ladybugs keep beetles in check.	Treat shoots and leaves with Sevin as beetles appear. Repeat as needed. Or use botanical spray: rotenone.	Widespread.
Plants eaten near the surface of soil.	cutworms	Garden cleanliness. Use oak leaf mulch. Plant tansy between asparagus rows. Place a cardboard collar around the stems. Push 1 inch into soil.	Spray the soil with Sevin or diazinon before shoots emerge.	Widespread.

Diseases

WHAT TO LOOK FOR	DISEASE	PREVENTION AND/OR NATURAL CONTROLS	CHEMICAL CONTROLS	GEOGRAPHICAL LOCATION
Yellow to orange to reddish brown pustles on stems and leaves.	rust (the most prevalent asparagus disease)	Plant resistant varieties: Mary Washington, Martha Washington (see Table 2-1).	Spray with maneb or zineb.	Widespread.
Tan to gray spots with reddish brown borders.	anthracnose	Use an all purpose fertilizer to keep the plants growing vigorously.	Spray with maneb or zineb.	Widespread.
Soft spots appear on tips and shoots.	crown rot	Dig out and destroy infected plants.	Apply PCNB to soil surface before the spears appear.	Widespread.
Plants stunted; plants wilt and die. Roots and shoot bases have reddish streaks.	root rot	Use treated seed only. Plant resistant varieties: Mary Washington (see Table 2-1).	Use captan on the seedbed.	Widespread.

BEANS

This includes garden (pole, bush, shell), lima, mung, scarlet runner, asparagus beans, and southern peas (similar to beans in its cultural requirements and susceptibility to insects). Generally beans will grow like topsy almost anywhere in the United States, even in average soil. They, however, have their share of problems. Here are the major ones you're likely to encounter.

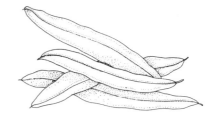

TABLE 9–4 **BEANS: All types**

Mother Nature's Puzzlers

WHAT TO LOOK FOR	POSSIBLE CAUSES	POSSIBLE CURES
Seedlings fail to emerge.	1 Soil temperatures of less than 55 to 60 degrees F. cause seeds to rot. Beans are a warm weather vegetable.	1 Delay planting until the soil has warmed above this temperature.
	2 Soil is heavy or crusted. Seedlings often break off or can't push through.	2 Apply a light mulch of compost, sawdust, or similar material over the bed to prevent crusting.
	3 Beans planted in the Spring 2 inches or more below ground often rot and fail to come up. Beans planted later, 1 inch or less deep, may dry out and die before emerging.	3 Plant beans about 1 inch deep in early Spring, 2 inches deep later in the season.
Poor flower and bean production.	1 Lack of nutrients in the soil. Beans must make strong, early growth before flowering starts.	1 Mix a good fertilizer (10-10-10) into the soil before planting.
	2 A few old pods left on the vines greatly reduces the development of new beans.	2 Keep snap beans picked off the vines during the young succulent stage.
Baldhead: Bean plants have no growing tips. The stem above the seed leaves (the cotyledons) is bare with no leaves or terminal bud (baldheads).	An injury to the seed has damaged the embryo. Can infrequently be caused by insect and disease attack (see below).	Buy seed from major seed growers. Remove plants from row and replant.

TABLE 9–4 BEANS (continued)

Mother Nature's Puzzlers

WHAT TO LOOK FOR	POSSIBLE CAUSES	POSSIBLE CURES
The first few seeds develop, the rest of the pod shrivels to a tail (polywogs).	A lack of moisture in the soil.	Place 2 to 3 inches of organic material on top of the bed to hold down loss of moisture. Water beans 2 to 3 hours at a time. Don't water again until the soil is dry to a depth of 4 to 5 inches. Check with a trowel.
Poor flower and bean production.	1 Lack of nutrients in the soil. Beans must make strong, early growth before flowering starts.	1 Mix a good fertilizer (10-10-10) into the soil before planting.
	2 A few old pods left on the vines greatly reduces the development of new beans.	2 Keep snap beans picked off the vines during the young succulent stage.
Vines flower, but flowers drop off without producing beans.	Temperature jumps from cool to 90 degrees F. and above or the weather is dry and especially windy.	Avoid planting Blue Lake, Kentucky Wonder, and pole limas. They are especially susceptible to blossom pod drop. Plant faster maturing varieties such as Spring Green, Bountiful, Stringless.
Sunscald: Reddish or pale brown spots and streaks appear on the pods.	Pods are exposed to the hot sun following cool, overcast weather.	Plant in well-drained soil.

Insects

WHAT TO LOOK FOR	PEST	PREVENTION AND/OR NATURAL CONTROLS	CHEMICAL CONTROLS	GEOGRAPHICAL LOCATION
Colonies of black sucking insects on stem leaves. Leaves can be curled and distorted. Sticky substance on leaves.	aphids	Companion plant with spearmint and garlic. Mulch with aluminum foil. Remove with blast from garden hose. Use a soap solution on the leaves. Control with lacewing flies, praying mantises, ladybugs.	Malathion, diazinon, pyrethrum, rotenone, or ryania.	Widespread.
Round or regular shaped holes in leaves.	bean leaf beetles	Garden cleanliness. Spade garden soil deeply to destroy larvae in early Spring. Companion plant with marigolds and rosemary. Pick off by hand.	Sevin, malathion, or diazinon.	Widespread.

TABLE 9–4 BEANS (continued)

Insects

WHAT TO LOOK FOR	PEST	PREVENTION AND/OR NATURAL CONTROLS	CHEMICAL CONTROLS	GEOGRAPHICAL LOCATION
Leaves riddled with tiny round holes.	flea beetles	Garden cleanliness. Companion plant with mint or wormwood. Spade garden soil deeply to destroy larvae in early spring. Pick off plants.	Diazinon, malathion, Sevin, pyrethrum, rotenone, or ryania.	Widespread.
Brown leaf margins.	leafhoppers		Sevin, malathion, pyrethrum, rotenone, or ryania.	Widespread, severe in eastern U.S.
Leaves appear skeletonized.	Mexican bean beetles	Plant bush rather than pole beans. Companion plant with rosemary, summer savor, and potatoes. Remove leaves with orange egg masses and destroy.	Sevin, or malathion.	Widespread east of the Rocky Mountains.
Bean plants have no growing tips. The stem above the seed leaves (the cotyledons) is a bare stem with no leaves or terminal bud.	seed corn maggot	Garden cleanliness.	Use diazinon as a soil treatment at time of planting.	Northern United States.
Fine webbing over the foliage. Mottled, speckled and wilting leaves.	spider mites	Use a soap solution on the leaves. Apply a light petroleum oil spray to the leaves. Use a forceful spray from garden hose.	Spray thoroughly with Kelthane or diazinon.	Widespread.

TABLE 9–4   BEANS (continued)

Insects

WHAT TO LOOK FOR	PEST	PREVENTION AND/OR NATURAL CONTROLS	CHEMICAL CONTROLS	GEOGRAPHICAL LOCATION
A cloud of white wings fly from plant when disturbed.	whiteflies	Companion plant with marigolds. They excrete substances that are absorbed by the roots of other plants and repel whiteflies. Use wasps to destroy whiteflies. Hose off with a stream of water. Trap whiteflies in tanglefoot on a bright yellow card.	Malathion or rotenone.	Widespread.
Plant growth stunted as worms bore into roots.	white grubs (the larvae of the June beetle), wireworms (the larvae of the click beetle)	Garden cleanliness.	Use diazinon as a soil treatment *before* planting.	White grubs are troublesome in the South and Midwest. Wireworms are widespread.

Diseases

WHAT TO LOOK FOR	DISEASE	PREVENTION AND/OR NATURAL CONTROLS	CHEMICAL CONTROLS	GEOGRAPHICAL LOCATION
Sunken reddish to black spots or blotches on pods.	anthracnose (fungal leaf spots)	Plant in well-drained soil. Keep down weeds.	Captan or dichlone. Insects spread the disease. Control them with both Sevin and malathion.	Widespread. More severe in dry areas in western states.
Brown or tan dead areas on leaves as spots or blotches, often with a yellow border.	bacterial blight	Plant certified disease-free seed. Keep weeds down. Grow in well-drained soil. Avoid overhead irrigation. Plant resistant varieties: Blue Lake strains, Great Northern strains, Kentudky Wonder strains, or tendergreen.	Sprays containing copper are effective during wet weather.	Widespread.

TABLE 9–4   BEANS (continued)

Diseases

WHAT TO LOOK FOR	DISEASE	PREVENTION AND/OR NATURAL CONTROLS	CHEMICAL CONTROLS	GEOGRAPHICAL LOCATION
Dark water-soaked spots on leaves, stems, and pods become covered with cottony mold.	blight (fungal)	Avoid overcrowding and overhead sprinkling. Keep down weeds. Plant wide rows in well-drained soil. Rotate with nonsusceptible crops such as onions or small grains. Dig up and burn affected plants before vines shade ground.	Apply captan or dichlone.	Widespread. More severe in humid, moist areas.
Seeds decay, seedlings wilt and collapse from rot at or below soil line.	damping off seed rot	Use crack-free seed. Plant when dry and warm (65 degrees F. or above) in well-drained soil. Practice rotation.	Treat soil with captan.	Widespread. More serious in cool weather.
Leaves puckered, brittle, stunted. Plants dwarfed and bunchy. Pods reduced in size and number.	curly top virus (transmitted by leafhoppers)	Immediately remove and destroy diseased plants when first noticed. Plant resistant varieties.	Control leafhoppers with malathion.	Western states.
Irregular patches of cottony mold on leaves.	lima bean downy mildew	Plant certified disease-free seed. Use 4-year rotation. Burn infested crops and crop debris after harvest.		Most serious along Atlantic Coast.
Downy white mold on pods (resembles cotton).		Avoid overhead irrigation. Plant downy mildew resistant varieties: New Fordhook lines, Piloy, Thaxter.	Treat weekly with maneb or zineb. Start just before bloom if disease is present.	Widespread.

TABLE 9–4   BEANS (continued)

Diseases

WHAT TO LOOK FOR	DISEASE	PREVENTION AND/OR NATURAL CONTROLS	CHEMICAL CONTROLS	GEOGRAPHICAL LOCATION
Leaves puckered, stunted, crinkled, irregular dark yellow or green streaking. Pods deformed.	mosaic-pod mottle (aphids and leafhoppers transmit virus)	Grow beans as far from alfalfa, clovers, and gladiolas as possible. Plant disease resistant varieties such as Blue Lake or Top Crop. Destroy diseased plants.	Spray with malathion or Sevin to control insects that transmit disease.	Widespread.
Whitish powdery patches on leaves, stems, and young pods.	powdery mildew	Rotate or plow under plant debris. Keep weeds down.	Apply sulfur or karathane 1 to 4 times at weekly intervals.	Widespread especially in the southern states and along the Pacific Coast.
Plants stunted yellowish and weak. Irregular swollen galls that are enlargements of roots.	root-knot nematodes	Rotate crops. Companion plant with marigolds.	Apply liquid or granular nematocide —see your local nursery.	Primarily in southern states in sandy soils.
Brown decayed areas on the lower stem. Decayed roots resulting in wilting, poor top growth, death.	root and stem rot	Plant crack-free seed in warm (65 degrees F. or above) soil. Plant in well-drained soil where beans have not grown in 6 years. Burn crop debris after harvest.	Use lanstan or PCNB in soil.	Widespread.
White, reddish brown to black pustles on underside of leaves, other parts.	rust	Keep weeds down. Grow plants in well-drained soil. Use resistant varieties such as Great Northern, Golden Wax.	Weekly applications of maneb or zineb.	Widespread.

TABLE 9–4   **BEANS** *(continued)*

Diseases

WHAT TO LOOK FOR	DISEASE	PREVENTION AND/OR NATURAL CONTROLS	CHEMICAL CONTROLS	GEOGRAPHICAL LOCATION
Small soft watery spots on stems, leaves, pods. Stems girdled causing plants to wilt and die. Sticky liquid on pods.	watery soft rot	Keep weeds down. Space plants farther apart. Rotate crops.	Treat soil with captan before planting.	Most prevalent in the western states and southern Florida.

BEETS

Beets are an extremely hardy vegetable that grow well in a wide range of soils and thrive in all parts of the country. Since beets produce their best quality in a cool climate, they are grown in the southern third of the United States in the Fall, Winter, and Spring; in the middle regions as early Summer or late Fall crops; and in the northern third as Summer and early Fall crops. Here are the problems to look for in your garden.

TABLE 9–5   **BEETS**

Mother Nature's Puzzlers

WHAT TO LOOK FOR	POSSIBLE CAUSES	POSSIBLE CURES
Stringy, tough roots; beets have a bland flavor.	1 Beets that have been exposed to temperatures of over 85 degrees F.	Grow in early Spring or Fall when temperatures are lower than 85 degrees F.
	2 Excessive competition from weeds or other beets.	Keep beds weeded. Space at a minimum of 2 to 3 inches apart.
	3 Soil has been allowed to dry out, slowing down growth. Beets need to grow at full speed without a single let-up.	Place 2 to 3 inches of organic material on top of the bed to reduce moisture loss. Water beets 2 to 3 hours at a time. Don't water again until the soil is dry to a depth of 4 to 8 inches. Check with a trowel.
	4 Beets left in the ground more than 10 days after obtaining edible size.	Harvest at about 2 inches in diameter.

TABLE 9–5   BEETS (continued)

Mother Nature's Puzzlers

WHAT TO LOOK FOR	POSSIBLE CAUSES	POSSIBLE CURES
Germination is spotty. Many seedlings fail to emerge.	Temperatures were too high when beets were planted. In extremely hot weather seeds fail to germinate.	If the weather turns unexpectedly hot, place an inch of compost or other organic material over the seedbed. Water twice a day, 2 to 3 hours at a time, until the seedlings are well established.
Red coloration on leaves that initially affects the margins or tips, then spreads to entire surface. Leaf tips die, middle and older leaves become crinkled. Corky spots at surface of beet or near growth rings.	Boron deficiency. Acid soil (pH 6.5 or below) makes beets especially sensitive to boron deficiency.	First check the pH level of the soil. If below 6.5, correct by adding 5 pounds of lime per 100 square feet for each pH unit (e.g., from 5.5 to 6.5 is one unit). Treat boron deficiency by mixing 1½ teaspoons borax in 15 gallons of water for every 100 square feet of garden. Sprinkle over soil surface.
"White ring," whitish rings inside the beet.	Drought or heavy rains which follow an extended period of high temperature.	No cure for heavy rains. Keep soil from drying out during drought conditions.

Insects

WHAT TO LOOK FOR	PEST	PREVENTION AND/OR NATURAL CONTROLS	CHEMICAL CONTROLS	GEOGRAPHICAL LOCATION
Colonies of sucking insects on underside of leaves. Leaves can be curled and distorted. Sticky substance on leaves.	aphids	Companion plant with spearmint and garlic. Mulch with aluminum foil. Remove with blast from garden hose. Use a soap solution on the leaves. Control with lacewing flies, praying mantises, ladybugs.	Malathion, diazinon, pyrethrum, rotenone, or ryania.	Widespread in U.S. and southern Canada.
Plants partially defoliated.	blister beetles	Garden cleanliness. Spade deeply in the Spring to kill the larvae. Pick beetles off by hand.	Spray or dust with Sevin, pyrethrum, rotenone, or ryania.	East of Rocky Mountains.

TABLE 9–5   BEETS *(continued)*

Insects

WHAT TO LOOK FOR	PEST	PREVENTION AND/OR NATURAL CONTROLS	CHEMICAL CONTROLS	GEOGRAPHICAL LOCATION
Irregular holes eaten in leaves.	cabbage loopers (occasional pest on beets)	Clean up and dispose of crop remnants each Fall. Remove weeds, especially mustard, peppergrass, and shepherd's purse. Pick off and smash worms. Use Bacillus thuringiensis.	Malathion, Sevin, or rotenone.	Widespread.
Plants eaten or cut off near the surface of the soil.	cutworms	Garden cleanliness. Companion plant with tansy between rows. Place cardboard collar around stems. Push 1 inch into soil.	Spray the soil with Sevin or diazinon before shoots emerge.	Widespread.
Leaves look like they have been shot through with tiny holes.	flea beetles	Garden cleanliness. Spade garden soil deeply to destroy larvae in early Spring. Pick off plants.	Use several applications of diazinon, malathion, Sevin, pyrethrum, rotenone, or ryania.	Widespread.
Pieces eaten from leaves. Webs among foliage.	garden (beet) webworm	Knock caterpillars off leaves into jar of water. Cut out and destroy protective webs.	Malathion, diazinon, or pyrethrum.	Widespread.
Plants partially defoliated.	grasshopper	Turn the soil under in Fall to bury the eggs so the young can't make their way to surface. Trap in quart jars filled with 1 part molasses and 9 parts water. Import praying mantises.	Sevin, malathion, diazinon, or rotenone.	Widespread. Especially destructive in the West and the Dakotas.
White threadlike tunnels within the leaf.	leaf miner	Deep spade before planting to help control maggots. Plant in Fall to lessen attack. Protect plants by covering with cheesecloth.	Control adult flies with diazinon or malathion. Repeat if necessary.	Widespread.

TABLE 9–5   BEETS (continued)

Insects

WHAT TO LOOK FOR	PEST	PREVENTION AND/OR NATURAL CONTROLS	CHEMICAL CONTROLS	GEOGRAPHICAL LOCATION
Trails of silver slime.	slugs, snails	Garden cleanliness. Use a shallow dish of beer with lip at ground level.	Control with a slug and snail bait (Slug-Geta) or try a dehydrating agent (Snail Snare).	Widespread.
Plant growth stunted as worms bore into roots.	white grubs (the larvae of the June beetle), wireworms (the larvae of the click beetle)	Garden cleanliness.	Use diazinon as a soil treatment before planting.	White grubs troublesome in the South and Midwest. Wireworms are widespread.

Diseases

WHAT TO LOOK FOR	DISEASE	PREVENTION AND/OR NATURAL CONTROLS	CHEMICAL CONTROLS	GEOGRAPHICAL LOCATION
Small round spots with brown centers. Spots may drop out leaving ragged holes.	cercospora leaf spot	Destroy the tops. Use a 3-year rotation.	Maneb or zineb.	Widespread in warm moist weather.
Thickened, rolled, dull green, crimped, or brittle leaves.	curly-top (virus) (transmitted by leafhoppers)	Keep down weeds. Destroy infected plants immediately.	Control leafhoppers with Sevin or malathion.	Serious in the western half of the United States.
Seeds rot, older plants wilt and collapse.	damping off, seed rot	Plant in deep, fertile, well-drained soil.	Treat seed with captan. Treat soil with captan, folpet, maneb.	Widespread.
Leaves mottled, leaf surfaces often crinkled and curled.	mosaics (carried by aphids)	Plant early in the season. Keep down weeds. Destroy infected plants.	Spray with malathion to control aphids.	Widespread.
Plants stunted and yellow. Veins conspicuously yellow.	yellows (transmitted by aphids)	Keep weeds out of garden area.	Spray with malathion to control aphids.	Widespread.

TABLE 9-5   **BEETS** *(continued)*

Diseases

WHAT TO LOOK FOR	DISEASE	PREVENTION AND/OR NATURAL CONTROLS	CHEMICAL CONTROLS	GEOGRAPHICAL LOCATION
Young leaves covered with violet or yellowish gray mold.	downy mildew	Use 3-year rotation. Keep down weeds.	Use zineb, maneb.	Widespread during cool, humid seasons.

BROCCOLI

Broccoli requires a cool growing season but can be grown almost anywhere in the United States. Most of the varieties grown in today's home garden have a large central head with many side branches, and continue to produce for long periods of time. Here are the problems you may find in your garden.

TABLE 9-6   **BROCCOLI**

Mother Nature's Puzzlers

WHAT TO LOOK FOR	POSSIBLE CAUSES	POSSIBLE CURES
Broccoli forms premature small scattered heads.	This often happens to young plants subjected to temperatures below 40 degrees F. before or shortly after planting.	Protect small plants with hot kaps or other protective devices.
Broccoli stops producing buds. Some older buds have little yellow flower buds.	As soon as some broccoli buds (heads) flower, the plant stops producing young buds.	Keep your broccoli crop harvested. Pick the developing buds as often as every 3 days as long as the plant continues to produce.
Broccoli flowers prematurely. It seems to be growing mightily, then suddenly the sprouts produce a number of yellow flowers.	1 Temperatures over about 85 degrees F. force broccoli to flower.	1 Plant early varieties: (Green Comet Hybrid, Spartan Early, Premium Early) to mature ahead of the heat. Or plant broccoli in mid-Summer for a Fall crop.

TABLE 9–6 **BROCCOLI** *(continued)*

Insects

WHAT TO LOOK FOR	PEST	PREVENTION AND/OR NATURAL CONTROLS	CHEMICAL CONTROLS	GEOGRAPHICAL LOCATION
Colonies of small green sucking insects on leaves. Leaves can be curled and discolored.	aphids	Companion plant with spearmint and garlic. Mulch with aluminum foil. Remove with blast from garden hose. Use a soap solution on the leaves. Control with lacewing flies, praying mantises, ladybugs.	Malathion, diazinon, pyrethrum, rotenone, or ryania.	Widespread.
Plants partially defoliated.	blister beetles	Garden cleanliness. Spade deeply in the Spring to kill larvae. Pick beetles off by hand.	Sevin, pyrethrum, rotenone, or ryania.	East of Rocky Mountains.
Irregular holes eaten in leaves.	cabbage loopers	Clean up and dispose of crop remnants each Fall. Remove weeds. Pick off and smash worms. Use Bacillus thuringiensis (Dipel).	Malathion, Sevin, or rotenone.	Widespread.
Damage to the buds of young plants.	cabbage webworm	Garden cleanliness. Pick off small worms. Use Bacillus thuringiensis.	Malathion, Sevin, or rotenone.	Especially prevalent in the South during Summer and Fall.
Brown root scars. Stunted, off-color plants. Some plants may be honeycombed with curving, slimy tunnels.	cabbage maggot (larva of cabbage root fly). Transmits spores of blackleg disease.	Cover plants with fine gauze to prevent flies from laying eggs on them. Dispose of damaged plants after harvest. Companion plant with mint and tomatoes. Put 4-inch circles of cardboard or tar paper around stems at ground level to prevent maggots from reaching roots.	Mix diazinon into the top 3 to 4 inches of the soil before planting. Repeat in 2 weeks.	Widespread. Most severe in the northern United States and southern Canada.

TABLE 9–6 BROCCOLI (continued)

Insects

WHAT TO LOOK FOR	PEST	PREVENTION AND/OR NATURAL CONTROLS	CHEMICAL CONTROLS	GEOGRAPHICAL LOCATION
Young plants cut off near the soil surface.	cutworms They hide in soil by day, feed at night.	Garden cleanliness. Use oak leaf mulch. Companion plant with tansy between rows. Place a cardboard collar around the stems, push 1 inch into soil.	Spray soil with Sevin or diazinon before transplanting into bed.	Widespread.
Leaves look like they have been shot through with tiny round holes.	flea beetles	Garden cleanliness. Spade garden soil deeply to destroy larvae in early Spring. Pick off plants.	Use several applications of diazinon, malathion, Sevin, pyrethrum, rotenone, or ryania.	Widespread.
Leaves chewed. Tunnels inside cabbage and cauliflower heads	imported cabbage worm (white cabbage butterfly)	Destroy all remains and weeds after harvest. Companion plant with mint. Use Bacillus thuringiensis (Dipel or Thurocide).	Malathion, Sevin, or rotenone.	Widespread.
Trails of silver slime.	slugs, snails	Reduce hiding places by keeping garden free of debris. Use a shallow dish of beer with lip at ground level.	Control with a slug and snail bait (Slug-Geta) or try a dehydrating agent (Snail Snare).	Widespread.
Brown root scars. Stunted off-color plants. Some plants may be honeycombed with curving slimy tunnels.	cabbage maggot (larva of cabbage root fly). Transmits spores of blackleg disease.	Cover plants with fine gauze to prevent flies from laying eggs on them. Dispose of damaged plants after harvest. Companion plant with mint and tomatoes. Put 4-inch circles of cardboard or tar paper around stems at ground level to prevent maggots from reaching roots.	Mix diazinon into the top 3 to 4 inches of the soil before planting. Repeat in 2 weeks.	Widespread. Most severe in the northern United States, southern Canada.

TABLE 9–6 BROCCOLI (continued)

Insects

WHAT TO LOOK FOR	PEST	PREVENTION AND/OR NATURAL CONTROLS	CHEMICAL CONTROLS	GEOGRAPHICAL LOCATION
White or yellow blotches on leaves where nymphs have sucked sap. Leaves can wilt.	stinkbug, harlequin bug	Destroy egg masses clustered on underside of leaves. Control with sabadilla.	Sevin, pyrethrum, or rotenone.	Extremely destructive to the cabbage clan in the southern half of the United States.
Plant growth stunted as worms bore into roots.	white grubs (the larvae of the June, beetle) wireworms (the larva of the click beetle)	Garden cleanliness.	Use diazinon as a soil treatment before planting.	White grubs troublesome in the South and Midwest. Wireworms are widespread.

Diseases

WHAT TO LOOK FOR	DISEASE	PREVENTION AND/OR NATURAL CONTROLS	CHEMICAL CONTROLS	GEOGRAPHICAL LOCATION
Slimy top foliage with a foul odor. Top falls away easily.	bacterial soft rot	Collect and burn compost or plant debris after harvest.		Widespread.
Light brown or gray spots on stem, leaves. Stem is girdled blackens and rots.	blackleg (spread by cutworms and cabbage root maggots)	Collect and burn tops after harvest. Use 4-year rotation.	Treat seed with captan.	Widespread east of the Rocky Mountains.
Seedlings turn yellow to brown, wilt, collapse. Yellow, brown or dark green V shaped areas with blackened veins. Leaves drop off.	black rot	Avoid overhead watering.		Widespread in warm, moist seasons.

TABLE 9–6 BROCCOLI (continued)

Diseases

WHAT TO LOOK FOR	DISEASE	PREVENTION AND/OR NATURAL CONTROLS	CHEMICAL CONTROLS	GEOGRAPHICAL LOCATION
Yellowish leaves that wilt on hot days. Roots greatly enlarged with warty growth.	clubroot	Keep weeds down.	Use Lanstan.	Widespread.
Pale green to yellow spotting on upper surface of leaves followed by purpling.	downy mildew	Avoid overcrowding plants. Don't water overhead. Pick off and burn infected plant parts.	Spray with maneb or fixed copper sprays.	Widespread during cool wet seasons.
Pale yellow, gray brown, dark green spots on leaves.	fungal spots	Collect and burn tops after harvest.	Spray seedbed with maneb or fixed copper sprays.	Widespread in wet weather.
Plants stunted, yellowish and weak. Irregular swollen galls that are enlargements of roots.	root-knot nematodes	Rotate crops.	Fumigate soil in the Fall with DBCP or telone.	Primarily in southern states in sandy soils.
Water soaked areas over the stems and leaves. Wilting of lower leaves followed by a collapse of the whole plant into a shapeless mass.	watery soft rot	Garden cleanliness. Rotate crops.		Common in the Gulf Coast region and the coastal valleys of the Pacific Coast.
Leaves turn dull yellow, curl, and die.	yellows (virus)	Destroy infected plants.		Widespread. Most serious when soil temperatures over 70 degrees F.

BRUSSELS SPROUTS

Brussels sprouts are a cool-season vegetable and do not grow well in areas with hot dry summers. Even in such places they can be grown as a Fall vegetable and can generally withstand October and November freezes even in northern areas. Here are the problems to look for.

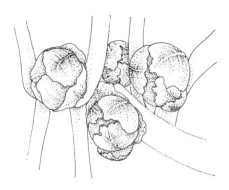

TABLE 9–7 **BRUSSELS SPROUTS**

Mother Nature's Puzzlers

WHAT TO LOOK FOR	POSSIBLE CAUSES	POSSIBLE CURES
Large, leafy "loose" sprouts.	Temperature too high. Brussels sprouts need temperatures of below 75 degrees F. to produce compact sprouts.	Plant so that your crop will mature in the cool temperatures of Fall.
Wart-like projections the size of a pinhead on the leaves and stems.	Injury to the tissue brought about by the blowing of soil particles against the leaves.	Protect plants on the windward side. Although the injury is quite conspicuous, it does not affect production.

Insects

WHAT TO LOOK FOR	PEST	PREVENTION AND/OR NATURAL CONTROLS	CHEMICAL CONTROLS	GEOGRAPHICAL LOCATION
Colonies of small green sucking insects on leaves. Leaves can be curled and discolored. Sticky substance on leaves.	aphids	Companion plant with spearmint and garlic. Mulch with aluminum foil. Remove with blast from garden hose. Use a soap solution on leaves. Control with lacewings flies, praying mantises, ladybugs.	Malathion, diazinon, pyrethrum, rotenone, or ryania.	Widespread.
Plants partially defoliated.	blister beetles	Garden cleanliness. Spade deeply in the Spring to kill larvae. Pick beetles off by hand.	Sevin, pyrethrum, rotenone, or ryania.	East of Rocky Mountains.
Irregular holes eaten in leaves.	cabbage loopers	Clean up and dispose of crop remnants each Fall. Remove weeds. Pick off and smash worms. Use Bacillus thuringiensis (dipel).	Malathion, Sevin, or rotenone.	Widespread.

TABLE 9–7   BRUSSELS SPROUTS (continued)

Insects

WHAT TO LOOK FOR	PEST	PREVENTION AND/OR NATURAL CONTROLS	CHEMICAL CONTROLS	GEOGRAPHICAL LOCATION
Brown root scars. Stunted off-color plants. Some plants may be honeycombed with curving, slimy tunnels.	cabbage maggot (larva of cabbage root fly). Transmits spores of blackleg disease.	Cover plants with fine gauze to prevent flies from laying eggs on them. Dispose of damaged plants after harvest. Companion plant with mint and tomato. Put 4-inch circles of cardboard or tar paper around stems at ground level to prevent maggots from reaching roots.	Mix diazinon into the top 3 to 4 inches of the soil before planting. Repeat in 2 weeks.	Widespread. Most severe in the northern United States, southern Canada.
Damage to the buds of young plants.	Cabbage web worms	Garden cleanliness. Pick off and smash worms. Use Bacillus thuringiensis.	Malathion, Sevin, or rotenone.	Especially prevalent in the South during Summer and Fall.
Young plants cut off near the soil surface.	Cutworms (they hide in soil by day, attack at night)	Garden cleanliness. Use oak leaf mulch. Plant tansy between rows. Place a cardboard collar around the stems, push 1 inch into soil.	Spray the soil with Sevin or diazinon before transplanting into bed.	Widespread.
Leaves riddled with tiny round holes.	flea beetles	Garden cleanliness. Spade garden soil deeply to destroy larvae in early spring. Pick off plants.	Use several applications of diazinon, malathion, Sevin, pyrethrum, rotenone, or ryania.	Widespread.
Leaves chewed. Tunnels inside cabbage and cauliflower heads.	Imported Cabbage worm (white cabbage butterfly)	Destroy all remains and weeds after harvest. Companion plant with mint. Use Bacillus thuringiensis (dipel or thuricide).	Malathion, Sevin, or rotenone.	Widespread.

TABLE 9–7 BRUSSELS SPROUTS (continued)

Insects

WHAT TO LOOK FOR	PEST	PREVENTION AND/OR NATURAL CONTROLS	CHEMICAL CONTROLS	GEOGRAPHICAL LOCATION
Trails of silver slime.	slugs, snails	Garden cleanliness. Use a shallow dish of beer with lip at ground level.	Control with a slug and snail bait (Slug-Geta) or try a dehydrating agent (Snail Snare).	Widespread.
White or yellow blotches on leaves where nymphs have sucked sap. Leaves can wilt.	stinkbug, harlequin bug	Destroy egg masses clustered on underside of leaves. Control with sabadilla.	Spray plants with Sevin, pyrethrum, and rotenone.	Extremely destructive to the cabbage clan in the southern half of the United States.
Plant growth stunted as worms bore into roots.	white grubs (the larvae of the June beetle), wireworms (the larvae of the click beetle)	Keep the garden free of refuse that could shelter beetle eggs.	Use diazinon as a soil treatment before planting.	White grubs troublesome in the South and Midwest. Wireworms are widespread.

Diseases

WHAT TO LOOK FOR	DISEASE	PREVENTION AND/OR NATURAL CONTROLS	CHEMICAL CONTROLS	GEOGRAPHICAL LOCATION
Slimy top foliage with a foul odor. Top falls away easily.	bacterial soft rot	Collect and burn compost or plant debris after harvest.		Widespread.
Light brown or gray spots on stem, leaves. Stem is girdled blackens and rots.	blackleg (spread by cutworms and cabbage root maggots)	Collect and burn tops after harvest. Use 4-year rotation.	Treat seed with captan.	Widespread east of the Rocky Mountains.
Seedlings turn yellow to brown, wilt, collapse. Yellow, brown or dark green V-shaped areas with blackened veins Leaves drop off.	black rot	Avoid overhead watering.		Widespread in warm, moist seasons.

TABLE 9–7   BRUSSELS SPROUTS (continued)

Diseases

WHAT TO LOOK FOR	DISEASE	PREVENTION AND/OR NATURAL CONTROLS	CHEMICAL CONTROLS	GEOGRAPHICAL LOCATION
Yellowish leaves that wilt on hot days. Roots greatly enlarged with warty growth.	clubroot	Keep weeds down.	Use Lanstan.	Widespread.
Pale green to yellow spotting on upper surface of leaves followed by purpling.	downy mildew	Avoid overcrowding plants. Don't water overhead. Pick off and burn infected plant parts.	Spray with maneb or fixed copper sprays.	Widespread during cool wet seasons.
Pale yellow, gray brown, dark green spots on leaves.	fungal spots	Collect and burn tops after harvest.	Spray seedbed with maneb or fixed copper sprays.	Widespread in wet weather.
Plants stunted, yellowish and weak. Irregular swollen galls that are enlargements of roots.	root-knot nematodes	Rotate crops.	Fumigate soil in the Fall with DBCP or telone.	Primarily in southern states in sandy soils.
Water soaked areas over the stems and leaves. Wilting of lower leaves followed by a collapse of the whole plant into a shapeless mass.	watery soft rot	Garden cleanliness. Rotate crops.		Common in the Gulf Coast region and the coastal valleys of the Pacific Coast.
Leaves turn dull yellow, curl, and die.	yellows (virus)	Destroy infected plants.		Widespread. Most serious when soil temperatures over 70 degrees F.

CABBAGE

Cabbage grows best where there is a cool, moist growing season and thrives in almost any type of soil. And Chinese cabbage performs well where it has a cool Fall growing season to develop. Collards, on the other hand, can withstand summer heat and does well in the South during the summer growing season. All suffer from the same insect and disease problems.

TABLE 9–8   CABBAGE (Collards, Chinese Cabbage)

Mother Nature's Puzzlers

WHAT TO LOOK FOR	POSSIBLE CAUSES	POSSIBLE CURES
Cabbage appears to be growing well, then suddenly starts to flower. Cabbage also sometimes flowers and goes to seed just before the harvest stage.	Exposure to 40 to 50 degree F. temperatures for 3 to 4 weeks. Cabbage planted to overwinter often flowers and fails to produce heads.	Plant slimmer pencil-sized transplants. This problem is especially serious when larger transplants are used or when cabbage is planted in the Fall to overwinter.
Cabbage heads start to split.	Plants have been allowed to dry out and have then been watered. As a result, the center and outer portions develop at different speeds. The heads of early varieties often split soon after they mature in warm weather.	Stop watering your cabbage. Or turn the whole plant about half a turn. This breaks off some of the roots and slows the growth.
Browning along margins of old leaves. The heads are bitter and tough. Water spots appear in the core and stem.	Boron deficiency.	Have the soil tested; then apply 8 ounces of borax for every 1000 square feet of garden space. Plant Wisconsin Ballhead, Wisconsin Hollander No. 8.
Multiple heading in early cabbage grown in northern climates.	Injury of the main growing tip by frost when the plants are young. Sometimes occurs when southern grown cabbage is transplanted or planted too early in northern gardens.	Plant locally grown seedlings.

TABLE 9–8   CABBAGE (continued)

Mother Nature's Puzzlers

WHAT TO LOOK FOR	POSSIBLE CAUSES	POSSIBLE CURES
Cabbages killed in a circular area in a cabbage patch. Plants die within a few days. Lightning scar found on surviving plants along edge of circle.	Lightning strikes the plants.	There is no cure for this unusual problem but understanding the cause keeps it from being confused with insect or disease damage.
Wartlike projections the size of a pinhead on the leaves and stems.	Injury to tissue caused by blowing of soil particles against the leaves.	Protect plants on the windward side by propping up a piece of plywood or something similar. The injury is often conspicuous, but does not affect production.

Insects

WHAT TO LOOK FOR	PEST	PREVENTION AND/OR NATURAL CONTROLS	CHEMICAL CONTROLS	GEOGRAPHICAL LOCATION
Colonies of small green sucking insects on leaves. Leaves can be curled and discolored. Sticky substance on leaves.	aphids	Companion plant with spearmint and garlic. Mulch with aluminum foil. Remove with blast from garden hose. Use a soap solution on leaves. Control with lacewing flies, praying mantises, ladybugs.	Malathion, diazinon, pyrethrum, rotenone, or ryania.	Widespread.
Plants partially defoliated.	blister beetles	Garden cleanliness. Spade deeply in the Spring to kill larvae. Pick beetles off by hand.	Sevin, pyrethrum, rotenone, or ryania.	East of Rocky Mountains.
Irregular holes eaten in leaves.	cabbage loopers	Clean up and dispose of crop remnants each Fall. Remove weeds. Pick off and smash worms. Use Bacillus thuringiensis (Dipel).	Malathion, Sevin, or rotenone.	Widespread.
Damage to the buds of young plants.	cabbage web worms	Garden cleanliness. Pick off and smash worms. Use Bacillus thuringiensis.	Malathion, Sevin, or rotenone.	Especially prevalent in the South during Summer and Fall.

TABLE 9–8 CABBAGE (continued)

Insects

WHAT TO LOOK FOR	PEST	PREVENTION AND/OR NATURAL CONTROLS	CHEMICAL CONTROLS	GEOGRAPHICAL LOCATION
Brown root scars. Stunted off-color plants. Some plants may be honeycombed with curving, slimy tunnels.	cabbage maggot (larva of cabbage root fly). Transmits spores of blackleg disease.	Cover plants with fine gauze to prevent flies from laying eggs on them. Dispose of damaged plants after harvest. Companion plant with mint and tomato. Put 4-inch circles of cardboard or tar paper around stems at ground level to prevent maggots from reaching roots.	Mix diazinon into the top 3 to 4 inches of the soil before planting. Repeat in 2 weeks.	Widespread. Most severe in the northern United States, southern Canada.
Young plants cut off near the soil surface.	cutworms (they hide in soil by day, attack at night)	Garden cleanliness. Use oak leaf mulch. Plant tansy between rows. Place a cardboard collar around the stems, push 1 inch into soil.	Spray the soil with Sevin or diazinon before transplanting into bed.	Widespread.
Leaves riddled with tiny round holes.	flea beetles	Garden cleanliness. Spade garden soil deeply to destroy larvae in early spring. Pick off plants.	Use several applications of diazinon, malathion, Sevin, pyrethrum, rotenone, or ryania.	Widespread.
Leaves chewed. Tunnels inside cabbage and cauliflower heads.	imported cabbage worm (white cabbage butterfly)	Destroy all remains and weeds after harvest. Companion plant with mint. Use Bacillus thuringiensis (Dipel or Thurocide).	Malathion, Sevin, or rotenone.	Widespread.
Trails of silver slime.	slugs, snails	Garden cleanliness. Use a shallow dish of beer with lip at ground level.	Control with a slug and snail bait (Slug-Geta) or try a dehydrating agent (Snail Snare).	Widespread.

TABLE 9–8   CABBAGE *(continued)*

Insects

WHAT TO LOOK FOR	PEST	PREVENTION AND/OR NATURAL CONTROLS	CHEMICAL CONTROLS	GEOGRAPHICAL LOCATION
White or yellow blotches on leaves where nymphs have sucked sap. Leaves can wilt.	stinkbug, harlequin bug	Destroy egg masses clustered on underside of leaves. Control with sabadilla.	Spray plants with Sevin, pyrethrum, and rotenone.	Extremely destructive to the cabbage clan in the southern half of the United States.
Plant growth stunted as worms bore into roots.	white grubs (the larvae of the June beetle) wireworms (the larva of the click beetle)	Keep the garden free of refuse that could shelter beetle eggs.	Use diazinon as a soil treatment before planting.	White grubs troublesome in the South and Midwest. Wireworms are widespread.

Diseases

WHAT TO LOOK FOR	DISEASE	PREVENTION AND/OR NATURAL CONTROLS	CHEMICAL CONTROLS	GEOGRAPHICAL LOCATION
Slimy top foliage with a foul odor. Top falls away easily.	bacterial soft root	Collect and burn compost or plant debris after harvest.		Widespread.
Light brown or gray spots on stem, leaves. Stem is girdled, blackens and rots.	blackleg (spread by cutworms and cabbage rot maggots)	Collect and burn tops after harvest. Use 4-year rotation.	Treat seed with captan.	Widespread east of Mountains.
Seedlings turn yellow to brown, wilt, and collapse. Yellow, brown or dark green V-shaped areas with blackened veins appear. Leaves drop off.	black rot	Avoid overhead watering.		Widespread in warm, moist seasons.

TABLE 9–8   CABBAGE (continued)

Diseases

WHAT TO LOOK FOR	DISEASE	PREVENTION AND/OR NATURAL CONTROLS	CHEMICAL CONTROLS	GEOGRAPHICAL LOCATION
Yellowish leaves that wilt on hot days. Roots greatly enlarged with warty growth.	clubroot	Keep weeds down.	Lanstan.	Widespread.
Pale green to yellow spotting upper surface of leaves followed by purpling.	downy mildew	Avoid overcrowding plants. Don't water overhead. Pick off and burn infected plant parts.	Maneb or fixed copper sprays.	Widespread during cool wet seasons.
Pale yellow, gray brown, dark green spots on leaves.	fungal spots	Collect and burn tops after harvest.	Spray seedbed with maneb or fixed copper sprays.	Widespread in wet weather.
Plants stunted, yellowing and weak. Irregular swollen galls that are enlargements of roots.	root-knot nematodes	Rotate crops. Companion plant with marigolds.	Apply liquid or granular nematocide— see your local nursery.	Primarily in southern states in sandy soils.
Water soaked areas on the stems and leaves. Wilting of lower leaves followed by a collapse of the whole plant into a shapeless mass.	watery soft rot	Garden cleanliness. Rotate crops.		Common in the Gulf Coast region and the humid valleys of the Pacific Coast.
Leaves turn dull yellow, curl, and die.	yellows (virus)	Grow the Early Snowball, resistant variety.		Widespread. Most serious when soil temperatures over 70 degrees F.

CARDOON

This native of the Mediterranean is related to the artichoke. It is a big thistle-like plant with deeply cut leaves. Cardoon is grown for the young leafstalks. Here are some problems you might encounter.

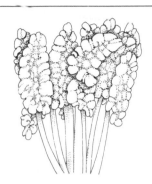

TABLE 9–9 CARDOON

Mother Nature's Puzzlers

WHAT TO LOOK FOR	POSSIBLE CAUSES	POSSIBLE CURES
Cardoon leafstalks become pithy and tasteless.	Slowed growth which creates tasteless leafstalks.	Keep fertilized with a complete vegetable fertilizer (10-10-10 will do. See Chapter 3). Keep the soil moist. Place a 2 to 3 inch layer of organic material over soil, or water the plant for 2 to 3 hours and not again until the soil dries out to a depth of 4 to 8 inches. Check with trowel.

Insects

WHAT TO LOOK FOR	PEST	PREVENTION AND/OR NATURAL CONTROLS	CHEMICAL CONTROLS	GEOGRAPHICAL LOCATION
Colonies of sucking insects on buds and leaves. Leaves can be curled and discolored. Sticky substance on stems and leaves.	aphids	Companion plant with spearmint and garlic. Mulch with aluminum foil. Remove with blast from garden hose. Use a soap solution on the leaves. Control with lacewing flies, praying mantises, ladybugs.	Malathion or diazinon, pyrethrum, rotenone or ryania.	Widespread.
Trails of silver slime.	slugs, snails	Garden cleanliness. Use a shallow dish of beer with lip at ground level.	Control with a slug and snail bait (Slug-Geta) or try a dehydrating agent (Snail Snare).	Widespread.
Heads and crown parts become slimy and foul smelling.	head/crown rot	Keep down weeds.	Apply a mixture of Captan and PCNB (sold as Terracap, Soil Treater "X," PCNB-Captan).	Widespread.

CARROTS AND PARSNIPS

Carrots will grow almost anywhere but do best in loose, sandy soil enriched with plenty of humus. Parsnips also like loose, sandy soil cultivated to a depth of about 18 inches. Both carrots and parsnips are in the same plant family and are attacked by many of the same insects and diseases.

TABLE 9–10 CARROTS AND PARSNIPS

Mother Nature's Puzzlers

WHAT TO LOOK FOR	POSSIBLE CAUSES	POSSIBLE CURES
Carrots Carrots come up in sparse clumps, or they don't come up at all.	1 Carrot seed isn't planted deeply enough. If the weather turns hot and dry, seed dries out and fails to germinate well.	1 Cover seed with 1 inch of vermiculite, compost, or sawdust. This keeps moisture in and allows full germination. Cover the seedbed with clear plastic to prevent evaporation. Remove the plastic as soon as the seedlings peek through the soil.
	2 The soil forms a hard crust that prevents the sprouting seed from breaking through.	2 Prevent the soil surface from drying out as above.
Twisted or forked carrot roots.	1 Rocks or clods in the soil cause the roots to twist around them or to fork.	1 Pick out rocks and clumps.
	2 Carrots are planted too close together. Those grown less than 1 inch apart tend to be misshapen and tough.	2 Space carrots 1 to 2 inches apart.
	3 Soil contains too much manure, causing rough-branching carrots.	3 Mix only fine, well rotted manure into the carrot bed.
Longitudinal cracks occur. In specific cases the leaves are yellow and malformed.	1 Boron deficiency.	1 Test the soil. If deficient apply about 2 ounces of borax per 1000 square feet.
	2 Dry weather is followed by heavy rain. Or the soil dries out completely and then is heavily watered again.	2 Place 2 or 3 inches of organic material on top of the soil to hold down moisture loss. Water carrots 2 to 3 hours at a time. Don't water again until the soil is dry to a depth of 4 to 5 inches. Check with a trowel.
The top of the carrot (the shoulder) turns green.	Too much exposure to light, causing chlorophyll to develop, making shoulder green and inedible.	Cover the shoulders with soil.

TABLE 9–10 CARROTS AND PARSNIPS (continued)

Mother Nature's Puzzlers

WHAT TO LOOK FOR	POSSIBLE CAUSES	POSSIBLE CURES
Carrot roots are long, thin and spindly, or short and stumpy.	Soil temperatures are too high or too low. Roots that develop at soil temperatures of 40 to 50 degrees F. become long and pointed. Roots that develop at soil temperatures of between 70 to 80 degrees F. produce short stumpy roots.	Plant and cultivate when soil temperatures are between 60 and 70 degrees F. If soil temperatures regularly rise above 70 degrees F., grow carrots during the cooler days of Spring or Fall.
Carrot roots develop a pale orange color.	Prolonged exposure to air temperatures of below 65 degrees F. Carrots grown under these conditions lose some of their nutritional value.	Plant later in the Spring so carrots can grow in temperatures of 65 degrees F. and above or grow them under protective devices.
Flower heads like Queen Anne's Lace begin to develop on your carrot plants.	Prolonged exposure to low temperatures (below 65 degrees F).	Plant later in the Spring. Or grow under protective devices.
Carrots have a bitter flavor.	Exposure to hot, dry weather conditions.	Place 2 to 3 inches of organic material over the soil to keep it cooler and to hold down moisture loss.
Carrots produce seed stalks early in the season.	Exposure to below freezing temperatures early in the season.	Protect young plants with hot kaps or other protective devices.
Parsnips Parsnips have poor flavor.	Insufficient exposure to below freezing temperatures. (Parsnip roots develop sweetness only under these conditions.)	Allow parsnips to remain in the ground until the second or third hard frost.

TABLE 9–10 CARROTS AND PARSNIPS (continued)

Insects

WHAT TO LOOK FOR	PEST	PREVENTION AND/OR NATURAL CONTROLS	CHEMICAL CONTROLS	GEOGRAPHICAL LOCATION
Colonies of sucking insects on leaves. Sticky substance on leaves.	aphids	Companion plant with garlic. Mulch with aluminum foil. Remove with blast from garden hose. Use a soap solution on the leaves. Control with lacewing flies, praying mantises, and ladybugs.	Malathion, diazinon, pyrethrum, rotenone, or ryania.	Widespread throughout U.S. and Canada.
Roots tunneled. Leaves can wilt and turn yellow.	carrot rust fly	Delay planting until late spring or summer if carrot rust fly is a problem in area. Companion plant with onion, rosemary. Place a fine gauze over carrot-bed.	Treat soil with diazinon.	Common in Eastern Canada, northern United States, Pacific Northwest.
Damage to leaves and roots. Roots tunneled by larvae with black heads.	carrot weevil	Spade the soil before planting. Companion plant with summer savory, tansy. Pick off beetles.	Sevin, malathion, or rotenone.	Widespread.
Leaves appear scorched and wilted.	leafhoppers	Spray with Sevin, malathion, pyrethrum, rotenone, or ryania when insects appear.		Widespread.

Diseases

WHAT TO LOOK FOR	DISEASE	PREVENTION AND/OR NATURAL CONTROLS	CHEMICAL CONTROLS	GEOGRAPHICAL LOCATION
Inner leaves and young leaves are yellow. Plants stunted and bunchy. Outer leaves may turn red or purple.	aster yellows (transmitted by leafhoppers)	Destroy infected plants. Keep weeds down.	Spray with malathion or Sevin to control leafhoppers.	Widespread.
Seedlings wilt and collapse.	damping off.	Avoid overcrowding carrots and parsnips.	Treat soil with captan.	Widespread.

TABLE 9–10   CARROTS AND PARSNIPS (continued)

Diseases

WHAT TO LOOK FOR	DISEASE	PREVENTION AND/OR NATURAL CONTROLS	CHEMICAL CONTROLS	GEOGRAPHICAL LOCATION
Yellow or brown spots on leaves. Entire top may be killed.	leaf blight	Use 3-year rotation. Keep down weeds. Burn or bury tops after harvest.	Spray with maneb or zineb 4 to 5 times at 10 day intervals when plants are 6 inches tall.	Widespread during wet seasons.
Leaves mottled light to dark green.	mosaics (spread by aphids)	Destroy infected plants. Keep weeds down.	Use malathion to control aphids.	Widespread.
Small gall-like swellings on roots. Taproot may be forked, twisted.	root-knot (nematode)	Rotate with corn or members of the cabbage clan. Companion plant with marigolds.	Apply liquid or granular nematocide— see your local nursery.	Southern states, occasionally in other areas.
Roots discolored and decayed. Plants stunted.	root rots (often follows attacks by carrot rust fly)	Plant in loose, well-drained soil. Plant resistant carrot varieties: Chantenay, Chantenay Red Cored.	Treat soil with diazinon to control insects.	Widespread.

CAULIFLOWER

Cauliflower does best where the weather is cool, frost free, yet sunny. It does not do well in very hot weather. Here are the principal problems to watch for.

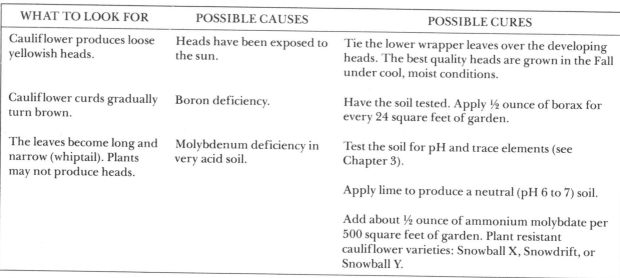

TABLE 9–11 CAULIFLOWER

Mother Nature's Puzzlers

WHAT TO LOOK FOR	POSSIBLE CAUSES	POSSIBLE CURES
Cauliflower produces loose yellowish heads.	Heads have been exposed to the sun.	Tie the lower wrapper leaves over the developing heads. The best quality heads are grown in the Fall under cool, moist conditions.
Cauliflower curds gradually turn brown.	Boron deficiency.	Have the soil tested. Apply ½ ounce of borax for every 24 square feet of garden.
The leaves become long and narrow (whiptail). Plants may not produce heads.	Molybdenum deficiency in very acid soil.	Test the soil for pH and trace elements (see Chapter 3). Apply lime to produce a neutral (pH 6 to 7) soil. Add about ½ ounce of ammonium molybdate per 500 square feet of garden. Plant resistant cauliflower varieties: Snowball X, Snowdrift, or Snowball Y.

Insects

WHAT TO LOOK FOR	PEST	PREVENTION AND/OR NATURAL CONTROLS	CHEMICAL CONTROLS	GEOGRAPHICAL LOCATION
Colonies of small green sucking insects on leaves. Leaves can be curled and discolored. Sticky substance on stems and leaves.	aphids	Companion plant with spearmint and garlic. Mulch with aluminum foil. Remove with blast from garden hose. Use a soap solution on the leaves. Control with lacewing flies, praying mantises, ladybugs.	Malathion, diazinon, pyrethrum, rotenone or ryania.	Widespread.
Plants partially defoliated.	blister beetles	Keep the garden area free of refuse. Spade deeply in the Spring to kill larvae. Pick beetles off by hand.	Sevin, pyrethrum, rotenone, or ryania.	East of Rocky Mountains.

TABLE 9–11   CAULIFLOWER (continued)

Insects

WHAT TO LOOK FOR	PEST	PREVENTION AND/OR NATURAL CONTROLS	CHEMICAL CONTROLS	GEOGRAPHICAL LOCATION
Irregular holes eaten in leaves.	cabbage loopers	Garden cleanliness. Remove weeds. Pick off and smash worms. Use Bacillus thuringiensis (Dipel).	Malathion, Sevin, or rotenone.	Widespread.
Brown root scars. Stunted off color plants. Some plants may be honeycombed with curving, slimy tunnels.	cabbage maggot (larva of cabbage root fly). Transmits spores of blackleg disease.	Cover plants with fine gauze to prevent flies from laying eggs on them. Dispose of damaged plants after harvest. Mint and tomato repel cabbage maggots. Put 4-inch circles of cardboard or tar paper around stems at ground level to prevent maggots from reaching roots.	Mix diazinon into the top 3 to 4 inches of the soil before planting. Repeat in 2 weeks.	Widespread. Most severe in the northern United States, southern Canada.
Damage to the buds of young plants.	cabbage webworm.	Garden cleanliness. Pick off and smash worms. Use Bacillus thuringiensis.	Malathion, Sevin, or rotenone.	Especially prevalent in the South during Summer and Fall.
Young plants cut off near the soil surface.	cutworms (they hide in soil by day, attack at night)	Garden cleanliness. Use oak leaf mulch. Plant tansy between rows. Place a cardboard collar around the stems, push 1 inch into soil.	Spray the soil with Sevin or diazinon before transplanting into bed.	Widespread.
Leaves riddled with tiny round holes.	flea beetles	Garden cleanliness. Spade garden soil deeply to destroy larvae in early Spring. Pick off plants.	Use several applications of diazinon, malathion, Sevin, pyrethrum, rotenone, or ryania.	Widespread.
Leaves chewed. Tunnels inside cabbage and cauliflower heads.	imported cabbage worm (white cabbage butterfly)	Destroy all remains and weeds after harvest. Companion plant with mint. Bacillus thuringiensis.	Malathion, Sevin, or rotenone.	Widespread.

TABLE 9–11 **CAULIFLOWER** *(continued)*

Insects

WHAT TO LOOK FOR	PEST	PREVENTION AND/OR NATURAL CONTROLS	CHEMICAL CONTROLS	GEOGRAPHICAL LOCATION
Trails of silver slime.	slugs, snails	Garden cleanliness. Use a shallow dish of beer with lip at ground level.	Control with a slug and snail bait (Slug-Geta) or a dehydrating agent (Snail Snare).	Widespread.
White or yellow blotches on leaves where nymphs have sucked sap. Leaves can wilt.	stinkbug, harlequin bug	Destroy egg masses clustered on underside of leaves. Control with sabadilla.	Sevin, pyrethrum, or rotenone.	Extremely destructive to the cabbage clan in the southern half of the United States.
Plant growth stunted as worms bore into roots.	white grubs (the larvae of the June beetle), wireworms (the larva of the click beetle)	Garden cleanliness.	Use diazinon as a soil treatment before planting.	White grubs troublesome in the South and Midwest. Wireworms are widespread.

Diseases

WHAT TO LOOK FOR	DISEASE	PREVENTION AND/OR NATURAL CONTROLS	CHEMICAL CONTROLS	GEOGRAPHICAL LOCATION
Slimy top foliage with a foul odor. Top falls away easily.	bacterial soft rot	Collect and burn compost or plant debris after harvest.		Widespread.
Light brown or gray spots on stem, leaves. Stem is girdled, blackens and rots.	blackleg (spread by cutworms and cabbage root maggots)	Collect and burn tops after harvest. Use 4-year rotation.	Treat seed with captan.	Widespread east of Rocky Mountains.
Seedlings turn yellow to brown, wilt, collapse. Yellow, brown, or dark green V-shaped areas with blackened veins. Leaves drop off.	black rot	Avoid overhead watering.	Widespread in warm, moist seasons.	

TABLE 9-11 CAULIFLOWER (continued)

Diseases

WHAT TO LOOK FOR	DISEASE	PREVENTION AND/OR NATURAL CONTROLS	CHEMICAL CONTROLS	GEOGRAPHICAL LOCATION
Yellowish leaves that wilt on hot days. Roots greatly enlarged with warty growth.	clubroot	Keep weeds down.	Lanstan.	Widespread.
Pale green to yellow spotting on upper surface of leaves followed by purpling.	downy mildew.	Avoid overcrowding plants. Don't water overhead. Pick off and burn infected plant parts.	Spray with maneb or fixed copper sprays.	Widespread during cool wet seasons.
Pale yellow, gray brown, dark green spots on leaves.	fungal spots	Collect and burn tops after harvest.	Spray seedbed with maneb or fixed copper sprays.	Widespread in wet weather.
Plants stunted, yellowing, and weak. Irregular swollen galls that are enlargements of roots.	root-knot nematodes	Rotate crops. Companion plant with marigolds.	Apply liquid or granular nematocide— see your local nursery.	Primarily in southern states in sandy soils.
Water-soaked areas on the stems and leaves. Wilting of lower leaves followed by a collapse of the whole plant into a shapeless mass.	watery soft rot	Garden cleanliness. Rotate crops.		Common in the Gulf Coast region and the humid valleys of the Pacific Coast.
Leaves turn dull yellow, curl, and die.	yellows (virus)	Grow the Early Snowball resistant variety.		Widespread. Most serious when soil temperatures over 70 degrees F.

CELERY

Celery and its relatives do well where the growing season is
fairly cool, especially in a highly fertile soil enriched with
organic material (compost, well rotted manure, peat moss).
The most common problems are as follows.

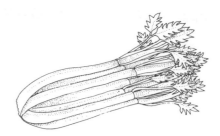

TABLE 9–12   CELERY

Mother Nature's Puzzlers

WHAT TO LOOK FOR	POSSIBLE CAUSES	POSSIBLE CURES
Ragged crosswise cracking of celery stems. The stems are stiff, brittle, sometimes bitter. The edges of the young leaves may be streaked. The leaves begin to turn brown.	Boron deficiency, especially prevalent in heavy, alkaline soils.	Test the soil. If deficient, apply 2 ounces of borax per 30 square yards. Plant resistant varieties of celery: Dwarf Golden Self-Blanching, Giant Pascal, Utah 52-70, Golden Self Blanching.
The tips and leaf margins of both celery and celeriac become streaked. They begin to look scorched.	Magnesium deficiency.	Have the soil tested. Use magnesium chelates. Follow manufacturer's instructions. Plant resistant celery varieties: Emerson Pascal, Utah 52-75.
Celery produces lots of leaves but no stalks.	Sudden fluctuations of temperature in the early stages of growth (up to about 4 inches high).	Protect plants by covering with translucent gallon milk jugs, hot kaps, or similar protective devices. Remove when the weather becomes warmer.

Insects

WHAT TO LOOK FOR	PEST	PREVENTION AND/OR NATURAL CONTROLS	CHEMICAL CONTROLS	GEOGRAPHICAL LOCATION
Colonies of sucking insects on leaves, stems. Discolored and curled leaves. Sticky substance on stems and leaves.	aphids	Companion plant with spearmint and garlic. Mulch with aluminum foil. Remove with blast from garden hose. Use soap solution on leaves. Spearmint and garlic help repel aphids. Mulch with aluminum foil.	Malathion, diazinon, pyrethrum, rotenone, or ryania.	Widespread throughout U.S. and Canada.
Holes chewed in leaves and stalks.	celery leaf tier	Control with lacewing flies, praying mantises, ladybugs.	Sevin or pyrethrum.	Widespread.

TABLE 9–12   **CELERY** *(continued)*

Insects

WHAT TO LOOK FOR	PEST	PREVENTION AND/OR NATURAL CONTROLS	CHEMICAL CONTROLS	GEOGRAPHICAL LOCATION
Irregular holes in foliage.	celery worm (larva of the black swallow-tail butterfly)	Pick off by hand. Spray with Bacillus thuringiensis (Dipel).	Sevin, pyrethrum, rotenone, or ryania.	
Plants partially defoliated.	blister beetles	Garden cleanliness. Spade deeply in the Spring to kill larvae. Pick beetles off by hand.	Spray or dust with Sevin, pyrethrum, rotenone, or ryania.	East of Rocky Mountains.
Irregular holes eaten in leaves.	cabbage loopers	Clean up and dispose of crop remains each fall. Remove weeds. Pick loopers off by hand. Use Bacillus thuringiensis (Dipel, Thurocide).	Malathion, Sevin, or rotenone.	Widespread.
Plant growth stunted as worms bore into roots.	white grubs (larvae of the June beetle), wireworms (larva of the click beetle)	Garden cleanliness.	Use diazinon as a soil treatment before planting.	White grubs troublesome in the South and Midwest. Wireworms are widespread.
Trails of silver slime.	slugs, snails	Garden cleanliness. Use a shallow dish of beer with lip at ground level.	Control with a slug and snail bait (Slug-Geta) or try a dehydrating agent (Snail Snare).	Widespread.

Diseases

WHAT TO LOOK FOR	DISEASE	PREVENTION AND/OR NATURAL CONTROLS	CHEMICAL CONTROLS	GEOGRAPHICAL LOCATION
Inner leaves yellowed, stunted, curled.	aster yellows (transmitted by leafhoppers)	Destroy infected plants. Keep weeds down.	Spray with malathion or Sevin to control leafhoppers	Widespread.

TABLE 9-12   CELERY *(continued)*

Diseases

WHAT TO LOOK FOR	DISEASE	PREVENTION AND/OR NATURAL CONTROLS	CHEMICAL CONTROLS	GEOGRAPHICAL LOCATION
Inner leaves die at tips and turn brown or black.	blackheart (associated with calcium deficiency)	Water according to instructions in Chapter 4. Plant resistant celery varieties: Cornell 19, Emerald, Emerson, Golden Pascal.	Spray with calcium chloride (¾ ounce to 1 gallon water).	Widespread in hot weather.
Seedlings shrivel and collapse.	damping off	Grow in well-drained soil.	Dust seed with captan. Apply maneb at weekly intervals during wet weather.	Widespread.
Plants turn pale green to golden yellow. Stalks brittle.	fusarium wilt	Plant resistant varieties of celery: Cornell No. 19, all the green celeries.		Widespread except in southern states.
Round to irregular yellowish brown to reddish black spots on leaves, stalks, stems.	leaf blight	Grow in well-drained soil. Keep weeds down. Rotate crops.	Apply maneb or zineb every 7 days.	Widespread.
Leaves spotted or striped-green and yellow zig-zag bands may develop.	mosaics	Destroy infected plants. Keep down all weeds.	Spray with malathion to destroy insects that may transmit mosaic.	Widespread.
Seedlings stunted, enlargements or small galls on roots.	root-knot (nematodes)	Rotate crops. Companion plant with marigolds.	Apply liquid or granular nematocide— see your local nursery.	Widespread.
Stems and leaf stalks may suddenly soften and wilt.	stem rot	Plant in well-drained soil. Keep weeds down.	Apply maneb or zineb every 7 days.	Widespread.

CORN

Corn grows best in a light sandy loam soil that warms up fast. It also likes a sunny warm growing season of about 3 months. In cooler climates, grow early or dwarf varieties.

TABLE 9–13 **CORN**

Mother Nature's Puzzlers

WHAT TO LOOK FOR	POSSIBLE CAUSES	POSSIBLE CURES
Ears are only partially filled with ripe kernels.	Each individual kernel must be pollinated. Kernels that don't receive pollen, simply don't fill out. Pollen from the male tassels floats down in the wind and pollinates the female cobs.	Plant corn in blocks of 2 to 3 rows rather than in a single row. This increases the likelihood of pollination.
Leaves develop purple margins starting with the leaves at the bottom of the plant. The entire plant may be dark green and stunted.	Phosphorus deficiency.	Fertilize soil with a commercial fertilizer rich in phosphorus (5-10-5 is especially good). Or sprinkle bonemeal on top of the bed before planting (2 to 3 pounds per 100 square feet). Sprinkle bonemeal on top of the bed before planting (2 to 3 pounds per 100 square feet).
Leaf edges roll inward.	Frequently means the plants don't have enough water. Corn needs to make rapid growth just as the ears start to mature. Lack of moisture in the soil will slow growth and affect ear size.	Place 2 to 3 inches of organic material on top of the bed to reduce moisture loss. Water corn 2 to 3 hours at a time, then don't water again until the soil dries out to a depth of 4 to 8 inches. Check with a trowel.
Stalks produce small ears.	Corn plants are spaced too close together.	Space early varieties at least 8 inches apart. Space later varieties 12 to 15 inches apart.
Popped kernel. The kernels look like popcorn.	Seedcoats break at the weakest point.	No cure. Plant another variety.

Insects

WHAT TO LOOK FOR	PEST	PREVENTION AND/OR NATURAL CONTROLS	CHEMICAL CONTROLS	GEOGRAPHICAL LOCATION
Leaves look like they have been shot through with tiny holes.	corn flea beetle (transmits Stewart's wilt)	Garden cleanliness. Spade garden soil deeply to destroy larva in early spring. Pick beetles off plant.	Diazinon, Malathion, Sevin, pyrethrum, rotenone, or ryania.	Widespread in the U.S. and southern Canada.

TABLE 9–13 **CORN** *(continued)*

Insects

WHAT TO LOOK FOR	PEST	PREVENTION AND/OR NATURAL CONTROLS	CHEMICAL CONTROLS	GEOGRAPHICAL LOCATION
Kernels at the tip of the ear are brown and eaten away.	corn earworm	Plant corn varieties with long, tight husks: Country Gentleman, Golden Security, Silver Cross Bantam. Apply 1 drop or 2 of mineral oil to the silks just inside the tip of each ear.	Dust with Sevin every 2 or 3 days until the silks turn brown. Spray with ryania.	Widespread in the United States and Canada. Most prevalent in the South.
Corn doesn't come up. Insides of seed and young plants eaten.	corn wireworm	Spade the corn bed and let lie fallow every third season. When replanting, spade between the rows in the early part of Summer.	Use diazinon as a soil treatment before planting.	Widespread.
Young plants eaten or cut off near the surface of the soil.	cutworms	Garden cleanliness. Companion plant with tansy between rows. Place a cardboard collar around the stems. Push 1 inch into soil.	Spray the soil with Sevin or diazinon before the young plants emerge.	Widespread.
Castings outside of tiny holes in the stalk. Broken tassels, bent stalks.	European corn borer	Clear plant debris and weeds out of the garden to prevent the adult from laying eggs near the garden.	Spray with Sevin as soon as the tassels are visible. Repeat at 5 day intervals.	Eastern U.S. Parts of the Rocky Mountains. South to Florida and Texas.
Plants partially defoliated.	grasshopper	Turn the soil under in the Fall to bury the eggs so the young cannot make their way to surface. Trap in quart jars filled with 1 part molasses and 9 parts water. Import praying mantises.	Spray or dust with Sevin, malathion, or diazinon. Or use rotenone.	Widespread. Especially destructive at times in the Dakotas, Montana, and Saskatchewan.
Brown leaf margins.	leafhoppers		Spray plants with Sevin and malathion when insects appear. Or use botanical sprays: pyrethrum, rotenone, ryania.	Widespread. More severe in eastern U.S.

TABLE 9–13   CORN (continued)

Diseases

WHAT TO LOOK FOR	DISEASE	PREVENTION AND/OR NATURAL CONTROLS	CHEMICAL CONTROLS	GEOGRAPHICAL LOCATION
Grayish green to tan or brown spots on lower leaves. Ears may be immature.	leaf blights (Helminthosporium)	Plant resistant varieties: Florigold 107, Gold Cup, Seneca. Bury or burn all corn debris after harvest. Avoid overhead sprinkling.	Spray with maneb or zineb at weekly intervals.	Widespread in humid areas.
Stalks rotted internally at base.	root and stalk rot (often associated with nematodes)	Grow in well drained soil. Rotate crops. Burn or bury stalks after harvest.	Use diazinon in soil to control soil insects that help spread the disease.	Widespread.
Yellowish orange to reddish brown pustules on both leaf surfaces	rusts	Burn or bury plant debris after harvest.	Spray with maneb or zineb.	Widespread.
Long white yellowish or pale green streaks in leaves that later turn brown.	bacterial wilt (Stewart's disease) (spread by flea beetles)	Plant resistant varieties: Aristogold, Bantam Evergreen, Atlas, Barbeque.	Spray with Sevin 2 to 4 times 3 to 5 days apart.	Widespread in eastern U.S.
Tassel looks like a large plumy mass. Tassel structures look like small leaves.	crazy top	Plant only in well-drained soil.	Widespread.	
Husks of ear appear bleached. Pink discoloration of kernel caps.	several kinds of ear rot	Plant resistant varieties.	Widespread.	
Silvery white galls which break, releasing dark brown to black sooty masses.	smuts	Cut out and burn galls before they break. Plant resistant varieties: Country Gentleman, Aristogold, Bantam Evergreen, Asgrow Golden 60, Golden Cross Bantam.		Widespread. Especially prevalent following hail or infestation of insects.

CUCUMBERS

Cucumbers are definitely a warm weather plant and the seeds need a warm soil (65 degrees F.) to sprout. They also are quite susceptible to frost. Given the proper conditions, however, the vines produce with a vengeance.

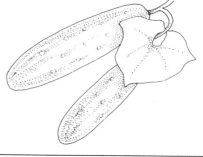

TABLE 9–14   CUCUMBERS

Mother Nature's Puzzlers

WHAT TO LOOK FOR	POSSIBLE CAUSES	POSSIBLE CURES
Early flowers don't produce fruit.	1 Female flowers (which are necessary for the actual production of cucumbers) may not have appeared. The first flowers are male. 2 An insufficient number of insects (mostly bees) to carry the pollen from the male flowers to the female. Where there is a shortage of bees, few cucumbers are produced.	1 A little patience. The plants will soon produce flowers of both sexes. You can also grow the all-female (gynoecious) cucumber hybrids. Every seed package contains a few seeds of male flower bearing plants. So there is something to pollinate the female blossoms. The seed package clearly states that the variety is an all-female hybrid. 2 Play bee. Pick off a male flower (the ones without the little cucumbers) and rub the fuzzy inside part on the tip of the tiny cucumbers.
Bitter tasting cucumbers	Some experts say the cause is uneven watering. The soil dries out completely, becomes saturated, then dries out again. Other experts say this happens when the temperature varies more than 20 degrees F. from day to day.	1 Place 2 to 3 inches of organic material on top of the bed to hold down moisture loss. Water 2 to 3 hours at a time. Don't water again until the soil has dried out to a depth of 4 to 8 inches. Check with a trowel. 2 Grow the variety Marketmore 70; it is a bitter-free cucumber.
Plants produce few cucumbers.	Cucumber plants are probably spaced too closely together.	Space cucumbers 8 to 12 inches apart. A Mississippi State University study shows that cucumber plants spaced closer or further apart than this produce fewer mature cucumbers.
Plants stopped producing.	Old cucumbers aren't being picked off. Even a few fruit left on the vine to mature will stop production cold.	Keep cucumbers picked from the vines as they reach useable size.

TABLE 9–14 **CUCUMBERS** *(continued)*

Insects

WHAT TO LOOK FOR	PEST	PREVENTION AND/OR NATURAL CONTROLS	CHEMICAL CONTROLS	GEOGRAPHICAL LOCATION
Colonies of sucking insects on leaves. Leaves can be curled and discolored. Sticky substance on stems and leaves.	aphids	Companion plant with spearmint and garlic. Mulch with aluminum foil. Remove with blast from garden hose. Use soap solution on the leaves. Control with lace-wing flies, praying mantises, ladybugs.	Malathion, diazinon, pyrethrum, rotenone, or ryania.	Widespread.
Plants eaten or cut off near the surface of the soil.	cutworms	Garden cleanliness. Companion plant with tansy. Place a cardboard collar around the stems. Push 1 inch into soil.	Spray the soil with Sevin or diazinon before the plants emerge.	Widespread.
Holes in leaves and flowers. Tunnels in vines and fruit.	pickleworm	Sevin, malathion, or rotenone.		Widespread, primarily in the South.
Affected leaves turn pale green. Dusty webs between vine and leaves.	spider mite	Use a strong spray from a garden hose to wash mites away. Ladybugs and lacewings— eat mites.	Diazinon or Kelthane.	Widespread, most severe in South.
Irregular holes chewed in leaves and shoots.	spotted cucumber beetle (carries bacterial wilt) (western spotted cucumber beetle in west)	Spade the soil before planting to destroy dormant beetles. Companion plant with radish, tansy. Pick off beetles.	Spray with Sevin or malathion. Or use the botanical spray rotenone.	Widespread.
Affected leaves wilt rapidly becoming black and crisp.	squash bug	Fertilize plants to keep growing vigorously. Nasturtium, tansy help repel squash bugs. Destroy squash bugs that collect under leaves at night. Use sabadilla (Doom).	Sevin malathion, pyrethrum, rotenone, or ryania.	Widespread.

TABLE 9–14   CUCUMBERS (continued)

Insects

WHAT TO LOOK FOR	PEST	PREVENTION AND/OR NATURAL CONTROLS	CHEMICAL CONTROLS	GEOGRAPHICAL LOCATION
Sudden wilting of runners. Holes in stems near base.	squash vine borer	Garden cleanliness. Slit the vine with a knife and take out the borer.	Dust with Sevin or malathion at weekly intervals as the vines start to grow.	Severe east of the Rocky Mountains.
Irregular holes chewed in leaves and shoots.	striped cucumber beetle (western striped cucumber beetle in the west)	Spade the soil before planting. Companion plant with Summer savory, radish, and tansy. Pick off beetles.	Sevin, malathion or rotenone.	Widespread.
Small plants turn yellow and break off.	southern corn rootworm (larvae of the spotted cucumber beetle)	Spade the soil before planting. Companion plant with savory, radish, tansy.	Sevin, malathion, pyrethrum, rotenone, ryania.	Especially prevalent in the South.

Diseases

WHAT TO LOOK FOR	DISEASE	PREVENTION AND/OR NATURAL CONTROLS	CHEMICAL CONTROLS	GEOGRAPHICAL LOCATION
Round to angular reddish brown to black spots on leaves. Spots may later dry and tear out.	anthracnose	Avoid overhead watering. Use 3- to 4-year rotation. Grow in well-drained soil. Burn plant debris. Keep down weeds.	Apply captan, maneb, or zineb at 10 day intervals.	Widespread in warm (65 to 85 degrees F.) humid weather.
Small angular spots on leaves. Round water-soaked spots on fruit.	bacterial spot or blight	Destroy plant debris after harvest.	Use fixed copper sprays.	Widespread.
Vines wilt rapidly and die starting with one or a few leaves on a vine.	bacterial wilt (transmitted by cucumber beetle)	Rotate crops each year. Pull and destroy wilted plants. Plant resistant varieties: Chicago Pickling.	Apply Sevin to control cucumber beetles that spread wilt.	Widespread.

TABLE 9–14 **CUCUMBERS** *(continued)*

Diseases

WHAT TO LOOK FOR	DISEASE	PREVENTION AND/OR NATURAL CONTROLS	CHEMICAL CONTROLS	GEOGRAPHICAL LOCATION
Yellowish to brownish areas on upper side of older leaves. Underside of leaves may show purplish gray mold.	downy mildew	Rotate cucumbers with other crops. Plant resistant varieties: Ashley, Dark Green Slicer, Early Marketer.	Apply maneb or zineb	Widespread.
Plants stunted and often yellow. Runners gradually die.	fusarium wilt	Collect and burn infected plants.		Widespread.
Yellow green and dark green mottling of leaves. Leaves often wrinkled and curled.	mosaics	Keep weeds out of garden area.	Use malathion to control aphids, cucumber beetles, and grasshoppers that transmit disease.	Widespread.
White or brownish mealy growth on leaves and young stems.	powdery mildew	Rotate cucumbers with other crops. Plant resistant varieties: Ashley, High Mark II, Pixie, Polaris.	Apply karathane 1 to 3 times 7 to 10 days apart.	Widespread.
Water soaked or pale green spots on leaves that turn white to gray to brown. Fruit crack.	scab	Plow under plants after harvest or burn. Grow in well-drained soil. Plant resistant varieties: Armour, Ashe, Crispy, Dark Green Slicer.	Apply maneb.	Widespread.

EGGPLANT

Eggplants grow well only in warm weather (60 to 85 degrees F.), will not tolerate frost, and prefer a well-drained, sandy soil. Here are the possible problems.

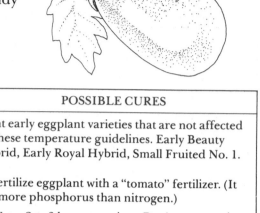

TABLE 9–15   EGGPLANT

Mother Nature's Puzzlers

WHAT TO LOOK FOR	POSSIBLE CAUSES	POSSIBLE CURES
Plant produces blossoms but they fall off without producing fruit.	Eggplant blossoms drop below 58 degrees F. and above 70 degrees F.	Plant early eggplant varieties that are not affected by these temperature guidelines. Early Beauty Hybrid, Early Royal Hybrid, Small Fruited No. 1.
Plants produce lush foliage, little fruit.	1 Too much nitrogen.	1 Fertilize eggplant with a "tomato" fertilizer. (It has more phosphorus than nitrogen.)
	2 Plants are receiving too much water.	2 Water 2 to 3 hours at a time. Don't water again until the soil has dried out to a depth of 4 to 8 inches. Check with a trowel.
Plants are stunted.	Temperature dips below 40 degrees F.	Set out the plants when the air temperatures are above 65 degrees F. Or protect the plants with plastic jugs with the bottoms cut out or other protective devices.

Insects

WHAT TO LOOK FOR	PEST	PREVENTION AND/OR NATURAL CONTROLS	CHEMICAL CONTROLS	GEOGRAPHICAL LOCATION
Colonies of sucking insects on leaves.	aphids	Companion plant with spearmint and garlic. Mulch with aluminum foil. Remove with blast from garden hose. Use a soap solution on the leaves. Lacewing flies, ladybugs, and praying mantises destroy aphids.	Malathion, diazinon, pyrethrum, rotenone, or ryania.	Widespread.
Plants partially defoliated.	blister beetles	Keep the garden free of refuse and weeds. Spade deeply in Spring to kill larvae. Pick beetles off by hand.	Spray or dust with Sevin, pyrethrum, rotenone, ryania.	East of Rocky Mountains.

TABLE 9–15   EGGPLANT (continued)

Insects

WHAT TO LOOK FOR	PEST	PREVENTION AND/OR NATURAL CONTROLS	CHEMICAL CONTROLS	GEOGRAPHICAL LOCATION
Leaves and shoots stripped.	Colorado potato beetle	Garden cleanliness. Companion plant with eggplant, flax, and green beans. Pick off beetles.	Malathion, Sevin, or rotenone.	Widespread in the U.S. and Canada except Nevada, California, and Florida.
Young plants cut off near soil surface.	cutworms; worms hide in the soil by day, feed at night	Garden cleanliness. Companion plant with tansy between the rows. Place a cardboard collar around the stems. Push 1 inch into soil.	Spray the soil with Sevin or diazinon before transplanting plants into beds.	Widespread.
Leaves look like they have been shot through with tiny round holes.	flea beetles	Garden cleanliness. Spade garden soil deeply to destroy larvae in early Spring. Companion plant with head lettuce, mint, wormwood. Pick beetles off plant.	Diazinon, malathion, Sevin, pyrethrum, rotenone, or ryania.	Widespread.
Leaves appear scorched and wilted.	leafhoppers	Spray with Sevin, malathion, pyrethrum, rotenone, or ryania when insects appear.		Widespread.
Fine webbing over the foliage. Mottled, speckled, and wilted leaves.	spider mites	Use a soap solution on the leaves. Apply a light petroleum oil spray to the leaves. Use a forceful spray from garden hose.	Spray thoroughly with diazinon or malathion every 7 to 9 days. Spray with Kelthane.	Widespread.
Insect eats into fruit.	tomato fruitworm (European corn borer)		Control worms when they are small with Sevin.	Widespread.
Plants partially defoliated.	tomato hornworm	Spade deeply in Fall to destroy larvae. Handpick and destroy caterpillars. Use Bacillus thuringiensis (Dipel, Thurocide).	Sevin.	Throughout U.S. and southern Canada.

TABLE 9–15   **EGGPLANT** *(continued)*

Insects

WHAT TO LOOK FOR	PEST	PREVENTION AND/OR NATURAL CONTROLS	CHEMICAL CONTROLS	GEOGRAPHICAL LOCATION
White spots on fruit. Leaf tips become distorted.	thrips (transmit spotted wilt virus)	Keep weeds out of garden area.	Treat with 2 or 3 applications of diazinon or malathion.	Widespread.
A cloud of white wings fly from plant when disturbed.	whiteflies	Companion plant with marigolds. Marigolds excrete a substance absorbed by roots of other plants that repel whiteflies. Use wasps to destroy whiteflies. Hose off with stream of water. Trap whiteflies in Tanglefoot on a bright yellow card.	Malathion or rotenone.	Widespread.

Diseases

WHAT TO LOOK FOR	DISEASE	PREVENTION AND/OR NATURAL CONTROLS	CHEMICAL CONTROLS	GEOGRAPHICAL LOCATION
Sunken water-soaked areas on fruit. Fruit may shrivel, become watery, collapse.	anthracnose	Destroy rotting fruit. Keep fruit off soil.	Spray with maneb or zineb.	Widespread.
Plants turn yellow starting at top. Plants stunted.	eggplant yellows	Destroy infected plants. Keep all weeds out of garden area.		Widespread.
Brown to almost black spots on leaves and lower stem. Leaves turn yellow to brown.	early blight	Garden cleanliness, with special attention to removing weeds.	Apply maneb or zineb.	Widespread.
Plants stunted, leaves wilt, wither, drop off. Brown to black streaks lower stem.	fusarium wilt	Crop rotation. Plant in well-drained soil.		Widespread.

TABLE 9–15 EGGPLANT (continued)

Diseases

WHAT TO LOOK FOR	DISEASE	PREVENTION AND/OR NATURAL CONTROLS	CHEMICAL CONTROLS	GEOGRAPHICAL LOCATION
Irregular greenish water-soaked spots on leaves and stems. Whitish-gray growth on the underside of leaves. Fruit corrugated.	late blight	Garden cleanliness. Keep weeds out of garden area.	Apply maneb, zineb, or fixed copper once a week.	Widespread in rainy season.
Plants stunted with galls on roots. Plants wilt in dry weather then recover.	root-knot (nematodes)	Rotate crops. Companion plant with marigolds.	Apply liquid or granular nematocide— see your local nursery.	Widespread in southern states.
Leaves have light to dark green streaks.	mosaic (tobacco mosaic spread by insects)	Destroy infected plants. Keep down all weeds in garden area. Avoid use of tobacco while working with plants. Smokers should wash hands before working in the garden.	Apply malathion to control insects that transmit this virus.	Widespread.
Lower leaves yellow and die. Stems discolored.	verticillium wilt	Crop rotation. Plant in well-drained soil.		Widespread.

KALE AND MUSTARD

Kale and mustard both like cool weather, although mustard has a greater tolerance for heat than kale. Both vegetables grow well in well-drained loam soil. Here's what to watch for.

TABLE 9–16 **KALE AND MUSTARD**

Mother Nature's Puzzlers

WHAT TO LOOK FOR	POSSIBLE CAUSES	POSSIBLE CURES
Kale Growth practically stops. Leaves lack "crisp, fresh" look.	Temperature rises above the high 60's.	Plant kale in mid or late Summer for a Fall crop. The flavor undergoes a noticeable improvement after a few nights of frost.
Mustard Mustard flowers and goes to seed.	Temperatures rise regularly above 80 degrees F.	Plant 2 weeks before the last frost in the Spring. Or if Spring temperatures regularly rise above 80 degrees F., plant in late Summer for a Fall crop.
Mustard leaves develop a pepper tang. This flavor is especially strong in older leaves.	Hot weather, with temperatures rising above 85 degrees F.	Grow mustard when the weather is cool (below 65 degrees F.) in the Spring and early Fall. Cool weather improves the flavor.

Insects

WHAT TO LOOK FOR	PEST	PREVENTION AND/OR NATURAL CONTROLS	CHEMICAL CONTROLS	GEOGRAPHICAL LOCATION
Colonies of small green sucking insects on underside of leaves. Leaves can be curled and discolored. Sticky substance on stems and leaves	aphids	Companion plant with spearmint or garlic. Mulch with aluminum foil. Remove with blast from garden hose. Use a soap solution on the leaves. Control with lacewing flies, praying mantises, ladybugs.	Malathion, diazinon, pyrethrum, rotenone, or ryania.	Widespread.
Plants partially defoliated.	blister beetle	Garden cleanliness. Spade deeply in the Spring to kill larvae. Pick off beetles by hand.	Sevin, pyrethrum, rotenone, or ryania.	Widespread.

TABLE 9-16   KALE AND MUSTARD (continued)

Insects

WHAT TO LOOK FOR	PEST	PREVENTION AND/OR NATURAL CONTROLS	CHEMICAL CONTROLS	GEOGRAPHICAL LOCATION
Irregular holes eaten in leaves.	cabbage looper	Garden cleanliness. Remove weeds. Pick off worms. Use Bacillus thuringiensis (Dipel, Thurocide).	Malathion, Sevin, or rotenone.	Widespread.
Young plants cut off near the soil surface.	cutworms; worms hide in soil by day, feed at night	Garden cleanliness. Place a cardboard collar around the stems. Push 1 inch into soil.	Spray the soil with Sevin or diazinon before transplanting plants into bed.	Widespread.
Leaves look like they have been shot through with tiny round holes.	flea beetles	Garden cleanliness. Spade garden soil deeply in early Spring to destroy larvae. Companion plant with mint, wormwood. Pick off plant.	Use several applications of diazinon, malathion, Sevin, pyrethrum, rotenone, ryania.	Widespread.
Holes in leaves.	imported cabbage worm (white cabbage butterfly)	Garden cleanliness. Companion plant with celery, mint, sage, thyme, tomato wormwood, and rosemary. Use Bacillus thuringiensis (Dipel or Thurocide).	Malathion, Sevin, or rotenone.	Widespread.
Brown root scars. Stunted off color plants. Some plants may be honeycombed with curving slimy tunnels.	cabbage maggot (larva of cabbage root fly); transmits spores of blackleg disease.	Cover plants with fine gauze to prevent flies from laying eggs on them. Garden cleanliness. Companion plant with tomatoes. Put 4-inch circles of cardboard around stems at ground level to prevent maggots from reaching roots.	Mix diazinon into the top 3 to 4 inches of the soil before planting. Repeat in 2 weeks.	Widespread. Most severe in the northern United States, southern Canada.

TABLE 9–16   **KALE AND MUSTARD** *(continued)*

Insects

WHAT TO LOOK FOR	PEST	PREVENTION AND/OR NATURAL CONTROLS	CHEMICAL CONTROLS	GEOGRAPHICAL LOCATION
white or yellow blotches on leaves where nymphs have sucked sap. Leaves can wilt.	stinkbug	Destroy egg masses clustered on underside of leaves. Control with sabadilla.	Sevin, rotenone, or pyrethrum.	Extremely destructive in the southern half of the United States.

Diseases

WHAT TO LOOK FOR	DISEASE	PREVENTION AND/OR NATURAL CONTROLS	CHEMICAL CONTROLS	GEOGRAPHICAL LOCATION
Slimy; foliage has a foul odor. Top falls away easily.	bacterial soft rot	Garden cleanliness.	Widespread.	
Light brown or gray spots on stems, leaves. Stem is girdled, blackens, and rots.	blackleg (spread by cutworms and cabbage root maggots)	Garden cleanliness. Use 4-year rotation for kale and mustard.	Treat seed with captan. Use diazinon in soil to control cutworms and maggots.	Widespread east of Rocky Mountains.
Seedlings turn yellow to brown, wilt, collapse. Yellow, brown, or dark green V-shaped areas with blackened veins. Leaves drop off.	black rot	Avoid overhead watering. Plant resistant varieties: kale— Dwarf Siberian; mustard— Florida Broadleaf.		Widespread in warm, moist seasons.
Yellowish leaves that wilt on hot days. Roots greatly enlarged with warty growth.	clubroot	Keep weeds down.	Drench soil with SMDC. Follow manufacturer's instructions. Use Terraclor.	Widespread.

TABLE 9–16   KALE AND MUSTARD *(continued)*

Diseases

WHAT TO LOOK FOR	DISEASE	PREVENTION AND/OR NATURAL CONTROLS	CHEMICAL CONTROLS	GEOGRAPHICAL LOCATION
Pale green to yellow spots on upper surfaces of leaves, followed by purpling of leaves.	downy mildew	Avoid overcrowding plants. Don't water overhead. Garden cleanliness.	Maneb or fixed copper sprays.	Widespread during cool wet seasons.
Pale yellow, gray brown, dark green spots on leaves.	fungal leaf spots	Plant resistant mustard: Southern curled giant.	Spray seedbed with maneb or fixed copper sprays.	Widespread in hot weather.
Leaves turn dull yellow, curl, and die.	yellows	Grow resistant varieties: kale— Siberian Kale.		Widespread. Most serious when soil temperatures are over 70 degrees F.

LETTUCE AND SALSIFY

You can grow lettuce almost anywhere. It likes 50 to 60 degree weather and does poorly in hot weather. Leafy types are better suited for warm weather than heading types, but different varieties vary greatly in their heat tolerance. In general, lettuce grows well in an "average" garden soil. Salsify is also a cool weather vegetable that takes up to 120 days to mature. Provide a deeply cultivated soil that gives the long root plenty of growing room.

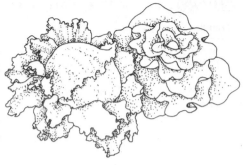

TABLE 9-17   LETTUCE AND SALSIFY

Mother Nature's Puzzlers

WHAT TO LOOK FOR	POSSIBLE CAUSES	POSSIBLE CURES
Lettuce seed planted in mid Summer for Fall harvest often fails to germinate well.	Temperatures are too high. Lettuce seed has a germination rate of 99 percent at 77 degrees F. This germination drops to 12 percent at 86 degrees F.	After planting, place a 2 to 3 inch layer of organic material over the seedbed to reduce the soil temperature. Or plant tolerant varieties: Progress, Great Lakes, Imperial 615. Black seeded simpson is extremely intolerant of high soil temperatures.
Lettuce flowers and goes to seed before it is ready to eat.	The long hot summer days and warm nights.	Plant in the Spring 2 weeks before the last frost. Or plant in late Summer for a Fall crop. Or shade the garden with lathe or gauze to reduce the light and heat. Plant heat resistant varieties: Great Lakes, Salad Bowl, Slowbolt.
The tips of the lettuce leaves turn brown and look burned.	High light intensities. This frequently happens in mid Summer when the lettuce garden receives full sun for the entire day.	Give your lettuce partial shade with lathes. Or plant where bushes will shade the lettuce bed part of the day.
Head lettuce fails to form good heads.	Plants have been crowded too close together.	Thin head lettuce to stand 12 to 14 inches apart.
Looseleaf varieties grow nothing but small bitter outside leaves. The tender material in the middle fails to form.	Plants are crowded too close to each other.	Thin looseleaf lettuce to stand 6 to 10 inches apart.
Romaine doesn't form hearts.	Romaine lettuce seed is planted too deep.	Drop seeds on seedbed and cover with ½ inch of soil only.

TABLE 9–17   LETTUCE AND SALSIFY (continued)

Insects

WHAT TO LOOK FOR	PEST	PREVENTION AND/OR NATURAL CONTROLS	CHEMICAL CONTROLS	GEOGRAPHICAL LOCATION
Colonies of sucking insects on underside of leaves. Leaves may be curled and discolored. Sticky substance on underside of leaves.	aphids	Companion plant with spearmint and garlic. Mulch with aluminum foil. Remove with blast from garden hose. Use a soap solution on the leaves. Control with lacewing flies, praying mantises, ladybugs.	Malathion, diazinon, pyrethrum, rotenone, or ryania.	Widespread.
Irregular holes eaten in leaves.	cabbage looper	Garden cleanliness. Remove weeds. Pick off worms. Use Bacillus thuringiensis (Dipel, Thurocide).	Malathion, Sevin, or rotenone.	Widespread.
Leaves eaten.	corn earworm	Pick off.	Sevin or ryania.	Widespread.
Leaves eaten by pincer bug.	earwigs	Trap in rolled up newspapers at night.	Commercial earwig bait.	Widespread.
Brown leaf margins.	leafhopper		Sevin, malathion, pyrethrum, rotenone, or ryania when insects appear.	Widespread. More severe in eastern U.S.
Trails of silver slime on leaves. Leaves eaten.	slugs, snails	Reduce hiding places by keeping garden free of debris. Use a shallow dish of beer with lip at ground level.	Control with a slug and snail bait (Slug-Geta) or try a dehydrating agent (Snail Snare).	Widespread.

TABLE 9–17   LETTUCE AND SALSIFY (continued)

Diseases

WHAT TO LOOK FOR	DISEASE	PREVENTION AND/OR NATURAL CONTROLS	CHEMICAL CONTROLS	GEOGRAPHICAL LOCATION
Center leaves become stunted, twisted, narrow and yellowed.	aster yellows (leafhoppers transmit virus)	Garden cleanliness. Destroy infected plants.	Apply Sevin or malathion at about 5 day intervals to control leafhoppers that transmit virus.	Widespread.
Leaf margins may rot and turn brownish black. Small yellowish brown to black spots	bacterial leaf spots	Avoid overhead watering. Garden cleanliness.	Fixed copper.	Widespread in wet weather.
Seedling wilt and collapse from rot at the soil line.	damping off	Plant in well-drained soil.	Treat soil with captan.	Widespread when soil is cold and wet.
Pale green to yellowish areas develop on upper leaf surface. Gray purple mold underneath.	downy mildew	Garden cleanliness. Resistant lettuce varieties: Arctic King, Big Boston, Salad Bowl, Imperial.	Maneb, zineb, or fixed copper.	Widespread.
Dark brown streaks inside stems and larger veins.	fusarium wilt (lettuce only)	Grow in well-drained soil. Destroy infected plants.		Widespread.
Grayish green or dark brown water-soaked areas on lower leaves.	gray-mold	Destroy infected plants.	Apply captan to soil before planting.	Widespread when weather is damp and overcast.
Leaf vein, swollen and light yellow. Leaves brittle.	big vein	Keep soil on the dry side.	Treat the soil with PCNB.	Widespread. Most severe during the cool seasons.

TABLE 9–17   **LETTUCE AND SALSIFY** *(continued)*

Diseases

WHAT TO LOOK FOR	DISEASE	PREVENTION AND/OR NATURAL CONTROLS	CHEMICAL CONTROLS	GEOGRAPHICAL LOCATION
Leaves mottled yellow and light green.	mosaics (transmitted by aphids)	Destroy infected plants. Garden cleanliness. Plant resistant lettuce varieties: Parris Island, Valmaine Cos.	Spray with malathion to control aphids.	Widespread.
Outer leaves start to rot. May become slimy and foul smelling.	rots (bottom and drop)	Garden cleanliness. Plant in well-drained soil. Keep soil surface as dry as possible.	Treat seedbed with captan.	Widespread.

MELONS

Melons do best in a well-drained sandy loam soil. They grow bountifully in areas with warm days, warm nights, and a long growing season (80 to 105 days). In cooler regions with shorter growing seasons, especially adapted varieties are available.

TABLE 9–18   **MELONS (Muskmelons, Cantaloupes, Persian, Honeydews, Crenshaws, Watermelon)**

Mother Nature's Puzzlers

WHAT TO LOOK FOR	POSSIBLE CAUSES	POSSIBLE CURES
Dark dry leathery areas on the blossom end of the fruit.	A sudden change in soil moisture. It is sometimes a problem where rains are followed by a dry spell.	Try to maintain an even supply of moisture in the soil. Place 2 to 3 inches of organic material on top of the soil to hold down moisture loss. Water melons 2 to 3 hours at a time. As with other crops, don't water again until the soil is dry to a depth of 4 to 8 inches. Check with a trowel.
Cantaloupes sometimes taste like mush or the taste is extremely bitter.	Uneven watering. Those gardeners who claim this happens because their cantaloupes cross pollinate with cucumbers are incorrect. Cucumbers and cantaloupes will not cross pollinate.	Maintain an even supply of moisture in the soil, following the instructions above.

TABLE 9–18 **MELONS** *(continued)*

Mother Nature's Puzzlers

WHAT TO LOOK FOR	POSSIBLE CAUSES	POSSIBLE CURES
Melons aren't ripe.	Whoever is harvesting hasn't looked for or isn't familiar with those subtle signs that the melons are ready to be picked.	Here are some clues: Cantaloupes: If the stem slips off easily, the cantaloupe nears maturity. The blossom end softens and the netting becomes corky.

Persian melons and *crenshaws:* Persians and crenshaws smell sweet when mature.

Watermelon: When the light spot on the underside of the watermelon turns from white to yellow the melon is probably ripe. The "thump" test is unreliable. |
| Melons fail to ripen before frost. | The melons haven't had sufficient time. Most require 75 warm (above 70 degrees F.) days or more to reach maturity. Persians, crenshaws and casabas require up to 115 days. | In short season areas grow "early" varieties: Alaska, Far North, Early Northern Queen Hybrid. |

Insects

WHAT TO LOOK FOR	PEST	PREVENTION AND/OR NATURAL CONTROLS	CHEMICAL CONTROLS	GEOGRAPHICAL LOCATION
Plants eaten or cut off near the surface of the soil.	cut worms	Garden cleanliness. Companion plant with tansy.

Place a cardboard collar around the stems. Push 1 inch into soil. | Spray the soil with Sevin or diazinon before the plants emerge. | Widespread. |
| Colonies of sucking insects on leaves. Leaves can be curled and discolored. Sticky substance on stems and leaves. | melon aphids | Companion plant with spearmint and garlic. Mulch with aluminum foil.

Remove with blast from garden hose. Use a soap solution on the leaves. | Malathion, diazinon, rotenone, or ryania. | Widespread. |
| Holes in leaves and flowers. Tunnels in vines and fruit. | pickle worm, melonworm | Pick off. Use Bacillus thuringiensis (Dipel, Thurocide). | Sevin, malathion, or rotenone. | Widespread. Most severe in Gulf and South Atlantic states. |

TABLE 9–18 MELONS (continued)

Insects

WHAT TO LOOK FOR	PEST	PREVENTION AND/OR NATURAL CONTROLS	CHEMICAL CONTROLS	GEOGRAPHICAL LOCATION
Affected leaves turn pale green. Dusty webs between vine and leaves.	spider mite	Use a strong spray from a garden hose. Ladybugs, lacewings eat spider mites.	Diazinon or Kelthane.	Most severe in the South.
Irregular holes chewed in leaves and shoots.	spotted cucumber beetle (carries bacterial wilt)	Spade the soil before planting to destroy dormant beetles. Pick off beetles.	Sevin, malathion, or rotenone.	Widespread.
Affected leaves wilt rapidly becoming black and crisp.	squash bug	Fertilize plants to keep growing vigorously. Companion plant with nasturtium. Destroy squash bugs that collect under leaves at night. Use sabadilla (Doom).	Sevin, malathion, pyrethrum, rotenone, ryania.	Widespread.
Sudden wilting of runners. Holes in stems near base.	squash vine borer	Garden cleanliness. Slit the vine with a knife and take out the borer.	Dust with Sevin or malathion at weekly intervals as the vines start to grow.	Severe east of Rocky Mountains.
Irregular holes chewed in leaves and roots.	striped cucumber beetle (carries bacterial wilt) western striped cucumber beetle in west.	Spade the soil before planting to destroy dormant beetles. Companion plant with Summer savory, radish, and tansy. Pick off beetles by hand.	Sevin, malathion or rotenone.	Widespread.

Diseases

WHAT TO LOOK FOR	DISEASES	PREVENTION AND/OR NATURAL CONTROLS	CHEMICAL CONTROLS	GEOGRAPHICAL LOCATION
Round to angular reddish brown to black spots on leaves. Spots may later dry and tear out.	anthracnose	Avoid overhead watering. Use 3- to 4-year rotation. Grow in well-drained soil. Burn plant debris. Keep weeds down.	Apply captan, maneb, or zineb at 10 day intervals.	Widespread when weather is warm (65 to 85 degrees F.) and humid.

TABLE 9-18 **MELONS** *(continued)*

Diseases

WHAT TO LOOK FOR	DISEASE	PREVENTION AND/OR NATURAL CONTROLS	CHEMICAL CONTROLS	GEOGRAPHICAL LOCATION
Small angular spots on leaves. Round water soaked spots on fruit.	bacterial spot or blight. (transmitted by insects)	Destroy plant debris after harvest.	Apply fixed copper.	Widespread.
Vines wilt rapidly and die starting with 1 or a few leaves on vine.	bacterial wilt (transmitted by cucumber beetle)	Rotate crops each year. Pull and destroy wilted plants.	Apply Sevin to control cucumber beetles that spread wilt.	Widespread.
Yellowish to brownish areas on upper side of older leaves. Underside of leaves may show purple-gray mold.	downy mildew	Rotate cucumbers with other crops. Plant resistant varieties: muskmelon: Early Market, Edisto, Florida No. 1	Apply maneb or zineb.	Widespread.
Plants stunted and often yellow. Runners gradually die.	fusarium wilt	Collect and burn infected plants.		Widespread.
Water soaked areas on stems of older plants turn into cracked brown cankers. Infected spots on fruits, become water soaked and dotted.	gummy stem blight (black rot on fruit)	Crop rotation.	Copper fungicide or zineb.	Widespread.
Yellow green to dark green mottling of leaves. Leaves often wrinkled and curled.	mosaics (transmitted by aphids, cucumber beetles, grasshoppers)	Keep weeds out of garden area.	Use malathion to control aphids, cucumber beetles, and grasshoppers that transmit mosaics.	Widespread.

TABLE 9–18   MELONS *(continued)*

Diseases

WHAT TO LOOK FOR	DISEASE	PREVENTION AND/OR NATURAL CONTROLS	CHEMICAL CONTROLS	GEOGRAPHICAL LOCATION
White or brownish mealy growth on leaves and young stems.	powdery mildew	Rotate melons with other crops. Plant resistant varieties: muskmelons—Campo, Desert Sun, Edisto.	Apply karathane 1 to 3 times 7 to 10 days apart.	Widespread.
Water soaked or pale green spots on leaves that turn white to gray to brown. Fruit crack.	scab	Destroy plants after harvest. Grow in well-drained soil. Plant resistant varieties: Edisto 47 muskmelon.	Apply maneb, captan, zineb.	Widespread.

OKRA

Okra is a tender vegetable that needs warm soil and air temperatures for germination and vigorous growth. It, however, does well in any average garden soil. Here are the problems, the causes, and possible cures.

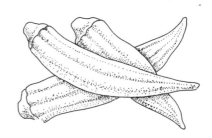

TABLE 9–19   OKRA

Mother Nature's Puzzlers

WHAT TO LOOK FOR	POSSIBLE CAUSES	POSSIBLE CURES
Okra seeds simply don't germinate. Plants fail to come up.	The soil wasn't warm enough (at least 70 degrees F.) at the time of planting. Otherwise, the seeds will rot.	Wait until the soil temperature has reached at least 70 degrees F. before planting. Sprouting can be improved by soaking seed in water at least 24 hours before planting.
The buds and flowers drop off before fruit (pods) start to form (bud drop).	Hot dry weather (above 95 degrees F.) or sudden temperature drops.	Simply wait until the weather becomes more conducive to pod formation.
Woody or tough okra.	Failure to pick pods regularly.	Pick plants clean of pods over 1½ to 2 inches long.

TABLE 9–19 OKRA (continued)

Insects

WHAT TO LOOK FOR	PEST	PREVENTION AND/OR NATURAL CONTROLS	CHEMICAL CONTROLS	GEOGRAPHICAL LOCATION
Holes eaten in pods.	corn earworms		Sevin or ryania.	Widespread in the United States and Canada. Most Prevalent in the South.

Diseases

WHAT TO LOOK FOR	DISEASE	PREVENTION AND/OR NATURAL CONTROLS	CHEMICAL CONTROLS	GEOGRAPHICAL LOCATION
Black blotches on stems, leaves. Center may drop out in leaves.	anthracnose	Keep weeds down.	Maneb and zineb.	Widespread.
Spots of varying colors on leaves. May be covered with dense mold.	leaf spots (gray-mold)	Grow in well-drained soil. Rotate with other crops.	Maneb or zineb.	Widespread.
Powdery white growth on leaves.	powdery mildew	Rotate okra with other crops.	Karathane or sulfur at 7 to 10 day intervals.	Widespread.
Small to large galls on roots. Plants stunted.	root-knot (nematode)	Rotate okra with other crops. Destroy infected plants. Companion plant with marigolds.	Apply liquid or granular nematocide— see your local nursery.	Primarily southern states.
Plants stunted, wilt, roots decayed.	root rots	Grow in well-drained soil. Rotate okra with other crops.	Apply captan to soil.	Widespread.
Small orange-yellow, to brown pustles on leaves and stems.	rust	Garden cleanliness.	Maneb or zineb at weekly intervals.	Widespread.
Decay of stem near soil line, later becomes covered with cottony mold.	stem canker crown rot	Grow in well-drained soil.	Treat soil with PCNB before planting.	Widespread.

THE ONION FAMILY

The onion and its relatives have been around so long, it's awfully hard to pin down just where they started. The Old Testament mentions onions. The pyramid builders dined on them in great quantity. And even General Grant ordered great quantities of them for his troops. Today there are literally several hundred varieties of onions available. Here are some problems to watch for in your garden.

TABLE 9–20   **THE ONION FAMILY (onions, garlic, leeks, shallots, chives)**

Mother Nature's Puzzlers

WHAT TO LOOK FOR	POSSIBLE CAUSES	POSSIBLE CURES
Onions go to seed and produce flabby, hollow bulbs. The nutrients that should go to bulb production go to seed production instead.	Onions were planted from sets (small bulbs) in late Fall or Winter.	Keep the flower bud picked off. Or harvest them as soon as you detect flower stalks and use them as green onions or leeks.
Onion bulbs split and sometimes look as if they might be trying to form two bulbs.	Uneven watering.	Place 2 to 3 inches of organic material on top of the bed to hold down moisture loss. Water onions 2 to 3 hours at a time. Don't water again until the soil has dried out to a depth of 4 to 8 inches. Check with a trowel.
Garlic plants produce many leaves but no bulbs.	Improper temperature conditions. Home-grown garlic cloves (divisions of the bulb) must be exposed to temperatures of 32 to 50 degrees F. for 1 to 2 months before planting to induce bulb formation.	Place garlic cloves in the refrigerator for a month before planting.
Garlic plants produce small bulbs.	The cloves that were planted were too small.	Plant the larger cloves from around the outside of the garlic bulb. Use the small slender cloves in the center for cooking.

TABLE 9–20   **THE ONION FAMILY** *(continued)*

Insects

WHAT TO LOOK FOR	PEST	PREVENTION AND/OR NATURAL CONTROLS	CHEMICAL CONTROLS	GEOGRAPHICAL LOCATION
Leaves become flabby and faded. Tunnels in onion bulbs.	onion maggot	Destroy all cull (disfigured, stunted) onions after harvest.	Spray with malathion during growing season to destroy flies. Spray diazinon on soil at planting time to control maggots.	Severe in northern U.S. Little damage in South.
White blotches on leaves. Leaf tips become distorted. Plant withers and turns brown.	onion thrips	Garden cleanliness.	Spray diazinon or malathion at 2 week intervals.	Widespread.
Plant growth stunted as worms bore into roots.	wireworms (the larvae of the click beetle)	Garden cleanliness.	Use diazinon as a soil treatment before planting.	Widespread.

Diseases

WHAT TO LOOK FOR	DISEASE	PREVENTION AND/OR NATURAL CONTROLS	CHEMICAL CONTROLS	GEOGRAPHICAL LOCATION
Bulb and leaves are water-soaked, then mushy and foul smelling.	bacterial soft rot	Destroy plant debris after harvest. Keep weeds down.	Treat soil with diazinon before planting to control insects that spread rot.	Widespread.
Soft spongy areas on bulb neck. Leaves may die.	neck rot	Destroy plant debris after harvest. Keep weeds down.		Widespread.
Leaves yellow and shrivel. Roots and bulbs decay.	bulb rot	Keep weeds down in garden area. Destroy plant debris after harvest. Plant resistant varieties: Elba, Globe, Grandee, Hickory.	Apply PCNB as dust or spray to soil for garlic and shallots.	Widespread.

TABLE 9–20   THE ONION FAMILY (continued)

Diseases

WHAT TO LOOK FOR	DISEASE	PREVENTION AND/OR NATURAL CONTROLS	CHEMICAL CONTROLS	GEOGRAPHICAL LOCATION
Sunken pale green to grayish areas develop in leaves. Later become covered with purplish-gray mold.	downy mildew	Garden cleanliness.	Spray with maneb or zineb.	Widespread.
Leaves die back from tips. Roots turn pink to red to yellow-brown.	pink root	Grow in well-drained soil. Plant resistant varieties: Sweet Spanish, Excel, Granex.		Widespread.
Stunted yellow and wilted foliage. Inner bulb swollen.	nematode (primarily onion, garlic, shallot)	Dig up and destroy plants when first found. Companion plant with marigolds.	Apply liquid or granular nematocide— see your local nursery.	Widespread.
Elongated blister like streaks occur in bulb scales or seedling leaves.	smut (garlic and chives are resistant)	Plant resistant varieties: Evergreen Bunching, White Welch, Winterbeck.	Treat onion seed with 1 ounce 75 percent captan for each 3 ounces of seed.	Most severe in northern states.
Small, pale, paper-like flecks or spots on leaves. Tips wilt and die back. Leaves may turn light tan, brown then collapse.	tip blight (blast)	Destroy plant debris after harvest. Keep all weeds down.	Spray weekly with maneb or zineb.	Widespread.

PEAS

Peas are a cool-season crop that thrive in soil and air filled with cool moisture (below 75 degrees F.). Although they will grow when the days become somewhat longer and warmer, they do not do well in hot dry weather. Generally, they are Spring planted in northern regions, Fall planted in warmer southern regions. They grow well in most types of soil.

TABLE 9–21   PEAS

Mother Nature's Puzzlers

WHAT TO LOOK FOR	POSSIBLE CAUSES	POSSIBLE CURES
Vines produce lush growth but few blossoms appear.	This is one of nature's mysteries.	Pinch back the growing tips of the stems. This usually slows down growth a little and encourages flower production.
Pea vines bloom in profusion but the blossoms simply don't produce pods.	Pollen isn't being transferred from the male parts of the flower to the female.	Shake the pods a little. While peas are self pollinating, they sometimes need a little help in the blossom stage.
The pods are hard; the peas woody.	The pods are left on the vines too long.	Pick peas just as they fill out, while they are still tender and succulent.
Brown cavity on inner surface of pea. Marsh spot.	Partial deficiency of available manganese on alkaline soils.	Spray the foliage with a 1 percent manganese sulfate solution at flowering time and 2 to 3 weeks later.
Scorched leaf margins.	Molybdenum deficiency.	Test soil. One teaspoon of ammonium molybdate per 1000 square feet.

Insects

WHAT TO LOOK FOR	PEST	PREVENTION AND/OR NATURAL CONTROLS	CHEMICAL CONTROLS	GEOGRAPHICAL LOCATION
Colonies of insects on upper parts of plant, flowers and pods. Shoots deformed.	pea aphids	Companion plant with spearmint and garlic. Mulch with aluminum foil. Remove with blast from garden hose. Use soap solution. Control with lacewing flies, praying mantises, ladybugs.	Malathion, diazinon, pyrethrum, rotenone, or ryania.	Widespread.

TABLE 9-21   PEAS (continued)

Insects

WHAT TO LOOK FOR	PEST	PREVENTION AND/OR NATURAL CONTROLS	CHEMICAL CONTROLS	GEOGRAPHICAL LOCATION
Blooms eaten, worms (larvae in pods and young peas)	pea weevil		Diazinon, malathion, or rotenone.	
Young plants fail to emerge from soil. If they emerge they are stunted.	root maggot		Treat the soil with diazinon before planting peas.	

Diseases

WHAT TO LOOK FOR	DISEASE	PREVENTION AND/OR NATURAL CONTROLS	CHEMICAL CONTROLS	GEOGRAPHICAL LOCATION
White to brown sunken spots with dark margins on leaves.	anthracnose	Destroy plant debris after harvest. Keep down weeds.	Apply maneb, zineb, or fixed copper during cool, wet periods.	Widespread.
Seedlings wilt and collapse from rot at soil line.	damping off	Rotate with other crops.	Treat soil with captan. Treat seed with captan before planting.	Widespread.
Irregular water soaked yellow to brown blotches on upper leaf surface. White gray brown or black mold underneath.	downy mildew	Grow in well-drained soil. Destroy plant debris after harvest. Use a 4-year rotation.	Apply maneb, zineb or fixed copper weekly during wet periods.	Widespread when weather is cool and damp.
Plants yellow, stunted. Lower leaves often wilt about blossoming time.	fusarium wilt	Grow resistant varieties: Alcross, Ace, Alaska.		Especially prevalent in northern states.

TABLE 9–21   **PEAS** *(continued)*

Insects

WHAT TO LOOK FOR	PEST	PREVENTION AND/OR NATURAL CONTROLS	CHEMICAL CONTROLS	GEOGRAPHICAL LOCATION
White powdery coating on leaves, pods, and stems.	powdery mildews	Rotate peas with other crops. Keep water off foliage as much as possible. Destroy debris after harvest.	Apply karathane or sulfur a week apart.	Widespread in areas of cool nights (below 50 degrees F).
Seedlings yellow, shrivel and die. Plants often wilt and die near flowering crown and roots discolored.	general rots — crown, roots	Plant in well-drained soil. Destroy infected plants. Plant resistant varieties: Green Admiral, Freezonian, Horal, Thomas Laxton 251, Wando.	Treat seed with captan. Use captan in seedbed.	Widespread.
Rings or brown or purple spots on leaves. Leaves distorted.	spotted wilt (ringspot) (virus transmitted by thrips)	Destroy infected plants. Keep weeds down in garden area.	Apply Sevin to control thrips that transmit the virus.	Widespread.
Light brown, black, or purplish streaks on stem. Sunken tan or dark spots on pods.	asochyta blights, septeria blights	Destroy plant debris after harvest. Plant resistant varieties: Creamette, Perfection.		Widespread during wet season.
Leaves streaked or spotted with yellow, light or dark green patterns. Plants may be stunted.	general pea viruses (transmitted by insects)	Keep down clovers. Plant resistant pea varieties: Bridger, Canner Prince.	Spray with malathion weekly to control insects that spread virus.	Widespread.

PEPPERS

Peppers are warm weather plants that like a well-drained sandy loam soil slightly on the acidic side (pH 5.5 to 6.8). Here are the problems to watch for.

TABLE 9–22 PEPPERS

Mother Nature's Puzzlers

WHAT TO LOOK FOR	POSSIBLE CAUSES	POSSIBLE CURES
The plant produces blossoms, but the blossoms fall off without producing fruit.	The temperature drops much below 60 degrees F. or it rises above 75 degrees F.	Plant early pepper varieties: Early Giant, Neapolitan, Early Niagara, Giant, Melrose.
Pepper plants produce few blossoms, few fruit.	Plants are blooming and producing fruit while they are too small. As a result, they remain stunted all their life and produce a poor yield of fruit.	Don't purchase small nursery seedlings that have started to bloom.
A dark leathery area appears on the blossom end of the fruit (blossom end rot).	Often caused by too much, then too little moisture in the soil. It is especially severe when temperatures rise above 90 degrees F. and when the fruit is exposed to full sun. Sometimes a calcium deficiency is a related cause.	Keep the soil moist at all times. Place 2 to 3 inches of organic material on top of the bed to hold down moisture loss. Water peppers 2 to 3 hours at a time. Don't water again until the soil is dry to a depth of 4 to 8 inches. Check with a trowel.
Plants produce lush foliage, little fruit.	1 Too much nitrogen.	1 Fertilize peppers with a "tomato" fertilizer (it has more phosphorus than nitrogen).
	2 Overwatering.	2 Keep soil moisture even by following instructions as above.
	3 Temperatures are too high or too low.	3 Increase night temperatures by placing plastic covers over wire cages.
	4 Insufficient pollination.	4 Sometimes it is possible to increase pollination and fruit production by lightly tapping or jarring the plants.
Sunscald: Light colored areas that are soft. Become sunken as they dry.	Peppers exposed to direct, "hot" sun.	Control leaf spot that causes leaf loss. Use shadecloth if peppers are being damaged, shade with lath screen.

TABLE 9–22   PEPPERS (continued)

Insects

WHAT TO LOOK FOR	PEST	PREVENTION AND/OR NATURAL CONTROLS	CHEMICAL CONTROLS	GEOGRAPHICAL LOCATION
Colonies of sucking insects on leaves. Leaves can be curled and discolored. Sticky substance on stems and leaves.	aphids	Spearmint and garlic help repel aphids. Mulch with aluminum foil. Remove with blast from garden hose. Use a soap solution on the leaves. Lacewing flies, ladybugs, and praying mantises destroy aphids.	Control with malathion or diazinon. Or use botanical sprays: Pyrethrum, rotenone, or ryania.	Widespread.
Plants partially defoliated.	blister beetles	Keep the garden free of refuse and weeds. Spade deeply in Spring to kill larvae. Pick beetles off by hand.	Spray or dust with Sevin. Or use botanical sprays: Pyrethrum, rotenone, ryania.	East of Rocky Mountains.
Leaves and shoots stripped.	Colorado potato beetle	Keep the garden area free of refuse. Eggplant, flax and greenbeans help repel the Colorado potato beetle. Pick off beetles.	Spray with malathion or Sevin. Or use the botanical spray rotenone.	Widespread in the U.S. and Canada except Nevada, California and Florida.
Young plants cut off near soil surface.	cutworms; worms hide in the soil by day, feed at night	Keep the garden area free of refuse. Plant tansy between the rows. Place a cardboard collar around the stems. Push 1 inch into soil.	Spray the soil with Sevin or diazinon before transplanting plants into beds.	Widespread.
Leaves look like they have been shot through with tiny round holes.	flea beetles	Keep the garden area free of refuse. Spade garden soil deeply to destroy larvae in early Spring. Head lettuce, mint, wormwood help repel flea beetles. Pick beetles off plant.	Use several applications of diazinon, malathion or Seven. Or use botanical sprays pyrethrum, rotenone, ryania.	Widespread.

TABLE 9-22   PEPPERS (continued)

Insects

WHAT TO LOOK FOR	PEST	PREVENTION AND/OR NATURAL CONTROLS	CHEMICAL CONTROLS	GEOGRAPHICAL LOCATION
Leaves appear scorched and wilted.	leafhoppers		Spray with Sevin, malathion, pyrethrum, rotenone, or ryania when insects appear.	Widespread
Holes in buds and blossoms. Small pods fall to ground. Larger pods become misshapen.	pepper weevil and grub	Spade the soil before planting. Pick off weevils and grubs by hand.	Sevin, malathion, or rotenone.	South, Southwest.
White spots on fruit. Leaf tips become distorted.	thrips (transmit spotted wilt virus)	Keep weeds out of garden area.	Treat with two or three applications of diazinon or malathion.	Widespread.
Insect eats into fruit.	tomato fruit worm (European corn borer)		Control worms when they are small with Sevin.	Widespread.
Plants partially defoliated.	tomato hornworm	Spade deeply in Fall to destroy larvae. Handpick and destroy caterpillars. Use Bacillus thuringiensis (Thurocide, Dipel).	Spray with Sevin.	Throughout U.S. and southern Canada.
A cloud of white wings fly from plant when disturbed.	whiteflies	Plant marigolds. Marigolds excrete a substance absorbed by roots of other plants that repel whiteflies. Use wasps to destroy whiteflies. Hose off with a stream of water. Trap whiteflies in Tanglefoot on a bright yellow card.	Spray plants with malathion or use rotenone.	Widespread.

TABLE 9–22   PEPPERS *(continued)*

Diseases

WHAT TO LOOK FOR	DISEASE	PREVENTION AND/OR NATURAL CONTROLS	CHEMICAL CONTROLS	GEOGRAPHICAL LOCATION
Sunken water-soaked areas on fruit. Fruit may shrivel, become watery, and collapse.	anthracnose	Destroy rotting fruit. Keep fruit off soil.	Spray with maneb or zineb.	Widespread.
Small yellowish raised spots on leaves turn brown and have water soaked appearance. Severe infection causes leaves to fall off.	bacterial leaf spot	Buy treated seed.	Spray with fixed copper spray when disease appears.	Widespread.
Circular, oblong spots on leaves, stems. Plants lose leaves.	cercospora leaf spot (fungus)		Zineb, Nabam.	Southern states.
Plants stunted, spindly. Cupping of leaves, leaf stems curve sharply downward.	curly top (transmitted by leafhoppers)	Destroy infected plants. Keep down all weeds.	Apply malathion to control leaf-hoppers that transmit virus.	Usually western half of United States.
Brown to almost black spots on leaves and lower stem. Spots have leaves turn yellow to brown.	early blight	Keep weeds down in garden area. Destroy plant debris after harvest.	Apply maneb or zineb.	Widespread.
Plants stunted leaves wilt, wither, drop off. Brown to black streaks lower stem.	fusarium wilt	Plant resistant varieties: college No. 6, Mexican chili No. 9.		Widespread.

TABLE 9–22   PEPPERS *(continued)*

Insects

WHAT TO LOOK FOR	PEST	PREVENTION AND/OR NATURAL CONTROLS	CHEMICAL CONTROLS	GEOGRAPHICAL LOCATION
Plants stunted with galls on roots. Plants wilt in dry weather, then recover.	root-knot (nematodes)	Crop rotation. Companion plant with marigolds.	Apply liquid or granular nematocide— see your local nursery.	Widespread in southern states.
Diseased plant drops leaves and wilts. Plants attacked at ground line.	southern blight	Crop rotation. Pull and burn infected plants.		Southeastern Gulf states.
Leaves curled, crinkled, streaked, and mottled.	tobacco mosaic (spread by insects)	Keep down all weeds in garden area. Destroy infected plants. Smokers should wash hands before working in the garden.	Apply malathion to control insects that transmit virus.	Widespread.
Lower leaves yellow and die. Stems discolored.	verticillium wilt	Widespread. Prevalent in northern states.		Widespread. Prevalent in northern states.

POTATOES

Potatoes will grow almost anywhere and like sandy, loam soils on the acid side (pH 4.8 to 6.3). They do best in cool weather. Plant early in the Spring. In mild Winter areas you can also plant in mid Summer for a Fall harvest. Here are the problems to watch for in your garden.

TABLE 9-23   POTATOES

Mother Nature's Puzzlers

WHAT TO LOOK FOR	POSSIBLE CAUSES	POSSIBLE CURES
Potatoes become knobby.	Lack of a steady supply of moisture. If the soil dries out for too long and then becomes moist, growth starts resulting in knobby potatoes.	Place 2 to 3 inches of organic material on top of the bed to hold down moisture loss. Water potatoes 2 to 3 hours at a time. Don't water again until the soil has dried out to a depth of 8 inches. Check with a trowel. Avoid planting varieties that tend to be excessively knobby: Green Mountain, Russet Burbank.

TABLE 9–23 **POTATOES** *(continued)*

Mother Nature's Puzzlers

WHAT TO LOOK FOR	POSSIBLE CAUSES	POSSIBLE CURES
Cavities occur near the center of the potato (hollow heart).	Rapid and uneven growth of potato tubers.	Space potatoes close together. Cut down on water. Avoid planting those varieties that develop hollow heart: Chippewa, Katahdin, Mohawk, Irish Cobbler, Sequoia, Russet Rural, or White Rose.
All tops and no potatoes.	Nights are too warm. Potatoes need cool nights below about 55 degrees F. for good tuber formation.	Plant so potatoes grow during cool weather. In hot Summer areas, plant in mid Summer to grow and mature in the cool Fall.
Potatoes turn green (sunburn).	Exposure to the sun during growth or after digging.	Keep covered with soil. Store in complete darkness.
Leaflets become light green, wilt, then dry up (Sunscald). Tubers become watery and turn brown to a considerable depth throughout the tuber.	Exposure of plant or potato tubers to hot sun and drying winds following cloudy weather.	Place sun screen over plants during extremely hot weather. Don't leave potato tubers in hot sun.
Yellowing of the tips and margins of leaflets. Gradual dying and browning or blackening of foliage. More than half the foliage may die (similar to leafhopper burn).	Excessive loss of moisture during hot, dry weather.	Place 2 to 3 inches of organic material on top of the bed to hold down moisture loss.
Irregular brown spots scattered throughout the flesh.	Hot, dry weather during growing season, lack of soil moisture.	Place 2 to 3 inches of organic material on top of bed to hold down moisture loss. Water potatoes 2 to 3 hours at a time; don't water again until the soil has dried to a depth of 4 to 8 inches.
Small marble-sized potatoes have grown directly from potato eye (sprout tubers).	Excessive concentration of cell sap in tubers.	Plant later in season. Don't store seed potatoes in light at temperatures 90 degrees F. or above.
Irregular dead streak on potato stems.	High levels of soluble manganese on acid soils.	Apply lime. (See Chapter 3.) Grow resistant varieties: Canso, Green Mountain, McIntyre.
Tissue on the potato tuber looks wet when dug and brought into warm area. Later it becomes infected with bacteria.	Injury is due to freezing.	Harvest crop before ground freezes.

TABLE 9–23 POTATOES (continued)

Mother Nature's Puzzlers

WHAT TO LOOK FOR	POSSIBLE CAUSES	POSSIBLE CURES
Dead tissue in the tuber (necrosis).	Potatoes left in hot soil after the vines begin to die.	Keep soil moist and shaded or dig tubers as soon as the vines begin to die.
Dark brown stippling of upper surface of leaf. Most severe on older leaves.	Ozone-air pollution damage.	No cure at present. Resistant varieties being developed.

Insects

WHAT TO LOOK FOR	PEST	PREVENTION AND/OR NATURAL CONTROLS	CHEMICAL CONTROLS	GEOGRAPHICAL LOCATION
Colonies of small sucking insects on leaves. Leaves can be curled and discolored. Sticky substance on stems and leaves.	aphids	Companion plant with spearmint, garlic. Mulch with aluminum foil. Remove with blast from garden hose. Use a soap solution on the leaves.	Malathion, diazinon, pyrethrum, rotenone, or ryania.	Widespread.
Leaves and shoots stripped.	Colorado potato beetle	Garden cleanliness. Companion plant with eggplant, flax and green beans. Pick off beetles.	Malathion, Sevin, or rotenone.	Widespread in the U.S. and Canada except Nevada, California and Florida.
Young plant cut off near the surface.	cutworms (they hide in soil by day, feed at night)	Garden cleanliness. Use oak leaf mulch. Companion plant with tansy between rows. Place a cardboard collar around the stems. Push 1 inch into soil.	Use diazinon as a soil treatment before planting.	Widespread.
Leaves look like they have been shot through with tiny round holes.	flea beetles	Garden cleanliness. Spade garden soil deeply in early Spring to destroy larvae. Companion plant with marigolds. Pick beetles off plant.	Several applications of diazinon malathion, Sevin, pyrethrum, rotenone, or ryania.	Widespread.

TABLE 9–23 **POTATOES** *(continued)*

Insects

WHAT TO LOOK FOR	PEST	PREVENTION AND/OR NATURAL CONTROLS	CHEMICAL CONTROLS	GEOGRAPHICAL LOCATION
Leaf margins turn brown.	leafhoppers		Spray plants with Sevin, malathion, pyrethrum, rotenone, or ryania.	Widespread. More severe in eastern U.S.
Fine webbing over the foliage. Mottled, speckled, and wilted leaves.	spider mites	Use a soap solution on the leaves. Apply a light petroleum oil spray to the leaves. Use a forceful spray from garden hose.	Spray thoroughly with diazinon or malathion every 7 to 9 days. Spray with Kelthane.	Widespread.
Plant growth stunted as worms bore into roots.	white grubs (the larvae of the June beetle), wireworms (the larvae of the click beetle)	Garden cleanliness.	Use diazinon as a soil treatment before planting.	White grubs troublesome in the South and Midwest. Wireworms are widespread.

Diseases

WHAT TO LOOK FOR	DISEASE	PREVENTION AND/OR NATURAL CONTROLS	CHEMICAL CONTROLS	GEOGRAPHICAL LOCATION
Plants gradually wilt and die. Stems turn brown at first only inside.	bacterial wilt (brown rot)	Plant certified disease-free potatoes.		Mostly in southern states.
Plants wilt. Stem base becomes dark brown, black, slimy. Tubers slimy brown to black on stem end.	blackleg (bacterial)	Plant certified disease-free potato tubers. Crop rotation. Cover potatoes shallowly to hasten emergence.	Streptomycin helps control blackleg.	Widespread.

TABLE 9–23 POTATOES *(continued)*

Diseases

WHAT TO LOOK FOR	PEST	PREVENTION AND/OR NATURAL CONTROLS	CHEMICAL CONTROLS	GEOGRAPHICAL LOCATION
Stems near the surface of the ground become covered with purplish, dirty grey fungus. Foliage curls, turns pinkish to yellowish.	black scruf	Plant certified disease-free potatoes. Rotate crops.	Treat soil with PCNB.	Widespread.
Rapidly enlarging round to irregular dark green to grayish purple water soaked areas on leaves, stems.	late blight	Destroy volunteer potatoes, culls, plant debris. Kill infected potato tops before harvest. Plant resistant varieties: Cherokee, Plymouth, Kennebec.	Apply maneb, zineb at 10-day intervals.	Widespread.
Lower leaflets cup or roll. Leaves may show light or dark green streaking.	leafroll (virus); transmitted primarily by green peach aphid	Keep down weeds. Plant certified seed potatoes. Plant resistant varieties: Cherokee, Houma, Merrimack. Destroy diseased plants.	Control aphids that spread virus with malathion, diazinon, pyrethrum, rotenone, or ryania.	Widespread.
Young leaves fail to enlarge, leaflets roll upward, reddish purple color, or topmost leaves become yellow.	purple-top wilt (virus spread by leafhoppers)	Plant certified disease-free seed potatoes. Take out and destroy diseased plants. Garden cleanliness.	Control leaf-hoppers with Sevin, malathion.	Most areas except in the South.
Small dark browned spots on leaves.	early blight (target spot)	Garden cleanliness. Crop rotation. Maintain vigor by fertilizing.	Apply maneb, zineb at 10 day intervals.	Widespread when weather is warm and humid.

TABLE 9–23 **POTATOES** *(continued)*

Insects

WHAT TO LOOK FOR	DISEASE	PREVENTION AND/OR NATURAL CONTROLS	CHEMICAL CONTROLS	GEOGRAPHICAL LOCATION
Plants stunted, gradually wilt. Yellowish-black streaks inside stems.	fusarium wilts	Plant certified disease-free potatoes. Collect and burn vines before harvest. Crop rotation. Plant resistant varieties: Irish Cobbler, Kennebec.		Widespread.
Stem end of potato rotted, wrinkled, sunken, brown to black.	jelly end rot	Maintain adequate moisture supply throughout growing season. Place 2 to 3 inches of organic material on top of bed to hold down moisture loss. Water potatoes 2 to 3 hours at a time. Don't water again until the soil has dried out to a depth of 8 inches.		Pacific Coast.
Wilting of stems, branches, leaves. Decay in tuber causes a "ring" appearance. Decayed tissue crumbly.	ring rot	Plant certified seed stock. Plant whole small potatoes. Practice crop rotation. Plant resistant varieties: Merrimack, Saranac, Teton.		Widespread.
Leaves dwarfed, mottled. Distinct crinkling of leaves.	rugose mosaic (transmitted by peach aphid)	Plant disease-free seed potatoes. Plant resistant varieties: Chippewa, Katahdin, Kennebec, Monona, and Snowflake.	Control aphids with malathion, diazinon, pyrethrum, rotenone, or ryania.	Widespread.
Raised or pitted corky areas on tuber (potato) surface.	scab (common or powdery)	Modify soil to obtain a pH of 4.8 to 5.2. Plant resistant varieties: Alamo, Arenac, Cherokee. Use long rotations.		Widespread in light sandy soils with little organic material.
Elongation of tuber. Eyes numerous and conspicuous. Sometimes deep growth cracks.	spindle tuber (virus transmitted by many insects)	Destroy plants early. Use certified disease-free seed.	Control insects with Sevin, malathion.	Widespread.

TABLE 9–23 POTATOES (continued)

Insects

WHAT TO LOOK FOR	DISEASE	PREVENTION AND/OR NATURAL CONTROLS	CHEMICAL CONTROLS	GEOGRAPHICAL LOCATION
Potatoes rot in field.	tuber rots	Harvest in dry weather. Destroy any potatoes that have started to rot. Avoid wounding potato tubers.		Widespread.
Plants somewhat stunted wilts. Lower leaves become streaked. Stem end of potato discolored around eyes.	verticilium wilt	Plant certified disease-free potatoes. Collect and burn vines before harvest. Plant resistant varieties: Houma, Cariboo, Red Beauty.		Widespread.
Plant produces many spindly cylindrical stems.	witches broom (virus)	Plant disease-free seed. Destroy diseased plants.		Pacific Northwest.
Yellow green foliage. Leaf margin rolls. Plants dwarfed, with rust colored spots. Growth cracks in potatoes. Small areas in flesh.	yellow dwarf (virus transmitted by leafhoppers)	Plant disease-free seed potatoes. Destroy diseased plants.	Control leafhoppers with Sevin, malathion.	Southeastern Canada, north central, north-east.

RADISHES

The radish is really an all-around performer. While they are a cool weather vegetable, they tolerate more heat than either peas or lettuce. They also grow well in almost any soil. But keep in mind that they do especially well in light sandy loam.

TABLE 9–24 **RADISHES**

Mother Nature's Puzzlers

WHAT TO LOOK FOR	POSSIBLE CAUSES	POSSIBLE CURES
Radishes have a hot taste.	Soil is too dry. Soil temperature rises above 90 degrees F.	Place 2 to 3 inches of organic material on top of the soil to keep it cooler. Water radishes 2 to 3 hours at a time. Don't water again until the soil has dried out to a depth of 4 to 8 inches. Check with a trowel.
Plants have leaves but bulbs fail to form.	Radishes are planted too close together.	Thin radishes to stand about 2 inches apart.
Radishes are woody and pithy.	Plants haven't been harvested at the proper time.	Dig your radishes as soon as the bulbs reach eating size.

Insects

WHAT TO LOOK FOR	PEST	PREVENTION AND/OR NATURAL CONTROLS	CHEMICAL CONTROLS	GEOGRAPHICAL LOCATION
Leaves look like they have been shot through with tiny holes.	flea beetles	Garden cleanliness. Spade garden soil deeply in early Spring to destroy larvae. Pick beetles off the plant.	Use several applications of malathion or Sevin, pyrethrum, rotenone, or ryania.	Widespread.
Leaves become flabby and faded. Tunnels in radish bulbs.	root maggots		Spray with malathion during growing season to destroy flies. Spray diazinon on soil at planting time.	

TABLE 9–24 **RADISHES** *(continued)*

Diseases

WHAT TO LOOK FOR	DISEASE	PREVENTION AND/OR NATURAL CONTROLS	CHEMICAL CONTROLS	GEOGRAPHICAL LOCATION
Light brown to gray spots on stem, leaves. Stem blackens and rots.	blackleg (spread by cutworms and root maggots)	Collect and burn tops after harvest. Use 4 year rotation.	Treat seed with captan.	Widespread east of Rocky Mountains.
Seedlings collapse from rot at soil line. Black scabby areas on roots.	damping off rhizoctonia disease	Collect and burn tops after harvest.	Treat soil with PCNB 75 and captan 50 (sold as Terra cap, PCNP-captan).	Widespread.
Pale green to yellow spotting on upper surface of leaves, followed by purpling, wilting.	downy mildew	Avoid overcrowding plants. Don't water overhead. Destroy infected plants.	Maneb or fixed copper.	Widespread during cool wet seasons.
Pale yellow, gray brown, dark green spots on leaves.	fungal leaf spots	Destroy tops after harvest.	Spray seedbed with maneb or fixed copper sprays.	Widespread in wet weather.
Leaves turn dull yellow, curl, and die.	yellows		Spray with Sevin or malathion to control leafhopper that spreads disease.	Widespread. Most serious when soil temperatures are over 70 degrees F.

SPINACH

Spinach will grow almost anywhere but likes cool weather best and prefers a good loam soil. Here are the problems to watch for.

TABLE 9–25   SPINACH

Mother Nature's Puzzlers

WHAT TO LOOK FOR	POSSIBLE CAUSES	POSSIBLE CURES
Leaves turn yellow. In severe cases, entire leaves have a sulfur yellow color.	Nitrogen deficiency. Spinach is very sensitive to a lack of nitrogen in the soil.	Add a fertilizer rich in nitrogen. Apply at the rate of 2.5 pounds per 100 square feet before planting.
Spinach rushes into flower before the leaves have reached eating size. This stops the production of usable foliage.	Long Spring days with temperatures in the 40s the first few weeks of growth, immediately followed by temperatures in the 80s.	Plant varieties that resist early flowering (bolting): Bloomsdale Long Standing, Big Crop, America. Or plant spinach in late Summer so the plants mature in the cool days of Fall.

Insects

WHAT TO LOOK FOR	PEST	PREVENTION AND/OR NATURAL CONTROLS	CHEMICAL CONTROLS	GEOGRAPHICAL LOCATION
Colonies of sucking insects on leaves. Leaves can be curled and discolored. Sticky substance on leaves.	aphids (yellow green aphid)	Companion plant with spearmint and garlic. Mulch with aluminum foil. Remove with blast from garden hose. Use a soap solution on the leaves. Spearmint and garlic help repel aphids. Control with lacewing flies, praying mantises, ladybugs.	Malathion, diazinon, pyrethrum, rotenone, or ryania.	Widepsread.
White thread-like tunnels within the leaf.	leaf-miner	Deep spade before planting to help control maggots. Plant in Fall to lessen attack. Protect plants by covering with cheesecloth.	Control adult flies with diazinon or malathion. Repeat if necessary.	Widespread.

TABLE 9–25 SPINACH (continued)

Diseases

WHAT TO LOOK FOR	DISEASE	PREVENTION AND/OR NATURAL CONTROLS	CHEMICAL CONTROLS	GEOGRAPHICAL LOCATION
Sunken reddish to nearly black spots or blotches on pods.	anthracnose (fungal leaf spots)	Plant in well-drained soil. Garden cleanliness.	Captan or dicholone. Insects spread the disease. Control them with both Sevin and malathion.	Widespread. Severe in dry areas in western states.
Small round spots with brown centers. Spots may drop out, leaving ragged holes.	cercospora leaf spot	Garden cleanliness. Use a 3-year rotation.	Maneb or zineb.	Widespread in warm moist weather.
Seedlings and older plants wilt and collapse.	damping off	Rotate spinach with other plants. Plant with well-drained soil.	Treat seedbed with captan.	Widespread.
Young leaves covered with violet or yellow gray mold.	downy mildew	Keep down weeds. Plant resistant varieties: Badger Savoy, Califlay, Dixie Market.	Maneb, zineb or copper containing fungicide.	Widespread during the cool humid seasons.
Young plants stunted. Leaves turn yellow, wilt.	fusarium yellows	Garden cleanliness. Destroy infected plants.		Widespread.
Plants stunted, veins in young leaves conspicuously yellow.	spinach blight (yellows)	Keep down weeds. Plant resistant varieties: Badger Savoy, Dixie Market, Viking.	Spray with fixed copper.	Widespread.

SQUASH

Squash is easy to grow, but it is a heat-lover and should not be set outdoors until night time temperatures regularly stay above 55 degrees F. Squash grows well in a good sandy loam enriched with rotted manure and compost. Here are the problems to watch for.

TABLE 9–26 SQUASH (summer squash, winter squash, pumpkins)

Mother Nature's Puzzlers

WHAT TO LOOK FOR	POSSIBLE CAUSES	POSSIBLE CURES
Some seeds fail to come up.	One of nature's inevitabilities. A certain percentage of all squash seeds are "hard," naturally resistant to water uptake that triggers sprouting.	Increase germination and slightly decrease sprouting time by soaking seeds in tepid water for 24 hours. Dry the seeds on a paper towel before planting.
Dark brown leathery areas appear on the blossom end of the squash fruit (blossom end rot).	Uneven soil moisture. If the soil is intermittently wet, then dries out for too long, it seems to promote blossom end rot.	Place 2 to 3 inches of organic material on top of the soil to hold down moisture loss. Water squash 2 to 3 hours at a time. Don't water again until the soil is dry to a depth of 4 to 8 inches. Check with a trowel.
Small squash start to form then rot or dry up.	1 Female flowers blossom before there are male flowers to pollinate the plants.	1 Some patience. Wait until male flowers start to blossom. They will then pollinate the female flowers and squash fruit will grow.
Too great an abundance of squash fruit on the plant.	2 The unpollinated fruit aborts in a self pruning process.	2 Keep the fruit of Summer squash (straight neck, crook neck, patty pan) picked to keep the plant producing. You will have to accept this limitation for Winter squash since the fruit cannot be picked until the shells become hard for Winter storage.
Few flowers form fruit, even when both male and female flowers are present.	Not enough bees to pollinate the squash and pumpkins. Recent research shows that the percentage of flowers setting (forming) fruit increases when these flowers are pollinated by many bees. The average size of the pumpkin or squash also increases when the vines are pollinated by numerous bees.	Use the chemical sprays diazinon, Sevin, and malathion *sparingly*. They kill not only harmful insects but bees as well.

TABLE 9–26   **SQUASH (summer squash, winter squash, pumpkins)** *(continued)*

Insects

WHAT TO LOOK FOR	PEST	PREVENTION AND/OR NATURAL CONTROLS	CHEMICAL CONTROLS	GEOGRAPHICAL LOCATION
Colonies of sucking insects on leaves. Leaves can be curled and discolored. Sticky substance on stems and leaves.	aphids	Companion plant with spearmint and garlic. Mulch with aluminum foil. Remove with blast from garden hose. Use a soap solution on the leaves. Control with lacewing flies, praying mantises, ladybugs.	Malathion diazinon, pyrethrum, rotenone, or ryania.	Widespread.
Plants eaten or cut off near the surface of the soil.	cut worms	Garden cleanliness. Companion plant with tansy. Place a cardboard collar around the stems. Push 1 inch into soil.	Spray the soil with Sevin or diazinon before the plants emerge.	Widespread. Most severe in Gulf and South Atlantic states.
Holes in leaves and flowers. Tunnels in vines and fruit.	pickle worms	Pick off. Use Bacillus thuringiensis (Dipel, Thurocide).	Sevin, malathion, or rotenone.	Widespread.
Affected leaves turn pale green. Dusty webs between vine and leaves.	spider mite	Use a strong spray from a garden hose. Ladybugs, lacewings eat spider mites.	Diazinon or Kelthane.	Widespread, most severe in South.
Irregular holes chewed in leaves and shoots.	spotted cucumber beetle (carries bacterial wilt)	Spade the soil before planting to destroy dormant beetles. Companion plant with radish, tansy. Pick off beetles.	Sevin, malathion, or rotenone.	Widespread.
Affected leaves wilt rapidly, becoming black and crisp.	squash bug	Fertilize plants to keep growing vigorously. Companion plant with nasturtium. Destroy squash bugs that collect under leaves at night. Use sabadilla (Doom).	Sevin, malathion, pyrethrum, rotenone, ryania.	Widespread.

TABLE 9–26   SQUASH (summer squash, winter squash, pumpkins) (continued)

Insects

WHAT TO LOOK FOR	PEST	PREVENTION AND/OR NATURAL CONTROLS	CHEMICAL CONTROLS	GEOGRAPHICAL LOCATION
Sudden wilting of runners. Holes in stems near base.	squash vine borer	Garden cleanliness. Slit the vine with a knife and take out the borer.	Dust with Sevin or malathion at weekly intervals as the vines start to grow.	Severe east of Rocky Mountains.
Irregular holes chewed in leaves and roots.	striped cucumber beetle (carries bacterial wilt)	Spade the soil before planting to destroy dormant beetles. Companion plant with summer savory, radish, and tansy. Pick off beetles by hand.	Sevin, malathion, or rotenone.	Widespread.

Diseases

WHAT TO LOOK FOR	DISEASE	PREVENTION AND/OR NATURAL CONTROLS	CHEMICAL CONTROLS	GEOGRAPHICAL LOCATION
Round to angular reddish brown to black spots on leaves. Spots may later dry and tear out.	anthracnose	Avoid overhead watering. Use 3- to 4-year rotation. Grow in well-drained soil. Burn plant debris. Keep weeds down.	Apply captan, maneb, or zineb at 10 day intervals.	Widespread when weather is warm (65 to 85 degrees F.) and humid.
Small angular spots on leaves. Round water-soaked spots on fruit.	bacterial spot or blight (transmitted by insects)	Destroy plant debris after harvest.	Apply fixed copper sprays.	Widespread.
Vines wilt rapidly and die starting with 1 or a few leaves on vine.	bacterial wilt (transmitted by cucumber beetle)	Rotate crops each year. Pull and destroy wilted plants.	Apply Sevin to control cucumber beetles that spread wilt.	Widespread.
Dense white fungus growth covers blossoms. Growth turns purplish-black. Young fruits also decay and die.	choanephora fruit rot	Crop rotation.	Copper fungicides, zineb, or ziram.	Widespread.

TABLE 9–26 **SQUASH (summer squash, winter squash, pumpkins)** *(continued)*

Diseases

WHAT TO LOOK FOR	DISEASE	PREVENTION AND/OR NATURAL CONTROLS	CHEMICAL CONTROLS	GEOGRAPHICAL LOCATION
Yellowish to brownish areas on upper side of older leaves. Undersides are purplish.	downy mildew	Rotate cucumbers with other crops.	Apply maneb or zineb.	Widespread.
Plants stunted and often yellow. Runners gradually die.	fusarium wilt	Collect and burn infected plants.		Widespread.
Water-soaked areas on stems of older plants turn into cracked brown cankers. Infected spots on fruits become water soaked and dotted.	gummy stem blight (black rot on fruit)	Crop rotation.	Copper fungicides or zineb.	Widespread.
Yellow to dark green streaking of leaves (leaves often wrinkled and curled).	mosaics (transmitted by aphids, cucumber beetles, grasshoppers)	Keep weeds out of garden area.	Use malathion to control aphids, cucumber beetles, and grasshoppers that transmit mosaics.	Widespread.
White or brownish mealy growth on leaves and young stems.	powdery mildew	Rotate melons with other crops.	Apply karathane or sulfur 7 to 10 days apart.	Widespread.
Water-soaked or pale green spots on leaves that turn white to gray to brown. Fruit crack.	scab	Destroy plants after harvest. Grow in well-drained soil.	Apply maneb.	Widespread.

SWEET POTATOES

Columbus first "discovered" the sweet potato growing in Central and South America and introduced it to Spain. Later early explorers of the "new world" carried the sweet potato around the world to the Philippines, Africa and Asia where it was cultivated extensively. Today it is grown in long, hot summer areas.

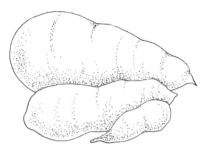

TABLE 9–27   SWEET POTATOES

Mother Nature's Puzzlers

WHAT TO LOOK FOR	POSSIBLE CAUSES	POSSIBLE CURES
Tubers are elongated, slender.	1 Too much water.	1 Water deeply for 2 to 3 hours then don't water again until the soil has dried out to a depth of 8 inches. This keeps the soil from becoming saturated.
	2 Heavy clay soils can cause the sweet potato roots to become long and stringy.	2 Put about 6 inches of organic material on top of your sweet potato bed and spade in.
Some transplanted sprouts die, fail to produce (slips) vines.	1 Thin succulent sprouts planted. Not enough moisture in sprouts to survive until roots form.	1 Plant larger sprouts with thick stems.
	2 Slips (sprouts) planted vertically.	2 Plant slips horizontally 2 to 3 inches with 5 nodes underground and only the tips showing.
Sweet potatoes have poor flavor.	Roots harvested after the soil temperature has dropped below 55 degrees F.	Harvest before the soil temperature dips below 55 degrees F. Check with a soil thermometer, or harvest on a mild day within a week or two of the first expected frost.
Roots rot after harvesting.	Harvest wounds at either end fail to close.	Lay sweet potatoes out in a room at about 75 degrees F. and cover with newspapers to keep the humidity high (between 80 to 90 percent). They'll be ready in about a week. Wrap the sweet potatoes in newspapers and store at about 55 degrees F.
Parts or all of sweet potato hard when cooked.	Sweet potato roots stored in near freezing temperatures, or in the refrigerator.	Store sweet potatoes at about 55 degrees F.

TABLE 9–27   SWEET POTATOES (continued)

Insects

WHAT TO LOOK FOR	PEST	PREVENTION AND/OR NATURAL CONTROLS	CHEMICAL CONTROLS	GEOGRAPHICAL LOCATION
Holes in leaves and roots.	sweet potato weevil	Spade the soil before planting. Companion plant with Summer savor, radish, tansy. Pick off beetles.	Sevin, malathion, or rotenone.	Sometimes a problem in South.

Diseases

WHAT TO LOOK FOR	DISEASE	PREVENTION AND/OR NATURAL CONTROLS	CHEMICAL CONTROLS	GEOGRAPHICAL LOCATION
Black enlarging sunken spots on underground stems and roots. Pale yellowish foliage.	black rot	Use only certified healthy slips. Keep down weeds. Plant resistant varieties: Norin No. 1, Allgold, Sunnyside.		Widespread.
Enlarging brown to black areas on stem near soil line. Rot of sweet potato at stem end.	foot rot (spread by sweet potato weevil)	Use only certified healthy slips.		Widespread.
Plants stunted. Leaves become yellow or brownish, wilt, and drop. Brown to black streaks inside stems.	fusarium wilt	Plant only certified healthy slips. Plant resistant varieties: Allgold, Coppergold, Dooley, Gem.		Widespread.
Round to angular spots on leaves.	leaf spots	Plant certified disease free slips.	Apply maneb or zineb 10 days apart.	Widespread.
Hard, corky islands in sweet potato flesh. Leaves mottled and yellowish along veins.	internal cork (transmitted by aphids)	Plant certified virus-free slips.	Apply malathion to control aphids that transmit virus.	Especially prevalent in southern states.

TABLE 9–27 **SWEET POTATOES** *(continued)*

Diseases

WHAT TO LOOK FOR	DISEASE	PREVENTION AND/OR NATURAL CONTROLS	CHEMICAL CONTROLS	GEOGRAPHICAL LOCATION
Small galls form on feder roots. Plants stunted, unhealthy.	root-knot (nematodes)	Plant nematode resistant varieties: heartogold, porto rico. Companion plant with marigolds.	Apply liquid or granular nematocide— see your local nursery.	Widespread.
Round, rusty brown to black spots and blotches on potato surface.	scurf	Plant certified disease-free slips.	Dip roots prior to planting in ferban or captan.	Widespread.

TOMATOES

The tomato is a warm weather vegetable that doesn't particularly like extremes in temperatures (either too hot or too cold). Nevertheless, it will grow almost anywhere, and does extremely well in an average garden soil enriched with a high potash fertilizer (such as 5-10-10). Here are the problems to watch for.

TABLE 9–28 **TOMATOES**

Mother Nature's Puzzlers

WHAT TO LOOK FOR	POSSIBLE CAUSES	POSSIBLE CURES
The plant produces blossoms, but the blossoms fall off without producing fruit (blossom drop).	Night temperatures are too low (below 55 degrees F.) or too high (much above 75 degrees F).	Increase night temperatures by using plastic covers over wire cages. Sometimes it is also possible to increase pollination and fruit production by lightly tapping or jarring the plants.
A dark leathery area appears on the blossom end of the fruit (blossom end rot).	Too much then too little moisture in the soil. It is especially severe when temperatures rise above 90 degrees F. and when the fruit is exposed to full sun. Sometimes also related to calcium deficiency.	Keep the soil moist at all times. Place 2 to 3 inches or organic material on top of the bed to hold down moisture loss. Water tomatoes 2 to 3 hours at a time. Don't water again until the soil is dry to a depth of 4 to 8 inches. Check with a trowel. Or mulch with black plastic to reduce moisture fluctuation. Test soil; if calcium deficient add soluble calcium.

TABLE 9–28 **TOMATOES** *(continued)*

Mother Nature's Puzzlers

WHAT TO LOOK FOR	POSSIBLE CAUSES	POSSIBLE CURES
Yellowish-patches on the fruit (sun scald). Later this forms a large grayish white spot.	Too much direct exposure to the sun and temperatures of between 90 and 100 degrees F.	Grow tomato varieties with heavy leaf cover like Vineripe, Star Fire, Marglobe, and Early Girl.
Tomato fruit are malformed with ugly scars between the segments (catfacing).	Cool and cloudy weather at the time of blossoming may cause the blossoms to stick to the small fruits and create tearing and distortion.	Pull blossoms off when the fruit is small. Plant tomato varieties like Big Set and Burpee's VF which resist catfacing.
Fruit is swollen and puffy with inner air spaces (puffiness).	Pollination occurring when the temperatures are below 55 degrees F. Sometimes puffiness also occurs when the fruit is pollinated at temperatures above 90 degrees F.	Increase temperatures by placing plastic covers over the cages. Provide shade in very hot weather.
Radial cracking occurs from the top toward the bottom of the fruit. Concentric cracking occurs in a circle around the fruit stem.	Uneven soil moisture—too dry or too wet. This occurs frequently during rainy periods when the temperatures are between 85 to 90 degrees F. Tomatoes exposed to full sun develop more cracks than those covered with good foliage.	Place 2 to 3 inches of organic material on top of the bed to hold down moisture loss. Water tomatoes 2 to 3 hours a time. Don't water again until the soil is dry to a depth of 4 to 8 inches. Check with a trowel. Mulch with black plastic to reduce fluctuations. Plant in well-drained soil.
Fruit takes on strange, distorted shapes (misshapen tomatoes).	Plants are exposed to temperatures below 55 degrees F. during blossoming.	Increase the night temperatures by placing plastic covers over the tomato cages. Grow early, lower temperature varieties: Early Girl, Rocket, Earliana.
A brown dashed scar appears down the side of the tomato (zipper streak).	Weather is too wet and cool causing the blossom to stick to the tiny fruit. The blossom tears and pulls away leaving a zipper-like scar. This scar enlarges as the fruit grows.	Pull off the flower parts when the fruit are tiny.

TABLE 9–28 **TOMATOES** (*continued*)

Mother Nature's Puzzlers

WHAT TO LOOK FOR	POSSIBLE CAUSES	POSSIBLE CURES
Blotchy, uneven ripening.	Too much exposure to intense sunlight. The exposed part of the fruits can become 20 degrees hotter than the shaded parts. This contributes to uneven ripening.	Plant varieties with good foliage for protection: Vineripe, Monte Carlo, Moreton Hybrid.
Plants produce lush foliage, little fruit.	1 Too much nitrogen.	1 Fertilize tomatoes with a "tomato" fertilizer (it has more phosphorus than nitrogen).
	2 Overwatering.	2 Water 2 to 3 hours at a time. Don't water again until the soil has dried out to a depth of 4 to 8 inches. Check with a trowel.
	3 Temperatures are too low.	3 Increase night temperatures by using plastic covers over wire cages.
	4 Inadequate pollination.	4 Sometimes it is possible to increase pollination and fruit production by lightly tapping or jarring the plants.
The edges of the leaves roll inward starting with the lower leaves. The leaves may cup and overlap (leaf roll).	Too much exposure to prolonged rains causing the moisture in the soil to accumulate.	Put black plastic over the bed to keep out excess moisture.
Gray to grayish-brown blotches that develop on surface of green fruit. Internal browning.	Low light intensity, low temperatures, high soil moisture, excessive compaction in soil.	Grow on well-drained soil. Avoid heavy fertilization that produces heavy foliage. Plant resistant varieties: Indian River, Ohio WR, Seven, Strain A Globe.

Insects

WHAT TO LOOK FOR	PEST	PREVENTION AND/OR NATURAL CONTROLS	CHEMICAL CONTROLS	GEOGRAPHICAL LOCATION
Colonies of sucking insects on leaves. Leaves can be curled and discolored. Sticky substance on stem and leaves.	aphids	Companion plant with spearmint and garlic. Mulch with aluminum foil. Remove with blast from garden hose. Use a soap solution on the leaves. Lacewing flies, ladybugs, and praying mantises destroy aphids.	Malathion, diazinon, pyrethrum, rotenone, or ryania.	Widespread.

TABLE 9-28 TOMATOES (continued)

Insects

WHAT TO LOOK FOR	PEST	PREVENTION AND/OR NATURAL CONTROLS	CHEMICAL CONTROLS	GEOGRAPHICAL LOCATION
Plants partially defoliated.	blister beetles	Garden cleanliness. Spade deeply in Spring to kill larvae. Pick beetles off by hand.	Sevin, pyrethrum, rotenone, ryania.	East of Rocky Mountains.
Leaves and shoots stripped.	Colorado potato beetle	Garden cleanliness. Companion plant with eggplant, flax, greenbeans. Pick off beetles.	Malathion, Sevin, rotenone.	Widespread in the U.S. and Canada except Nevada, California, and Florida.
Young plants cut off near soil surface.	cutworms worms hide in the soil by day, feed at night	Garden cleanliness. Companion plant with tansy between rows. Place a cardboard collar around the stems. Push 1 inch into soil.	Spray the soil with Sevin or diazinon before transplanting plants into beds.	Widespread.
Leaves look like they have been shot through with tiny round holes.	flea beetles	Garden cleanliness. Spade garden soil deeply to destroy larvae in early Spring. Companion plant with head lettuce, mint, wormwood. Pick beetles off plant.	Use several applications of diazinon, malathion or Sevin. Or use botanical sprays pyrethrum, rotenone, ryania.	Widespread.
Leaves appear scorched and wilted.	leafhoppers		Sevin, malathion, pyrethrum, rotenone, or ryania when insects appear.	Widespread.
Insect eating into fruit.	tomato fruit worm (European corn borer)		Control worms when they are small with Sevin.	Widespread.
Plants partially defoliated.	tomato hornworm (especially destructive to tomatoes)	Spade deeply in Fall to destroy larvae. Handpick and destroy caterpillars. Use Bacillus thuringiensis (Thurocide, Dipel).	Sevin.	Throughout U.S. and southern Canada.

TABLE 9–28 **TOMATOES** *(continued)*

Insects

WHAT TO LOOK FOR	PEST	PREVENTION AND/OR NATURAL CONTROLS	CHEMICAL CONTROLS	GEOGRAPHICAL LOCATION
White spots on fruit. Leaf tips become distorted.	thrips (transmit spotted wilt virus)	Garden cleanliness.	Treat with 2 or 3 applications of diazinon or malathion.	Widespread.
A cloud of white wings fly from plant when disturbed.	whiteflies	Companion plant with marigolds. Marigolds excrete a substance absorbed by roots of other plants that repel whiteflies. Use wasps to destroy whiteflies. Hose off with a stream of water. Use tanglefoot on a bright yellow card to trap whiteflies.	Malathion or rotenone.	Widespread.

Diseases

WHAT TO LOOK FOR	DISEASE	PREVENTION AND/OR NATURAL CONTROLS	CHEMICAL CONTROLS	GEOGRAPHICAL LOCATION
Sunken water-soaked areas on fruit. Fruit may shrivel, become watery, collapse.	anthracnose	Destroy rotting fruit. Keep fruit off soil. Use 3 to 4 year rotation.	Maneb, zineb, or ziram.	Widespread.
Wilting of leaflets on one side of plant. Light-colored streak on stems, streaks break open to form cankers.	bacterial canker	Plant certified disease-free seed.		Widespread.
Leaflets show small (⅛ inch), irregular, dark greasy looking spots. Water soaked spots on fruit become raised and enlarged.	bacterial spot	Purchase certified disease-free seed.	Fixed copper fungicides.	Widespread in seasons with frequent rainy seasons.

TABLE 9–28 TOMATOES (continued)

Diseases

WHAT TO LOOK FOR	DISEASE	PREVENTION AND/OR NATURAL CONTROLS	CHEMICAL CONTROLS	GEOGRAPHICAL LOCATION
Rapid wilting and death of entire plant, yellowing or spotting of leaves.	bacterial wilt	Do not grow in beds where the disease has occurred. Rotate crops.		Southern states.
Plants stunted, spindly. Cupping of leaves. Flowers often distorted.	curly top (transmitted by leafhoppers)	Garden cleanliness. Shade individual plants under slatted or muslin-covered frames to ward off leaf hoppers that transmit disease.	Apply malathion to control leaf hoppers that transmit virus.	Usually western half of United States.
Roots of seedlings severely damaged. Stem girdled at ground line.	damping off	Do not grow seedlings in poorly drained soil.	Captan.	Widespread.
Brown to almost black spots on leaves and lower stem. Spots have rings. Leaves turn yellow to brown.	early blight	Garden cleanliness.	Maneb or zineb.	Widespread.
Plants stunted with galls, on roots. Plants wilt in dry weather then recover.	root-knot (nematodes)	Plant resistant varieties: Apollo, Better Boy, Pelican, Vigor Boy. Companion plant with marigolds.	Apply liquid or granular nematocide— see your local nursery.	Widespread. Serious in southern states.
Water-soaked spots on leaves. Spots become circular with gray centers.	septorial leaf spot	Garden cleanliness. Rotate crops.	Fixed copper fungicides.	Severe in mid-Atlantic and central states.

TABLE 9–28   TOMATOES *(continued)*

Diseases

WHAT TO LOOK FOR	DISEASE	PREVENTION AND/OR NATURAL CONTROLS	CHEMICAL CONTROLS	GEOGRAPHICAL LOCATION
Brown sunken spot where tomatoes touch ground. Spot enlarges, becomes dark brown. The center breaks open. Concentric rings evident.	soil rot	Stake plants. Use black plastic under plants.		Widespread.
Plants stunted. Leaves wilt, wither, drop off. Brown to black streaks lower stem.	fusarium wilt	Plant resistant tomato varieties: Alamo, Blackhawk, Morcross, Roma VF.		Widespread.
Numerous brown spots on older leaves. When spots numerous, the leaves yellow and wither.	gray leaf spot	Garden cleanliness. Use 3- to 4-year rotation. Plant resistant varieties: Manalee, Marion, Manapal, Floradel, Floralou, Indian River, Tecumesh.	Maneb or zineb.	Southeast.
Irregular greenish water soaked spots on leaves and stems. Whitish gray growth underside of leaves, fruit corrugated.	late blight	Garden cleanliness.	Maneb, zineb, or fixed copper once a week.	Widespread in rainy season.
General drooping of leaves. Plant dies without yellowing.	southern blight	Garden cleanliness. Crop rotation.		Across the South.

TABLE 9–28   TOMATOES (continued)

Diseases

WHAT TO LOOK FOR	DISEASE	PREVENTION AND/OR NATURAL CONTROLS	CHEMICAL CONTROLS	GEOGRAPHICAL LOCATION
Leaves curled, crinkled, streaked and mottled.	tobacco mosaic (spread by insects)	Garden cleanliness. Destroy infected plants. Smokers should wash hands before working in the garden.	Apply malathion to control insects that transmit virus.	Widespread.
Wilting of lower leaves which yellow and die. Stems discolored.	verticillium wilt	Plant resistant varieties: Ace 55, Early Pak, Highlander.		Widespread. Most prevalent in northern states.

TURNIPS, RUTABAGAS, KOHLRABI

Turnip, rutabaga, and kohlrabi are cool weather crops that thrive in average soil enriched with a high phosphate fertilizer or rock phosphate. Here are the situations you might find in your garden.

TABLE 9–29 TURNIPS, RUTABAGAS, KOHLRABI

Mother Nature's Puzzlers

WHAT TO LOOK FOR	POSSIBLE CAUSES	POSSIBLE CURES
Turnips and rutabagas go to seed before good roots form.	Exposure for too many days of 40 degree temperatures causes the plants to flower, making the roots unusable.	Plant in the Spring 4 to 6 weeks before the last frost. In areas where late Spring and Summer have many 80-plus degree days, plant for a Fall harvest.
Turnips and kohlrabi become pithy, fibrous, and bitter.	Allowing the plants to remain in the ground too long. Woody fibers appear in both turnips and kohlrabi as they become older.	Harvest both turnips and kohlrabi when they are about 2 inches in diameter.

TABLE 9–29 **TURNIPS, RUTABAGAS, KOHLRABI** *(continued)*

Insects

WHAT TO LOOK FOR	PEST	PREVENTION AND/OR NATURAL CONTROLS	CHEMICAL CONTROLS	GEOGRAPHICAL LOCATION
Colonies of small green sucking insects on leaves. Leaves can be curled and discolored. Sticky substances on stems and leaves.	aphids	Companion plant with spearmint and garlic. Mulch with aluminum foil. Remove with blast from garden hose. Use a soap solution on the leaves. Control with lacewing flies, praying mantises, ladybugs.	Malathion, diazinon, pyrethrum, rotenone, or ryania.	Widespread.
Plants partially defoliated.	blister beetle	Garden cleanliness. Spade deeply in the Spring to kill larvae. Pick off beetles by hand.	Sevin, pyrethrum, rotenone, or ryania.	Widespread.
Irregular holes eaten in leaves.	cabbage looper	Garden cleanliness. Pick off worms. Use Bacillus thuringiensis (Dipel, Thuricide).	Malathion, Sevin, or rotenone.	Widespread.
Young plants cut off near the soil surface.	cutworms; worms hide in soil by day, feed at night.	Garden cleanliness. Place a cardboard collar around the stems. Push 1 inch into soil. Plant tansy between rows.	Spray the soil with Sevin or diazinon before transplanting plants into bed.	Widespread.
Leaves look like they have been shot through with tiny round holes.	flea beetles	Garden cleanliness. Companion plant with head lettuce, mint, wormwood. Pick off plant.	Use several applications of diazinon, malathion, Sevin, pyrethrum, rotenone, or ryania.	Widespread.
Holes in leaves.	imported cabbage worm (white cabbage butterfly)	Garden cleanliness. Companion plant with mint, sage, thyme, tomato, wormwood, rosemary. Use Bacillus thuringiensis (Dipel or Thurocide).	Malathion, Sevin, or rotenone.	Widespread.

TABLE 9–29   TURNIPS, RUTABAGAS, KOHLRABI (continued)

Insects

WHAT TO LOOK FOR	PEST	PREVENTION AND/OR NATURAL CONTROLS	CHEMICAL CONTROLS	GEOGRAPHICAL LOCATION
Brown root scars. Stunted off-color plants. Some plants may be honeycombed with curving slimy tunnels.	cabbage maggot (larva of cabbage root fly). Transmits spores of blackleg disease.	Cover plants with fine gauze to prevent flies from laying eggs on them. Dispose of damaged plants after harvest. Put 4-inch circles of cardboard around stems at ground level to prevent maggots from reaching roots. Mint repels the cabbage maggot.	Mix diazinon into the top 3 to 4 inches of the soil before planting. Repeat in 2 weeks.	Widespread. Most severe in the northern United States, southern Canada.
White or yellow blotches on leaves where nymphs have sucked sap. Leaves can wilt.	stinkbug	Destroy egg masses clustered on underside of leaves. Control with sabadilla.	Sevin, rotenone, or pyrethrum.	Extremely destructive to turnips, rutabaga, and kohlrabi in the southern half of the United States.

Diseases

WHAT TO LOOK FOR	DISEASE	PREVENTION AND/OR NATURAL CONTROLS	CHEMICAL CONTROLS	GEOGRAPHICAL LOCATION
Light brown to gray spots on stem, leaves. Stem blackens and rots.	blackleg (spread by cutworms and root maggots)	Garden cleanliness. Rotate with other crop. Wait 4 years before replanting in same area.	Treat seed with captan. Use diazinon in soil to control cutworms and maggots.	Widespread east of Rocky Mountains.
Yellowish leaves that wilt on hot days. Roots greatly enlarged and distorted.	clubroot	Keep weeds down. Plant resistant varieties: turnip—Bruce, Dale's Hybrid. Rutabagas—American Purple top, Willhemsburger.		Widespread.
Seedlings collapse from rot at soil line. Black scabby areas on roots.	damping off	Destroy tops after harvest.	Treat soil with PCNB 75 and captan 50 (sold as Terra cap, PCNP-captan).	Widespread.

TABLE 9–29   TURNIPS, RUTABAGAS, KOHLRABI *(continued)*

Diseases

WHAT TO LOOK FOR	DISEASE	PREVENTION AND/OR NATURAL CONTROLS	CHEMICAL CONTROLS	GEOGRAPHICAL LOCATION
Pale green to yellow spotting on upper surface of leaves followed by purpling, wilting.	downy mildew	Avoid overcrowding plants. Don't water overhead. Destroy infected plants.	Maneb or fixed copper sprays.	Widespread during cool wet seasons.
Pale yellow, gray brown, dark green spots on leaves.	fungal leaf spots	Destroy tops after harvest.	Spray seedbed with maneb or fixed copper sprays.	Widespread in wet weather.
Leaves turn dull yellow, curl and die.	yellows			Widespread. Most serious when soil temperatures over 70 degrees F.

ZUCCHINI

Zucchini (the "Z" in our A to Z account) is a summer squash and a warm weather vegetable that grows almost anywhere, develops quickly, and keeps churning out fruits until you holler "uncle." Surprisingly, although we tend to think of zucchini as a single vegetable, there are at least 50 popular varieties you can plant in your garden. Here are the situations you might encounter.

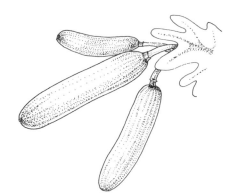

TABLE 9–30   ZUCCHINI

Mother Nature's Puzzlers

WHAT TO LOOK FOR	POSSIBLE CAUSES	POSSIBLE CURES
Some seeds fail to come up.	One of nature's inevitabilities. A certain percentage of all squash seeds are "hard" naturally resistant to water uptake that triggers sprouting.	Increase germination and slightly decrease sprouting time by soaking seeds in tepid water for 24 hours. Dry the seeds on a paper towel before planting.

TABLE 9–30 ZUCCHINI *(continued)*

Mother Nature's Puzzlers

WHAT TO LOOK FOR	POSSIBLE CAUSES	POSSIBLE CURES
Dark brown leathery areas appear on the blossom end of the squash fruit (blossom end rot).	Uneven soil moisture. If the soil is intermittently wet, then dries out, it seems to produce blossom end rot.	Place 2 or 3 inches of organic material on top of the soil to hold down moisture loss. Water 2 to 3 hours at a time. Don't water again until the soil is dry to a depth of 4 to 8 inches. Check with a trowel.
Small zucchini start to form, then rot or dry up.	Female flowers blossom before there are male flowers to pollinate the plants.	Have some patience. Wait until male flowers start to blossom. They will pollinate the female flowers and zucchini fruit will grow.
Too great an abundance of squash fruit on the plant.	The unpollinated fruit aborts in a self-pruning process.	Keep the fruit of zucchini picked to keep the plant producing.
Few flowers form fruit, even when both male and female flowers are present.	Not enough bees to pollinate the zucchini. Recent research shows that the percentage of flowers increases when these flowers are pollinated by many bees.	Use the chemical sprays diazinon, Sevin, and malathion *sparingly*. They kill not only harmful insects but bees as well.

Insects

WHAT TO LOOK FOR	PEST	PREVENTION AND/OR NATURAL CONTROLS	CHEMICAL CONTROLS	GEOGRAPHICAL LOCATION
Colonies of sucking insects on leaves. Leaves can be curled and discolored. Sticky substance on stems and leaves.	aphids	Companion plant with spearmint and garlic. Mulch with aluminum foil. Remove with blast from garden hose. Use a soap solution on the leaves. Control with lacewing flies, praying mantises, ladybugs.	Malathion, diazinon, pyrethrum, rotenone, or ryania.	Widespread.
Plants eaten or cut off near the surface of the soil.	cut worms	Garden cleanliness. Companion plant with tansy. Place a cardboard collar around the stems. Push 1 inch into soil.	Spray the soil with Sevin or diazinon before the plants emerge.	Widespread. Most severe in Gulf and South Atlantic states.
Holes in leaves and flowers. Tunnels in fruit.	pickle worms	Pick off. Use Bacillus thuringiensis (Dipel, Thurocide).	Sevin, malathion or rotenone.	Widespread, especially prevalent in South.

TABLE 9–30   ZUCCHINI (continued)

Insects

WHAT TO LOOK FOR	PEST	PREVENTION AND/OR NATURAL CONTROLS	CHEMICAL CONTROLS	GEOGRAPHICAL LOCATION
Affected leaves turn pale green. Dusty webs between vine and leaves.	spider mite	Use a strong spray from a garden hose. Ladybugs, lacewings eat spider mites.	Kelthane or diazinon.	Most severe in South.
Irregular holes chewed in leaves and shoots.	spotted cucumber beetle (carries wilt)	Spade the soil before planting to destroy beetles. Companion plant with radish and tansy. Pick off beetles.	Sevin, malathion, or rotenone.	Widespread.
Affected leaves wilt, rapidly becoming black and crisp.	squash bug	Fertilize plants to keep growing vigorously. Companion plant with nasturtium. Destroy squash bugs that collect under leaves at night. Use sabadilla (Doom).	Sevin, malathion, pyrethrum, rotenone, or ryania.	Widespread.
Sudden wilting of runners. Holes in stems near base.	squash vine borer	Garden cleanliness. Slit the vine with a knife and take out the borer.	Dust with Sevin or malathion at weekly intervals as the vines start to grow.	Severe East of Rocky Mountains.
Irregular holes chewed in leaves and roots.	stripped cucumber beetle (carries wilt)	Spade the soil before planting to destroy dormant beetles. Companion plant with Summer savor, radish, and tansy. Pick off beetles by hand.	Sevin, malathion, or rotenone.	Widespread.

TABLE 9–30 ZUCCHINI

Diseases

WHAT TO LOOK FOR	DISEASE	PREVENTION AND/OR NATURAL CONTROLS	CHEMICAL CONTROLS	GEOGRAPHICAL LOCATION
Round to angular reddish brown to black spots on leaves. Spots may later dry and tear out.	anthracnose	Avoid overhead watering. Use 3 to 4 year rotation. Grow in well drained soil. Garden cleanliness.	Apply captan, maneb, or zineb at 10 day intervals.	Widespread when weather is warm (65 to 85 degrees F.) and humid.
Small angular spots on leaves. Round water-soaked spots on fruit.	bacterial spot or blight (transmitted by insects)	Garden cleanliness.	Apply fixed copper sprays.	Widespread.
Vines wilt rapidly and die starting with one or a few leaves on vine.	bacterial wilt (transmitted by cucumber beetle)	Rotate crops each year. Garden cleanliness.	Apply Sevin to control cucumber beetles that spread wilt.	Widespread.
Dense white fungus growth covers blossoms. Growth turns purplish-black. Young fruits decay and die.	Choanephora fruit rot	Crop rotation.	Copper fungicides, zineb or ziram.	Widespread.
Yellowish to brownish areas on upper side of older leaves. Undersides purplish. Plants stunted and often yellow. Runners gradually die.	down mildew	Rotate cucumbers with other crops.	Apply maneb or zineb.	Widespread.
Plants stunted and often yellow. Runners gradually die.	fusarium wilt	Collect and burn infected plants.		Widespread.

TABLE 9–30 **ZUCCHINI** *(continued)*

Diseases

WHAT TO LOOK FOR	DISEASE	PREVENTION AND/OR NATURAL CONTROLS	CHEMICAL CONTROLS	GEOGRAPHICAL LOCATION
Water soaked areas on stems of older plants turn into cracked brown cankers. Infected spots on fruits become water soaked and dotted.	gummy stem blight (black rot on fruit)	Crop rotation.	Copper fungicides or zineb.	Widespread.
Yellow to dark green streaking of leaves (leaves often wrinkled and curled).	mosaics (transmitted by aphids, cucumber beetles, grasshoppers)	Garden cleanliness.	Use malathion to control aphids, cucumber beetles, and grasshoppers that transmit mosaics.	Widespread.
White or brownish mealy growth on leaves and young stems.	powdery mildew	Practice crop rotation.	Apply karathane or sulfur 7 to 10 days apart.	Widespread.
Water-soaked or pale green spots on leaves that turn white to gray to brown, fruit cracks.	scab	Destroy plants after harvest. Grow in well drained soil.	Apply maneb.	Widespread.

Just What the Doctor Ordered

So now you have a basic guide to better, healthier vegetable gardening that you can put to instant use. Just understanding some of the problems will allow you to prevent them. For instance, a gardener who knows that bean rot in cool soil (below 65 degrees F.) will wait to plant until the soil warms up so most of the seed will germinate. Or the gardener who can't get blossoming tomato plants to form fruit will shake the plants by hand each day to increase the "set."

I'm sure you have also noticed that a number of the best gardening practices were repeated over and over again—for example, avoiding uneven moisture conditions in your soil by watering properly. As you garden, you will soon master the basic ins and outs of diagnosis and cure, of providing good soil, giving your plants adequate moisture and nutrients, following good cultural practices, and in general simply giving mother nature a hand here and there when the garden gets out of balance.

Rx for Vegetable Gardens was written to show you how to prevent, live with, or eliminate the major garden problems that are the inevitable lot of many home growers. It can help you grow healthier vegetables in a more vigorous, productive garden from the very first season on.

APPENDIX A

COOPERATIVE EXTENSION SERVICES

ALASKA
Cooperative Extension Service
University of Alaska
Fairbanks, AK 99701

ALABAMA
Cooperative Extension Service
Auburn University
Auburn, AL 36830

ARIZONA
Cooperative Extension Service
University of Arizona
College of Agriculture
Tucson, AZ 85721

ARKANSAS
Cooperative Extension Service
University of Arkansas
P.O. Box 391
Little Rock, AR 72203

CALIFORNIA
Agricultural Extension Service
University of California
College of Agriculture
Berkeley, CA 94720

COLORADO
Cooperative Extension Service
Colorado State University
Fort Collins, CO 80521

DELAWARE
Cooperative Extension Service
University of Delaware
College of Agricultural Sciences
Newark, DE 19711

DISTRICT OF COLUMBIA
Cooperative Extension Service
The Federal City College
1424 K Street, N.W.
Washington, DC 20005

FLORIDA
Cooperative Extension Service
University of Florida
Institute of Food and
    Agricultural Sciences
Gainesville, FL 32601

GEORGIA
Cooperative Extension Service
University of Georgia
College of Agriculture
Athens, GA 30601

HAWAII
Cooperative Extension Service
University of Hawaii
2500 Dole Street
Honolulu, HI 96822

IDAHO
Cooperative Extension Service
University of Idaho
College of Agriculture
Moscow, ID 83843

ILLINOIS
Cooperative Extension Service
University of Illinois
College of Agriculture
Urbana, IL 61801

INDIANA
Cooperative Extension Service
Purdue University
West Lafayette, IN 47907

IOWA
Cooperative Extension Service
Iowa State University
Ames, IA 50010

KANSAS
Cooperative Extension Service
Kansas State University
Manhattan, KS 66506

KENTUCKY
Cooperative Extension Service
University of Kentucky
College of Agriculture
Lexington, KY 40506

LOUISIANA
Cooperative Extension Service
State University
A & M College
University Station
Baton Rouge, LA 70803

MAINE
Cooperative Extension Service
University of Maine
Orono, ME 04473

MARYLAND
Cooperative Extension Service
University of Maryland
College Park, MD 20742

MASSACHUSETTS
Cooperative Extension Service
University of Massachusetts
Amherst, MA 01002

MICHIGAN
Cooperative Extension Service
Michigan State University
East Lansing, MI 48823

MINNESOTA
Agricultural Extension Service
University of Minnesota
Institute of Agriculture
St. Paul, MN 55101

MISSISSIPPI
Cooperative Extension Service
Mississippi State University
State College, MS 39762

MISSOURI
Cooperative Extension Service
University of Missouri
Columbia, MO 65201

MONTANA
Cooperative Extension Service
Montana State University
Bozeman, MT 59715

NEBRASKA
Cooperative Extension Service
University of Nebraska
College of Agriculture and
    Home Economics
Lincoln, NB 68503

NEVADA
Cooperative Extension Service
University of Nevada
College of Agriculture
Reno, NV 89507

NEW HAMPSHIRE
Cooperative Extension Service
University of New Hampshire
College of Life Sciences and
    Agriculture
Durham, NH 03824

NEW JERSEY
Cooperative Extension Service
College of Agriculture and
    Environmental Science
Rutgers—The State University
New Brunswick, NJ 08903

NEW MEXICO
Cooperative Extension Service
New Mexico State University
Box 3AE, Agriculture Bldg.
Las Cruces, NM 88003

NEW YORK
Cooperative Extension Service
Cornell University
State University of New York
Ithaca, NY 14850

NORTH CAROLINA
Cooperative Extension Service
North Carolina State Universit
P.O. Box 5057
Raleigh, NC 27607

NORTH DAKOTA
Cooperative Extension Service
North Dakota State University
    of Agriculture and Applied
    Science
University Station
Fargo, ND 58102

OHIO
Cooperative Extension Service
Ohio State University
Agriculture Administration
    Bldg.
2120 Fyffe Road
Columbus, OH 43210

OKLAHOMA
Cooperative Extension Service
Oklahoma State University
201 Whitehurst
Stillwater, OK 74074

OREGON
Cooperative Extension Service
Oregon State University
Corvallis, OR 97331

PENNSYLVANIA
Cooperative Extension Service
The Pennsylvania State
    University
College of Agriculture
323 Agricultural
    Administration Bldg.
University Park, PA 16802

RHODE ISLAND
Cooperative Extension Service
University of Rhode Island
Kingston, RI 02881

SOUTH CAROLINA
Cooperative Extension Service
Clemson University
Clemson, SC 29631

SOUTH DAKOTA
Cooperative Extension Service
South Dakota State University
College of Agriculture
Brookings, SD 57006

TENNESSEE
Agricultural Extension Service
University of Tennessee
Institute of Agriculture
P.O. Box 1071
Knoxville, TN 37901

TEXAS
Agricultural Extension Service
Texas A & M University
College Station, TX 77843

UTAH
Cooperative Extension Service
Utah State University
Logan, UT 84321

VERMONT
Cooperative Extension Service
University of Vermont
Burlington, VT 05401

VIRGINIA
Cooperative Extension Service
Virginia Polytechnic Institute
Blacksburg, VA 24061

WASHINGTON
Cooperative Extension Service
College of Agriculture
Washington State University
Pullman, WA 99163

WEST VIRGINIA
Cooperative Extension Service
West Virginia University
Morgantown, WV 26506

WISCONSIN
Cooperative Extension Service
University of Wisconsin
412 N. Lake Street
Madison, WI 53706

WYOMING
Agricultural Extension Service
University of Wyoming
College of Agriculture
University Station, Box 3354
Laramie, WY 82070

APPENDIX B

SUPPLIERS OF PREDATOR INSECTS

ALLAN'S AQUARIUM &
EXOTIC BIRDS
845 Lincoln Blvd.
Venice, CA 90291

Ladybugs

BIO-CONTROL CO.
Route 2, Box 2397
Auburn, CA 95603

Ladybugs
Praying mantises

W. ATLEE BURPEE CO.
Philadelphia, PA 19132
Clinton, IA 52732
Riverside, CA 92502

Ladybugs
Praying mantises

CALIFORNIA GREEN
LACEWINGS INC.
P.O. Box 2495
Merced, CA 95340

Lacewing flies
Trichogramma wasps

CONNECTICUT VALLEY
BIOLOGICAL SUPPLY CO.
Valley Rd.
South Hampton, MA 01073

Damselfly nymphs
Dragonfly nymphs

EASTERN BIOLOGICAL
CONTROL CO.
Route 5, Box 379
Jackson, NJ 08527

Praying mantises

GOTHARD INC.
P.O. Box 370
Canutillo, TX 79835

Praying mantises
Trichogramma wasps

GURNEY SEED AND
NURSERY CO.
Yankton, SD 57079

Ladybugs
Praying mantises

KING LABS
P.O. Box 69
Limerick, PA 19468

Praying mantises
Green lacewing

LAKELAND NURSERY SALES
340 Poplar
Hanover, PA 17331

Ladybugs
Praying mantises

ORGANIC CONTROL INC.
P.O. Box 25382
W. Los Angeles, CA 90025

Ladybugs
Praying mantises

RINCON VITOVA INSECTARIES INC. P.O. Box 95 Oak View, CA 93022	Fly parasites Lacewing flies Ladybugs Scale parasites Trichogramma wasps
ROBERT ROBBINS 424 N. Courtland St. East Stroudsburg, PA 18301	Praying mantises

APPENDIX C

WHERE TO FIND HELP

COOPERATIVE EXTENSION SERVICE

The best place to go for help, no matter where you live, is to your County Extension Service, Cooperative Extension Service, or Agricultural Service. (These are just different names for the same thing.) They are usually listed in the phone directory under county government offices. Your county agent can often answer questions, help you with soil testing, and provide useful gardening booklets.

You can also obtain a catalog of available garden publications by writing directly to your State Cooperative Extension Service. Some of the available publications are:

Bitterness in Cucumbers: Washington State University EM 2450

Control of Diseases and Nematodes in the Home Garden: Oklahoma State University F 7314

Garden Insect Control Without Synthetics: Washington State University EM 3439

Suggestions for Insect Control in Home Gardens: Oklahoma State University CR- 7313

Weed Control Guide For Vegetable Crops: Michigan State University E 433

Check your own State Cooperative Extension Service for others.

The U.S. Department of Agriculture (USDA) also has several thousand publications available on nearly every subject. Many are free. For a complete list write:

Office of Information
U.S. Department of Agriculture
Washington, D.C.

MASTER GARDENERS

In 1972, Dr. David Gibby, King County Washington Extension Agent, and Dr. Arlen Davison, Washington State Extension Agent, established a Master Gardener Program to help answer the tremendous number of requests for gardening information. Experienced local amateur gardeners were recruited and given 60 hours of instruction from extension agents on basic botany, vegetable gardens, plant disease, insect damage, pesticide safety, and more. Master Gardeners then set up clinics at branch libraries, local nurseries, shopping centers, and booths at garden shows and county fairs. When the answers to questions require a microscope and more technical training, plant specimens are forwarded to the state extension office where they are examined by fully trained experts. Currently Master Gardener Programs operate in 21 states: Alaska, Arizona, California, Colorado, Connecticut, Hawaii, Idaho, Illinois, Massachusetts, Michigan, Minnesota, Montana, Nevada, New York, Ohio, Oregon, Rhode Island, Utah, Virginia, Washington, and Wisconsin. More programs are contemplated. Contact your County Extension Service for information.

TELETIPS

California now has a teletips program developed through the state cooperative extension service which provides phone information on vegetable gardens, houseplants, insects, chemicals, food preservation, and more. Tape-recorded messages on nearly 300 subjects provide basic information and answer the most frequently asked questions. A complete listing of teletapes is available from the California State Cooperative Extension Service.

COMMERCIAL SOURCES

Some seed catalogs are almost gardening primers. Here are some of the more informative ones:

Burpee Seed Co.
Warminster, PA 18991
  or
Clinton, IA 52732
  or
Riverside, CA 92502

H.G. Hastings Co.
P.O. Box 4274
Atlanta, GA 30302

Herbst Brothers Seedsmen, Inc.
100 N. Main Street
Brewster, NY 10509

Johnny's Selected Seeds
 Albion, MA 04910

Kilgore Seed Company
1400 West First St.
Sanford, FL 32771

Thompson & Morgan Inc.
P.O. Box 100
Farmingdale, NJ 07727

Manufacturers of garden products often offer informational booklets on a wide variety of garden subjects. Sample booklets include:

The New Vigoro Vegetable Garden Book—How to Grow Your Own Vegetables; Swift, Agricultural Chemicals Corp., Vigoro Division, 111 W. Jackson Boulevard, Chicago, IL 60604
A Summary of Sevin—Complete crop and insect listings with appropriate rates and limitations for Sevin (carbaryl insecticide).
Union Carbide Corporation
Agricultural Products Division
P.O. Box 1906
Salinas, CA 93901
Chacon Horticultural Guide
2600 Yates Avenue
City of Commerce, CA 90040

The Chevron Chemical Company: Ortho Division, 575 Market Street, San Francisco, CA 94510, regularly publishes a small magazine or booklet, Ortho *Lawn and Garden Book,* that covers every garden subject from A to Z. This publication can be picked up free of charge at most garden centers that carry Ortho products. I highly recommend it. Ask your garden center about other manufacturer garden guides.

Some community colleges also offer gardening courses and frequently garden club members will answer gardening questions. You can contact these clubs through announcements of their activities in the local paper. Finally, most local nurseries have a knowledgeable staff that will be glad to answer gardening questions. The sources for local gardening information, especially through the cooperative extension services, are now rapidly expanding, and in the future many more should be available to help make gardening troubles much easier to solve.

RECOMMENDED READING

Brooklyn Botanic Garden. *Handbook on Biological Control of Plant Pests.* BBG: 1974.

Bebach, Paul. *Biological Control by Natural Enemies.* Cambridge University Press, 1974.

Dillon, Elizabeth S., and Lawrence S. Dillon. *A Manual of Common Beetles of Eastern North America Vol. II.* New York: Dover Publications, 1972.

Jacobson, Martin and D. G. Crosby, Eds. *Naturally Occurring Insecticides.* New York: Marcel Dekker Inc., 1966.

National Academy of Sciences. *Principles of Plant and Animal Pest Control Vol. 1.* Washington D.C.: Plant Disease Development and Printing and Publishing Office, 1968.

Newcomb, Duane G. *The Postage Stamp Garden Book*. Los Angeles: J. P. Tarcher, 1975.

———. *Growing Vegetables the Big Yield/Small Space Way*. Los Angeles: J. P. Tarcher, 1981.

Rodale, J. I. and Staff. *The Encyclopedia of Organic Gardening*. Emmaus, PA: Rodale Press, Inc., 1970.

———. *The Organic Way to Plant Protection*. Emmaus, PA: Rodale Press, Inc., 1972.

Stevens, Neil E., and Russell B. Stevens. *Disease in Plants*. Chronica Botanica Company, 1952.

Tyler, Hamilton. *Organic Gardening Without Poisons*. New York: Van Norstrand Reinhold, 1970.

Westcott, Cynthia. *The Gardener's Bug Book*. New York: Doubleday and Company Inc., 1973.

———. *Plant Disease Handbook*. New York: Van Nostrand Reinhold Company, 1971.

BULLETINS, CIRCULARS, PAMPHLETS

Aphids of Leafy Vegetables. Farmers' Bulletin No. 2149. U.S. Department of Agriculture.

Controlling the Japanese Beetle. Home and Garden Bulletin No. 159. U.S. Department of Agriculture, 1976.

Home and Garden Insect Control Guide. New Mexico State University Cooperative Extension Service, 1977.

Insects and Diseases of Vegetables in the Home Garden. Bulletin No. 380. U.S. Department of Agriculture, 1975.

Organic Soil Conditioners. University of Wisconsin Extension Leaflet A 2305, 1972.

INDEX

Rx for Your Vegetable Garden was set in Baskerville
by Transtype, Los Angeles.
Manufactured by The Haddon Craftsmen.